Mr Hodson

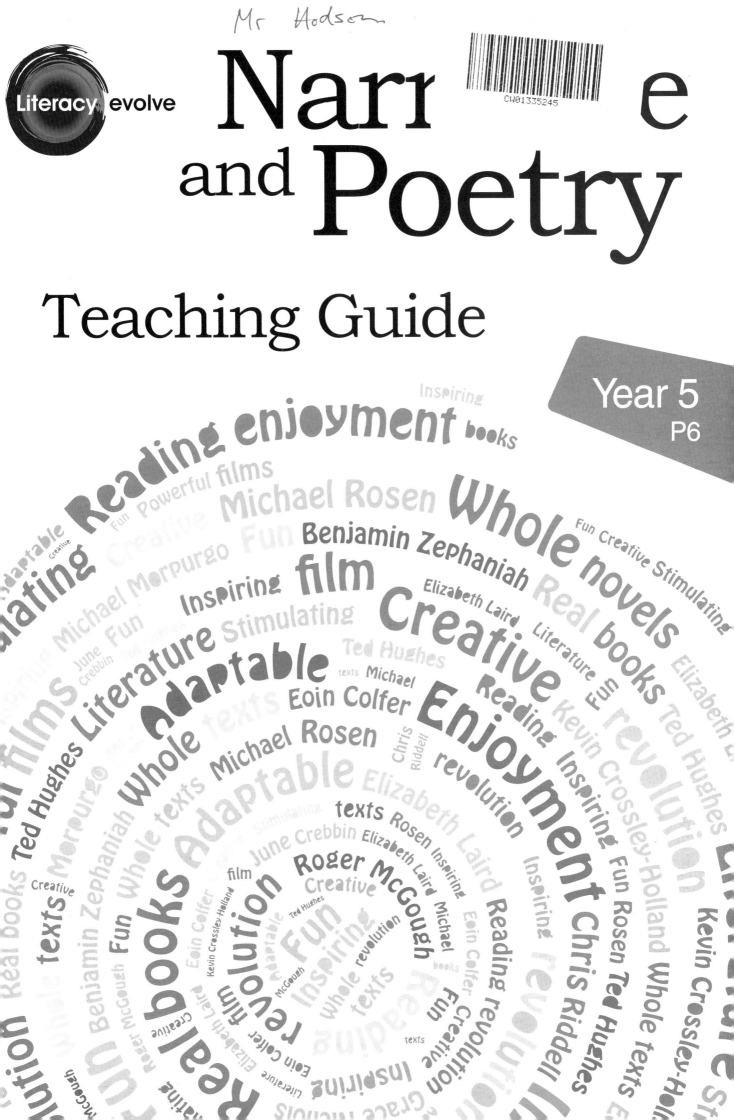

Literacy evolve

Narre and Poetry

Teaching Guide

Year 5
P6

Heinemann is an imprint of Pearson Education Limited, a company incorporated in England and Wales, having its registered office: Edinburgh Gate, Harlow, Essex, CM20 2JE. Registered company number: 872828

www.pearsonschools.co.uk

Heinemann is the registered trademark of Pearson Education Limited.

Text © Pearson Education Limited 2009

First published 2009

12 11 10 09

10 9 8 7 6 5 4 3 2 1

British Library Cataloguing in Publication Data
A catalogue record for this book is available from the British Library.

Literacy Evolve Year 5 Teaching Guide

ISBN 978-0435035761

Authors: Rachael Sutherland, Rebecca Harris, Michael Lockwood

Series editor: Janice Pimm

Series Consultant: Michael Rosen

Illustrated by Luke Finlayson

Typeset by Phoenix Photosetting, Chatham, Kent

Printed in the UK by Ashford Colour Press

Acknowledgements

The publisher gratefully acknowledges permission to reproduce copyright material in this book:
Extract from 'Friend or Foe' Text © Michael Morpurgo, Egmont UK Ltd 1977; Extract from 'The Pied Piper of Hamelin' by Robert Browning; Extract from 'The Pied Piper of Hamelin' by The Brothers Grimm; Extract from 'The Children of Hamelin' by Pie Corbett taken from Writing Models Year 5, Pie Corbett, Copyright © 2009 Heinemann. Reproduced by permission of Taylor & Francis Books UK; 'I'm The Youngest In Our House …' reprinted from WOULDN'T YOU LIKE TO KNOW (Scholastic 1996) copyright © Michael Rosen 1996; 'Rodge Said …' reprinted from YOU TELL ME (Puffin 1981) copyright © Michael Rosen 1981; 'Harrybo' reprinted from THE HYPNOTISER (André Deutsch 1988) copyright © Michael Rosen 1988; 'Mary, Mary Magdalene', 'By St. Thomas Water', 'As I Went Down Zig-Zag', reprinted from COLLECTED POEMS FOR CHILDREN (Macmillan 1996) copyright © Charles Causley 1996.

The publisher would like to thank Egmont UK Ltd for illustrations by Trevor Stubley, from 'Friend or Foe' and Penguin Books Ltd for illustrations by Eve Garnett from 'The Family from One End Street'.

Adaptation of scenes from the film *The Book,* by Haydn Middleton.

We would like to thank Coppetts Wood Primary School, Winchcombe Abbey Primary, St Mary Magdalen's Catholic Primary, Dorridge Junior School, Fourlanesend CP School, Brookside Primary School, Archbishop of York's CE Jnr School, Lady Modiford's CofE School, Hursthead Jnr School, The Deans Primary School and St Peter's CE Primary School for their invaluable help in the development and trialling of this programme.

The author and publisher would like to thank the following individuals and organisations for permission to reproduce photographs:

© Alamy / Paul Bernhardt

Every effort has been made to contact copyright holders of material reproduced in this book. Any omissions will be rectified in subsequent printings if notice is given to the publishers.

To find the latest information about *Literacy Evolve* visit:

www.pearsonschools.co.uk/literacyevolve

Contents

Welcome to *Literacy Evolve*

"If all we mean by literacy is just being able to read one word after another, we're living in a terrible, impoverished world."

Michael Rosen

Sometimes literacy can feel like little more than reading one word after another. *Literacy Evolve* offers a more inspiring way to approach the subject. It is a whole-class resource for narrative and poetry with enjoyment at its heart. It has been influenced by the ideas of former Children's Laureate Michael Rosen and uses whole, 'real' novels, powerful short films and 'single-voice' poetry collections to ignite children's interest in communication and language. If this passion and enjoyment can be inspired at school, then children are likely to read more for pleasure in their own time which in turn will lead to a greater facility with language, increased vocabulary, critical-thinking, personal development and other benefits across the curriculum (UNESCO PISA Report, 2000).

The teaching support has been designed to help you teach literacy in a creative and exciting way. The notes are written by teachers who are passionate about literacy and are packed with ideas that will spark children's creativity and provide imaginative contexts in which to apply their developing literacy skills. The sessions aim to be lively and interactive with an emphasis on speaking and listening, talk for writing and drama. 'Open-ended' questions are used frequently to stimulate meaningful discussion and develop children's confidence in talking about books and ideas. Additionally, its use of film and highly visual books allows great scope for developing children's visual literacy skills.

The units seek to immerse the children in the stimulus piece and move from reading and analysing through to responding and writing. Word and sentence level skills are covered along the way as appropriate to the unit, though the expectation is that a separate spelling programme will also be in place. Assessment for learning practices are embedded throughout, content is matched to Assessment Focuses to help you with Assessing Pupils' Progress, and our interactive planner (I-Planner Online) allows you to track progress.

Welcome to *Literacy Evolve*

Literacy Evolve is correlated to all UK curricula including the new Proposed Primary Curriculum and the Renewed Primary Framework. At Year 5 there are 24 weeks of teaching divided into units of between 1 and 4 weeks. The teaching sessions are intended to last around 1 hour to 1 ½ hours, but they can be extended or contracted as appropriate to the needs of individual classes and timetables.

Progression is built in across the units and therefore, within the narrative or poetry section it is advisable to use the units in the numbered order. However, I-Planner Online allows you to reorder the units and customise them if you so wish.

Literacy Evolve is not a one-size-fits-all programme. I-Planner allows you to teach your way and according to the needs of your class. You can customise the lesson plans as you wish, including moving units around, changing the day-to-day detail of the weekly plans, allocating different independent tasks, evaluating children and changing your future plans according to assessments.

Read on to find out more about what *Literacy Evolve* has to offer.

Literacy Evolve components

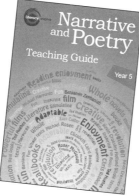

Meet the team

Michael Rosen (Series Consultant)

When I ask myself how I got into this world of children's books it all goes back to my mum and dad, who were teachers. One of the most amazing memories I have from my childhood was of when we were on a camping holiday in Yorkshire. Every night we gathered in the tent, my dad pumped up a little lamp and he read us the whole of *Great Expectations* with all the voices and actions. The voices and gestures live with me even now. It's this kind of power - literature in action - that I believe in. It's these 'Golden Moments' that teachers cherish. Every child is entitled to that level of engagement and delight that my father gave us.

A real 'Golden Moment' for me was when I was reading the story of Persephone to my 8 year-old daughter, when we came across the word 'pity'. Here is a difficult, abstract idea but when enacted in the Persephone myth it becomes accessible and concrete. Suddenly we were able to think of other examples of pity from her life and mine and also to juggle it with other abstract words like sympathy, compassion or callousness.

Literature is the most pleasurable way we have access to these difficult ideas, but we will never reach them if we quiz children too closely with closed-ended questions. Literature is a way of opening up a conversation between equals: there is no difference between my daughter's right to talk about 'pity' and mine. So here we have this enormous treasure house of literature stretching back thousands of years, giving us the greatest wisdom that the human race can put together, accessible to all.

Literacy Evolve has evolved out of the ideas that I'm expressing here, so I'm delighted to be a part of the project and hope that teachers and children will enjoy finding their way through its stories and poems. No-one involved in the project is claiming that this is an end in itself - what matters with reading and young people is that we get them hooked, and *Literacy Evolve* strikes me as a great way to do just that. It reaches out into that vast world of books that can never exhaust.

Rachael Sutherland

I have been passionate about the power of books, first as a Primary teacher, and then as a literacy consultant in South East London for 12 years. More recently I have rediscovered the joy of reading aloud to my own children. I currently juggle parenthood with work as a freelance writer, and have contributed to many projects for the Literacy Strategy, particularly *Early Literacy Support* and *Year 3 Literacy Support*. *Literacy Evolve* brings brilliant whole books to the heart of literacy teaching and it has been exciting to work on these materials.

Golden Moment

It was the last day of the Spring term and I had been reading *Krindlekrax* by Philip Ridley to my Year 5 class. They were so desperate to know how the story ended that they couldn't bear to wait all through the Easter break. They begged me to read on through playtime. I could hardly believe it - even those football-mad boys who just lived for their playtimes had got lost in the world of the book. It was magical, reading aloud as they hung on every word.

Meet the team

Rebecca Harris

I trained as a KS1 and Foundation Stage teacher but have ended up spending most of my career in KS2. I'm sure that the creative and practical way I was taught to approach learning with younger children has made my teaching in KS2 more successful. I started teaching part time at my present school in 2003 and I'm now the head there. Over the years I have seen many changes in teaching practices, but the one that has had the most impact on the children and their progress has been that of using film and drama to enhance the teaching of writing. The difficulty with this is how time-consuming it can be trawling through numerous films to find a clip to match a learning objective. It has been very exciting working on *Literacy Evolve* to help teachers have easy access to quality short films. This resource will save teachers hours of time.

Golden Moment

One of the children I was teaching had produced a fantastic story and I asked him what had helped him to achieve that. He explained that he had used visualisation and had played it through in his mind like a film; then it was simple, he explained, because we'd had so many lessons in how to put films into words. The success criteria was achieved: reading his story put the film he had visualised very clearly in my head. Isn't that the whole point of story writing?

Michael Lockwood

I was a teacher for nearly 10 years, specialising in KS2 and literacy. I've always believed in the power of whole texts read aloud to hook children into books, with or without the special effects. Since leaving the classroom, I've lectured in teacher training, working with the next generation of teachers to develop their strategies for bringing children and texts together. I've also been able to research and write about the teaching of English. In my most recent book, *Promoting Reading for Pleasure in the Primary School* (Sage 2008), I try to show teachers how they can inspire the reading habit and just how important that is. Poetry has always been a special interest of mine and the chance to work on this strand of Literacy Evolve was too good to miss.

Golden Moment

I was reading aloud Mildred Taylor's *Roll of Thunder, Hear My Cry* to a Year 6 class. I'd reached the climax of the novel where the storm in the title happens – and lo and behold the heavens opened outside and a real thunderstorm broke out. I've never had a more spellbound audience. Even the caretaker who was passing by stayed to listen!

Novels

"When a book is written, it's written whole. The point of a book is that it should be fun, it should be exciting, it should tell you more about the world around you, it should open your eyes and open your heart, it should make you joyful, it should make you sad — and you can't get this from just taking little snippets from it."

Michael Morpurgo

The joy of reading whole novels aloud to children is central to *Literacy Evolve*. As the stories spark their imagination and interest, children will feel more confident about reading for themselves – another book by the same author, or a story with a similar theme. As they listen to the story unfold and see characters develop, children are encouraged to ask questions and explore the answers for themselves. This is 'comprehension' in its truest sense.

The novels in *Literacy Evolve* have been selected by children's literature experts and trialled in classrooms across the country. They have been selected for their quality, power and teaching potential.

Literacy Evolve assumes that you will read the book to the children in the first instance and has time built in for reading during the sessions. (It is also recommended that teachers read the novel themselves before sharing in class.) If timetable restrictions occasionally mean that a book has to be read independently, simply written chapter summaries in I-Planner Online have been included for children who may have difficulty accessing the text for themselves.

Year 5 (P6) novels

Friend or Foe by Michael Morpurgo

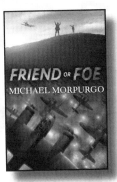

The Germans are bombing London and every day people are dying in the Blitz. Everyone hates them, especially David because they killed his father and caused him to be sent to the country to live with strangers. So when a German soldier rescues David and asks him for help, he is faced with a dilemma …

A classic novel with universal appeal from the master-storyteller, Michael Morpurgo.

Oranges in No Man's Land by Elizabeth Laird

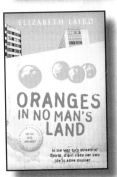

Ayesha lives in a battle-scarred building with her granny. Outside, the Lebanese civil war is ripping the city apart – and before long Ayesha herself is forced to make the forbidden journey across no man's land.

A serious but ultimately positive story by acclaimed author Elizabeth Laird about war, prejudice, courage and growing up.

Shortlisted for the Sheffield Award and winner of the Hull KS2 Award.

*Tales of the Family from One End Street** by Eve Garnett

There's never a dull moment in the lively Ruggles family. The seven children are experts at finding fun, adventure and mischief! The book's universal appeal still delights children 70 years after it was written and it is now also a fascinating insight into the values, traditions and culture of a former time.

Eve Garnett's classic book won the Carnegie when it was published and has recently been judged to be one of the 10 most important children's books of the last 70 years.

Winner of the Carnegie Medal, 1937.

* Tales of the Family from One End Street contains 6 of the 10 original stories from Family from One End Street.

Poetry Collections

"With the Literacy Evolve project, what we've got are poets talking about why they wrote a poem, how they wrote a poem and where they come from. So we get the possibility of the child engaging with the poet and the poem and that's very, very important."

Michael Rosen

Literacy Evolve doesn't offer just another yearly anthology of poetry. Instead, the whole collection is dedicated to the voice of one poet, such as Benjamin Zephaniah, Grace Nichols or Ted Hughes.

This 'single voice' collection approach means that children get to know the poets as individuals: they understand their views and their style. Additionally, the collections have a 'personal journal' feel to them, with the poets giving insights into their backgrounds and the inspiration behind their poems. All this helps to bring poetry to life for children and increases their understanding and enjoyment.

There are two poetry collections a year (both contained in a single 'flipover' volume).

"I think it's important that children look at and enjoy a volume of poetry by one poet; then they get the voice and they get the point of view. Rather than, you know, a hundred poems about hedgehogs . . . "

Roger McGough

Films

Literacy Evolve harnesses the power of film to engage children. Research (UKLA/PNS Report Raising Boys' Achievement in Writing, 2004) has shown that film can inspire even reluctant readers and writers to perform well. Short, whole films have been expertly sourced for *Literacy Evolve*. They have been chosen for their quality and teaching potential. They are all supplied on our Interactive Teaching Resource, meaning that they benefit from clear display, a whole range of annotation tools, the ability to create markers, and a saving facility.

Year 5 (P6) films

The Book

A young girl discovers a book in an old library while on on a school visit. It tells of a secret hidden in the library, a secret that is still protected by ghostly monks who want no one to find out.

A spooky and mysterious short film that uses camera trickery and suggestion to create a sense of tension.

Magik Circus

A young girl enters a circus tent where she stumbles across a genie in a lamp, who tries to entice the girl to be his assistant and help with a new trick he is working on. After a series of failed attempts to persuade her, the girl chooses a trick where the genie turns himself into an acrobatic flying frog, with great success for the girl, not so much for the genie.

A slick animation that has a lot of texture and detail, *Magik Circus* has a humorous and light-hearted feel. The story is told through actions and expressions without relying on dialogue.

News and adverts

Three factual clips that tackle the topic of animal extinction. The first is an extract from *BBC News* and shows the different elements a factual script contains. A segment from the popular children's news programme *Newsround* follows. Its youthful presenting style and exciting, colourful graphics contrast to the *BBC News* clip and show different presenting styles.

Finally, a short film from the Born Free Foundation charity appeals for people to adopt an endangered animal to help save it from extinction. The video's visual effects, camera work and language will all be key elements in the study of factual presentation scripts and their intended audience.

The stimulus materials

Unit stimuli

This chart shows the main stimulus pieces across *Literacy Evolve* Key Stage 2 (P4-P7) and how they are matched to units.

Year 3/P4

   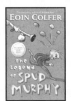  

Narrative Unit 1: *Storm* – novel (Settings)

Narrative Unit 2: *Dragon Slayer* – film (Myths and legends)

Narrative Unit 3: *Ottoline and the Yellow Cat* – novel (Mystery)

Narrative Unit 4: *The Legend of Spud Murphy* – novel (Author study)

Narrative Unit 5: *Dragon Slayer* – film (Play and film scripts)

Poetry Units 1, 2 and 3: Gina Douthwaite, Roger McGough

Year 4/P5

Narrative Unit 1: *Invasion* – novel (Historical settings)

Narrative Unit 2: *The Spiderwick Chronicles* – novel (Fantasy)

Narrative Unit 3: *Christophe's Story* – novel (Other cultures)

Narrative Unit 4: *Lard* – film (Issues)

Narrative Unit 5: *Bicho* – film (Play and film scripts)

Poetry Units 1 and 2: Grace Nichols, James Carter

Year 5/P6

Narrative Unit 1: *Friend or Foe* – novel (Author study)

Narrative Unit 2: *The Book* – film (Traditional stories)

Narrative Unit 3: *Oranges in No Man's Land* – novel (Other cultures)

Narrative Unit 4: *Tales of the Family from One End Street* – novel (Classic literature)

Narrative Unit 5: *Magik Circus* – film (Film narrative)

Narrative Unit 6: *News and adverts* – film (Media scripts)

Poetry Units 1, 2 and 3: Michael Rosen, Charles Causley

Year 6/P7

Narrative Unit 1: *Fantastic, Funny, Frightening!* – stories (Genres)

Narrative Unit 2: *Planet Prision* – multi-media text (Multi-modal reading)

Narrative Unit 3: *Millions* – novel (Author study)

Narrative Unit 4: *Eye of the Wolf* – novel (Narrative technique)

Narrative Unit 5: *Fantastic, Funny, Frightening!* – stories (Revision)

Poetry Units 1, 2 and 3: Benjamin Zephaniah, Ted Hughes

The teaching approach

Visual literacy
A focus on visual literacy skills gives children another access point to understanding and responding to the texts.

Open questions
Open-ended questions stimulate meaningful discussion and develop children's confidence in talking about books and ideas.

Active strategies and talk for writing
Talk for writing, speaking, listening and drama strategies mean that the children are active and engaged all through the lesson and are continually preparing for writing. The strategies are highlighted and a glossary is provided on page xvii.

Differentiation
Where appropriate, tasks are differentiated three ways, with three dots indicating tasks for the more able. Often the differentiation ideas are offered in the supporting T/TA notes on I-Planner Online.

Session 12

We are learning to ...	Resources
• use drama to explore characters • understand different points of view and how this affects characters' behaviour (PNS Strands 4.1, 7.2) **Assessment Focuses** AF (R): 3	*Lard* (film) PCM 4.11

Shared teaching
• Share the learning objectives.
• Review Thought Tracking from Session 11 to recap Jake's thoughts and motives in *Lard*.
• Recap the thinking point from Session 11. Take feedback.
• Organise a Forum Theatre activity to show how the other characters in the film felt. Explain that the film follows the main character Jake, but the children will focus on the viewpoint of the other characters.
• Watch the film again. Ask the children to nominate peers to act out the roles of the characters in the film: the two boys, Jake's mum, the neighbour, the old man, the young girl and the shopkeepers. The rest of the children act as directors and explain to the characters what they should do. Use props if appropriate.
• Guide the children while the Forum Theatre takes shape and remind them of the ground rules for large group work. If possible, film the activity to review in the plenary.
• After the Forum Theatre, use Hot-Seating to focus on the two boys. Show 'Quality questions' (PCM 4.11) as a prompt to ask the children playing those characters to explain how they felt and what they thought about what Jake did.

Independent and Guided
• In small groups, Hot-Seat the rest of the characters in *Lard*: Jake's mum, the shopkeepers, the young girl, the neighbour and the old man.
ooo Take turns to play a character and answer questions from the rest of the group to explain what they saw and what they thought about it.
oo As above. Focus on Jake's mum and the shopkeepers first. (TA+)
o As above. Use PCM 4.11 as a prompt. (T)

Plenary
• Remind the children that their actions can be perceived differently by different people, depending on their point of view.
• Recap the learning objectives.
• If you filmed the Forum Theatre activity, show the highlights.
• Discuss the viewpoints of the other characters in the film. *Were you surprised by what they thought? Have you changed your view of what happened in the film? How did the hot-seating help you explore the characters?*
• Explain that in Session 13, the children will look more closely at the other characters and what they know about them.

Assessment pointers
• S&L: drama activities will show how far the children can sustain roles and understand the characters.
• AF3 (R): the forum theatre and hot-seating activities show how well children can interpret information and events from different viewpoints.

Session 13

We are learning to ...	Resources
• explore shots, music, words and images in film • explore how film directors use film techniques • choose words and images for particular effects (PNS Strands 2.2, 8.3, 9.5) **Assessment Focuses** AF (R): 5, 6; AF (W): 1, 7	*Lard* (film) ITP 4.10, 4.11, 4.12 PCM 4.12

Shared teaching
• Show 'Film shots' (ITP 4.10) to recap film vocabulary learned in Year 3.
• Share the learning objectives. Explain that this session will focus on how the director made the film in order to convey meaning to the viewer, e.g. the choices made about what camera shots and music to use, how the characters should speak and look, etc.
• Watch *Lard* from the beginning to Marker 1. *What do you notice about the way the clip is filmed? How does the director portray the tall boy playing football?* Focus on the way the director films the ball rolling across the road. *Why is the ball rolling filmed at ground level? What effect does this have? What is the effect of the colour of the ball?*
• As an author how might you write about the ball rolling? Reflect on work from Phase 1 about expressive and figurative language. Encourage the children to suggest adverbs.
• Watch *Lard* from Marker 1 to Marker 2. Note the camera angles, the close-up of the boy's face and the way he walks towards Jake. *What is the effect of these shots?*
• Show 'How does Jake feel?' (ITP 4.11). Ask for words to describe how Jake felt about the ball while he watched the other boys playing. *Jake obviously wanted to play with the ball. Why? How does he feel when he is bouncing the ball? How does he feel after the ball is flattened?*

• Explain that you're going to put the film sequence into written words. Use Modelled Writing to create a model text or show 'The golden ball' (ITP 4.12) example text.
• Use Think Alouds to show your thought processes while developing the model text, e.g. *Jake was very excited about the ball ... how can I convey that? How could I describe the ball? What does it look like? Sound like?* Show or create your own model text.

Independent and Guided
• The children watch *Lard* from Marker 3 to Marker 4 and describe the scene in written words.
ooo Write a description of the incident in the shop from the moment Jake enters until he leaves.
oo As above. Use prompts from 'Jake's dilemma in the shop' (PCM 4.12) to structure writing. (T)
o As above. Use PCM 4.12 as a writing frame (TA)

Plenary
• Take feedback and ask for volunteers to share their writing.
• Recap the learning objectives and explain that just like a film director, an author makes choices to get the reader to think and feel certain things. *What tools can an author use?* (E.g. powerful vocabulary, suspense, descriptive and expressive language, etc.)
• Discuss the tools a film director has to work with. *How do music, sound, images and different camera shots change how you feel when watching a film?*

Assessment pointers
• AF5, 6 (R): shared discussions will indicate how far the children understand the effect an author's choice of language has on a reader.
• AF1, 7 (W): written outcomes show how far the children can write imaginatively and use effective vocabulary.

Narrative Unit 4: *Lard*

The teaching approach

The teaching approach

Objectives
Clear objectives for sharing with the class and evaluating against. Assessment Focuses are also clearly flagged.

PHASE 3: PLANNING AND WRITING A STORY WITH A DILEMMA (7 DAYS)

Session 14

We are learning to …	Resources
• plan writing using planning tools	ITP: (4.1)
• work together to plan writing (PNS Strands 9.1)	PCM: (4.1, 4.2)
Assessment Focuses	
AF (W): 3	

Shared teaching

Recall annotated 'Story mind map' (ITP 4.1). Remind the children of the work they did when they planned their oral stories. *How did the storymaker cards help you to plan?*

Share the learning objectives. Explain that the children are going to write a story with issues based on a structure like *Lord*, so that the ending opens up another issue or dilemma and leaves the main character on a cliffhanger.

Discuss what the story should include, e.g. a beginning, middle, end and twist.

Discuss the audience for the children's stories, e.g. their peer group, and the purpose of a story with a dilemma, e.g. to make people think carefully about the issues raised as well as to entertain.

As a starting point for ideas, read through the dilemmas collected on the Learning Wall and recall dilemmas in films and stories from earlier sessions.

Independent and Guided

The children plan in groups, pairs or individually, using a technique of their own choice, e.g. Mind Mapping, Improvisation, etc. Give the children time to explore dilemmas and solutions and provide support according to their needs.

Use 'Storymaker cards 1' (PCM 4.1) and 'Storymaker cards 2' (PCM 4.2) to plan a new dilemma story.
As above. (TA+)
As above. (T+)

Plenary

• Play Just a Minute. Talk Partners take turns to tell the rough sequence of their story.
• Encourage the children to give positive verbal feedback about what they liked in each other's story and why.
• Ask the children to give peer assessment, using thumbs up, down, or half way. *Has your partner got a clear idea of their own story with a dilemma?* Make a note of any thumbs down and support these children in Session 15.
• Recap the learning objectives. *How did you plan your story? Did anyone help you develop your ideas? How?*

Assessment pointers

• S&L: group or pair work will show how far the children can adopt group roles, drawing ideas together and promoting effective discussion.
• AF3 (W): peer assessment and independent planning work will show how far the children can generate imaginative ideas and structure their stories.

Session 15

We are learning to …	Resources
• plan writing using planning tools	ITP: 4.13
• choose words and images for particular effects (PNS Strands 9.1, 9.5)	PCM: (4.1, 4.2), 4.13, 4.14
Assessment Focuses	
AF (W): 3, 4, 7	

Shared teaching (1)

Share the learning objectives. Explain that in this session, the children will continue to develop plans for their stories with a dilemma. Explain that they will need to have a clear plan for your story and know the order in which things happen in the plot before you start writing.

Recap the notes made in the independent and guided activity in Session 14 and explain that the children are going to take these notes and develop a story plan.

Independent and Guided (1)

• The children work independently to complete 'Dilemma story planner' (PCM 4.13), using notes from 'Storymaker cards 1' (PCM 4.1) and 'Storymaker cards 2' (PCM 4.2). Encourage the children to add figurative and expressive language and adverbs to the plan, that they can use in their story.

Use PCM 4.13. Complete all sections, including the final 'Twist'.
As above. Provide support with the 'Vocabulary' column. (TA+)
As above. If necessary, allow the children to draw scenes from their story plan instead of writing. (T+)

Shared teaching (2)

Remind the children of the work they did on story structure in Session 10. *How did the director structure the film to make it interesting?*

• Show 'Story plan' (ITP 4.13). Ask for a volunteer to share their ideas from PCM 4.13. Model how to transfer these ideas onto the first screen of ITP 4.13, thinking about the order in which events happen. *What comes next, after I have opened my story and set the scene?*
• Discuss chapters in a story and how they are used. Explain that each step on ITP 4.13 could form a chapter.
• Model completing the second screen of ITP 4.13. Show the children how to use the Learning Wall and other sources to find interesting opening sentences and connectives to use.

Independent and Guided (2)

• The children use annotated PCM 4.13 to complete their 'Story plan' (PCM 4.14).

Complete PCM 4.14 and start thinking about openings and connectives to use in their story. (T)
As above, thinking about openings to use in their story.
As above, concentrating on completing their story plans. (TA+)

Plenary

• Talk Partners peer review each other's plans using thumbs up, down or half way. *Does the story build up to the most exciting part?* Allow the children time to respond to the feedback.
• Recap the learning objectives. *What opening sentences and connectives have you made a note of?*

Assessment pointers

• S&L: pair work will show how well the children can express and respond to opinions.
• AF3, 4, 7 (W): story plans will show how far the children can sequence and structure their stories.

Reference to the Interactive Teaching Resource
Interactive teaching pages which support and enliven your shared teaching are clearly referenced.

Teaching Assistant or Teacher notes
(T) or (TA) indicates the recommended support for each Independent Activity. A + sign indicates that additional notes are available on I-Planner Online.

Assessment Pointers
Assessment pointers identify relevant evidence for each Assessment Focus, including Speaking and Listening, and help with APP.

Assessment for Learning
Assessment for learning is embedded throughout, including peer review, self-review, marking ladders and success criteria.

Interactive Teaching Resource

The Interactive Teaching Resource (ITR) is the one-stop shop for all the supporting materials you will need to use *Literacy Evolve*. All resources are accessed using a 'player' which provides a range of annotation and editing tools.

The ITR contains:

- Films (up to three per year for Key Stage 2 (P4–P7))
- Videos of author interviews
- Videos of poetry performances by the original poet
- Additional stimulus materials (short stories, extracts, photos, artwork, audio, etc.)
- PDF versions of PCMs (editable versions can be found on I-Planner)
- A wealth of interactive teaching pages which structure and support your lesson in an engaging and interactive way

Navigating the DVD

The ITR is very simple to navigate. You will find references to the pages you require in the teaching notes. These are the Interactive Teaching Pages (ITPs).

To access your desired electronic resource:

1) Simply choose the unit that you are studying. This screen is broken down into columns, one for narrative units and one for poetry.

2) Once you have opened your chosen unit, you can then select the resource type that you require (as indicated in the lesson plans). From this screen you can access video resources, ITPs and electronic versions of PCMs. (Please note that the Storybooks option is only available for Key Stage 1 units.)

3) When you have clicked on the type of resource that you need, you can then select the specific ITP, film or PCM that you require by checking the relevant number and name of the resource against the lesson plan. Once clicked, the resource will load automatically and is ready to use. You can then navigate to the previous menus via the 'breadcrumb' navigation toolbar at the bottom of the screen.

Interactive Teaching Resource

Toolbar

At the bottom of any activity or video, you will find a toolbar full of features for you to use to annotate the screen.

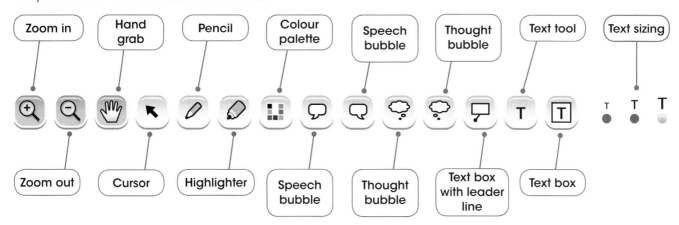

Film Tools (situated next to the annotation toolbar)

There are also a range of film tools available, including film markers, which let you add your own stop/start points to the film.

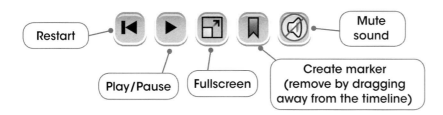

Printing

There is a print button located in the top right-hand corner of the player. Clicking this button will print the current page in view. You simply need to select the printer you wish to use from the list, as with your normal operating system.

Loading

To load a previously saved screen, simply click the open button in the top right-hand corner of the player. This will then bring up a list of locations on your computer. Find the file that you wish to use and open as normal. This new file will then replace the screen currently open.

Saving

To save your work on a current screen, click the save button located in the top right-hand corner of the player. You can then save the screen to a desired location on your computer.

Save

Exit

This button will close the program completely.

Assessment and I-Planner

Assessment for Learning practices are embedded through *Literacy Evolve*. Objectives are shared and reviewed at the beginning and end of every session. There are many opportunities for self- and peer-assessment, and success criteria are used for children to evaluate their work at each stage of its development.

All the lesson content is matched to Assessment Focuses. Assessment pointers are provided for every session which help you to identify what evidence has been identified for each Assessment Focus. This matches the approach of Assessing Pupil Progress and will help fulfil the requirements of this initiative.

I-Planner Online allows you to record evaluations of your children's learning, and from this will generate 'alerts' to remind you when your assessments are next relevant to your planning.

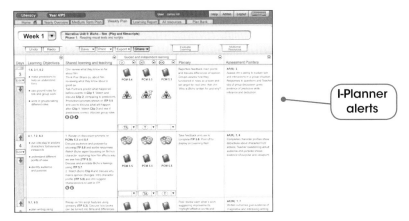

I-Planner alerts

In addition, I-Planner will create an ongoing Learning Report to summarise where the class are and which pupils you have identified as needing further support or extension.

Detailed information on how I-Planner works can be found on the Help tab of I-Planner.

The Learning Report is based on the Renewed Framework objectives. Underneath each of the Framework objectives are the *Literacy Evolve* 'We are learning to …' statements or learning objectives. These break down the broader Framework objectives into smaller chunks. You can use the Evaluate Learning feature in I-Planner Online to quickly assess these objectives and the Learning Report will then show at a glance how much progress your pupils are making towards the overall Framework objectives.

Teaching strategy glossary

Babble Gabble: The children work in pairs to retell a story they have just listened to. One child retells the story as fast as they can, whilst still including as much detail as possible, changing after a minute so their partner continues the tale.

Conscience Alley: One child takes on the role of the character whilst the other children create each side of the alley, putting forth their opposing views as the character walks down. The child in role listens to his 'conscience' before making a decision about the course of action to take.

Envoys: One member of each group moves between the other groups, sharing information and collecting ideas.

Expert Groups: Groups each focus on a specific subject, researching and discussing to become experts on it. (Leads to Jigsawing.)

Fortunately/Unfortunately: players take it in turns to tell a story which begins alternately with these words, e.g. unfortunately I lost my dinner money on the way to school. Fortunately I don't like school dinners!

Forum Theatre: A small group of children act out a scene, while the rest of the class work as directors.

Freeze Frame: A drama activity where the children use their bodies to form a still image to illustrate a specific incident or event.

Grammar Poetry: Groups try to make up nonsense sentences consisting of an adjective, noun and verb all beginning with the same letter or sound, e.g. angry aardvarks amble.

Hot-Seating: A drama technique where a child takes on the role of a character in the 'hot seat', while the other children ask the character either prepared or improvised questions.

Improvisation: A drama activity that is not planned in any way. The children take on roles and make up the dialogue, actions, etc. as they go along.

Jigsawing: Home groups are given a task to complete. Each member is then given a number and groups of children with the same number are formed (i.e. all the number 1s together) to undertake investigations, discuss their work and agree on the main points to report back to the home group.

Just a Minute: The children speak for one minute on a chosen subject, trying not to hesitate or repeat themselves.

Learning Wall: A place where key ideas, information and success criteria are stored in the classroom, so that children can easily refer to it throughout the sessions.

Mind Map: The children think of ideas about a particular topic, such as the personality traits of a character, the features of a story type, etc. Then they write down these ideas, usually in the form of a diagram.

Modelled Writing: The teacher models the writing process by orally rehearsing before writing, making and explaining out loud decisions and changes, while encouraging the children to share the writing process.

Rainbowing: Discussion is paused and each group is given a different colour. The class is reorganised into colour groups so that the children share ideas with children from other groups.

Role Play: The children take on the roles of different characters to act out a scene.

Role on the Wall: Key words and phrases are placed inside and outside an outline of a character, e.g. character's thoughts placed inside, other characters' opinions on the outside.

Signifier: A drama technique where a prop or item of clothing is used to signify a role being played.

Snowballing: Pairs discuss a subject then join with another pair to form a group and share ideas. Two groups then join together and so on until there is a whole-class discussion.

Statement Game: The children are given a set of cards on which statements are written. They then use the cards to discuss in groups or with a partner to decide how to categorise the statements.

Talk Partners: Pairs talk through and develop ideas together.

Teacher in Role: The teacher takes on the role of a character who is being focused on, in order to introduce, control or develop drama activities.

Think Alouds: Out loud, the teacher explains their thought processes during the writing process. This also includes aspects such as rereading the text to check for sense and making changes to the text, e.g. crossing out, improving words for effect.

Think-Pair-Share: The children are given think time, then talk though ideas with a partner, before sharing ideas with a larger group or the rest of the class.

Think Time: The children are given a brief amount of time to think about a question before answering.

Thought Tracking: The action in a novel or a film is frozen at a key moment and the thoughts of the character are spoken aloud, either by the child in role or by the rest of the group.

Two Stars and a Wish: When reviewing each other's work, the children identify two positive aspects and one negative aspect to feed back on.

Walking Bus: Music is played while the children walk around the classroom. When the music stops, the teacher asks a question which the children discuss with those nearest to them.

Word Tennis: In pairs, each child takes it in turn to say one word or phrase. This either makes up a continuous sentence or is used as a form of word association.

Understanding English, communication and languages curriculum progression

LATER	Narrative						Poetry		
	Unit 1 *Friend or Foe* (Author study)	Unit 2 *The Book* (Traditional stories)	Unit 3 *Oranges…* (Other Cultures)	Unit 4 *…One End Street* (Classic literature)	Unit 5 *Magik Circus* (Film narrative)	Unit 6 *News and adverts* (Media scripts)	Unit 1 Rosen/ Causley (Poetic voice)	Unit 2 Rosen/ Causley (Narrative)	Unit 3 Rosen/ Causley (Performance)
1. Speaking and listening									
Convey complex ideas, using different techniques for clarity and effect	✔	✔	✔	✔	✔	✔	✔	✔	✔
Select relevant ideas and use appropriate vocabulary to engage and maintain the interest of listeners	✔	✔	✔	✔	✔	✔	✔	✔	✔
Organise and adjust what they say, including the use of spoken standard English, according to the formality of the context, the needs of their listeners and any communication technology being used	✔	✔	✔	✔	✔	✔	✔	✔	✔
Evaluate their own and others' speech and identify how it varies				✔	✔	✔	✔	✔	✔
Sustain different roles, deal with disagreement and vary contributions in group discussion	✔	✔	✔	✔	✔	✔	✔	✔	✔
Extend and justify their opinions and ideas, building on what they have heard	✔	✔	✔	✔	✔	✔	✔	✔	✔
Use dialogue and discussion to build up and refine ideas, move groups on and reach agreement collaboratively	✔	✔	✔	✔	✔	✔	✔	✔	✔
To identify differences between spoken and written language, both on paper and on screen, taking account of context, purpose and audience.	✔	✔		✔		✔		✔	✔
2. Reading									
Use inference and deduction to understand layers of meaning	✔	✔	✔	✔	✔	✔		✔	✔
Make connections and comparisons between different parts of a text and with other texts they have read	✔	✔	✔	✔	✔	✔	✔	✔	✔
Verify the accuracy and reliability of information, including from online sources, detect bias and distinguish evidence from opinion									
Search for information using ICT and other methods and make choices about the appropriateness of the information	✔			✔					
Evaluate techniques used by writers and poets commenting on how effective they are	✔	✔	✔	✔	✔	✔	✔	✔	✔
Recognise and use some conventions for conveying meaning in moving-image and multimodal texts		✔			✔	✔			
Evaluate structural and organisational features, including the use of different presentational devices, layouts and combinations of formats, and their effects	✔	✔	✔	✔	✔	✔	✔	✔	✔

Understanding English, communication and languages curriculum progression

LATER	Narrative						Poetry		
	Unit 1 Friend or Foe (Author study)	Unit 2 The Book (Traditional stories)	Unit 3 Oranges… (Other Cultures)	Unit 4 …One End Street (Classic literature)	Unit 5 Magik Circus (Film narrative)	Unit 6 News and adverts (Media scripts)	Unit 1 Rosen/ Causley (Poetic voice)	Unit 2 Rosen/ Causley (Narrative)	Unit 3 Rosen/ Causley (Perform-ance)
Evaluate ideas and themes that broaden perspectives and extend thinking	✔	✔	✔	✔		✔	✔	✔	
Express and justify preferences by referring to the texts	✔	✔		✔		✔	✔	✔	✔
Identify the use of specialist vocabulary and of structures and techniques associated with different forms and purposes of writing	✔	✔		✔	✔	✔	✔	✔	
Critique views, opinions and arguments	✔								
Reflect on viewpoints in narratives and distinguish between those of the characters and those of the author	✔	✔	✔	✔	✔	✔	✔	✔	✔
3. Writing									
Plan, create, shape and review their work, knowing when and how to improve it including the use of ICT	✔	✔	✔	✔	✔	✔	✔	✔	✔
Select form, content, style and vocabulary to suit particular purposes and readers	✔	✔	✔	✔	✔	✔	✔	✔	✔
Combine written text and illustration, moving image and sound, integrating different effects to add power to the words and meanings					✔	✔			
Synthesise ideas using ICT by combining a variety of information from different sources									
Communicate and collaborate with others remotely and in locations beyond the school by selecting and using appropriate ICT									
Use features of layout, presentation and organisation effectively in written and on-screen media		✔		✔	✔		✔		
Understand how paragraphs, bullets, hyperlinks, screen layout and headings are used to organise and link ideas, and to use these in their own work	✔	✔	✔	✔	✔	✔			
Explore how ideas are linked within and between sentences	✔	✔	✔	✔	✔	✔			
Function of punctuation within sentences and how to use it to clarify structure and development in what they write	✔	✔	✔	✔	✔	✔			
Recognise and apply common spelling patterns for regular and irregular words, using conventions and spellchecking techniques as well as their knowledge of the origins of words and how spelling has changed over time					✔		✔		
Gain fluency in handwriting and keyboard use		✔		✔	✔	✔	✔	✔	

Curriculum Correlation – Primary Framework

LATER	Narrative						Poetry		
	Unit 1 Friend or Foe (Author study)	Unit 2 The Book (Traditional stories)	Unit 3 Oranges… (Other Cultures)	Unit 4 …One End Street (Classic literature)	Unit 5 Magik Circus (Film narrative)	Unit 6 News and adverts (Media scripts)	Unit 1 Rosen/ Causley (Poetic voice)	Unit 2 Rosen/ Causley (Narrative)	Unit 3 Rosen/ Causley (Perform-ance)
1. Speaking									
Tell a story using notes designed to cue techniques, such as repetition, recap and humour	✔	✔			✔				
Present a spoken argument, sequencing points logically, defending views with evidence and making use of persuasive language									
Use and explore different question types and different ways words are used, including in formal and informal contexts	✔	✔			✔		✔		
2. Listening and responding									
Identify different question types and evaluate impact on audience									
Identify some different aspects of talk which vary between formal and informal occasions				✔					
Analyse the use of persuasive language									
3. Group discussion and interaction									
Plan and manage a group task over time using different levels of planning	✔					✔			
Understand different ways to take the lead and support others in groups	✔					✔			
Understand the process of decision making									
4. Drama									
Reflect on how working in role helps to explore complex issues	✔	✔	✔	✔	✔		✔	✔	
Perform a scripted scene making use of dramatic conventions		✔	✔			✔		✔	✔
Use and recognise the impact of theatrical effects in drama						✔			✔
5. Word recognition (objectives covered by the end of Year 2)									
6. Word structure and spelling									
Spell words containing unstressed vowels									
Know and use less common prefixes and suffixes, e.g. im-, ir, -ian									
Group and classify words according to their spelling patterns and their meanings							✔		
7. Understanding and interpreting texts									
Make notes on and use evidence from across a text to explain events or ideas	✔	✔	✔	✔	✔	✔	✔	✔	
Infer authors' perspectives from what is written and from what is implied	✔	✔	✔	✔	✔	✔			
Compare different types of narrative and information texts and identify how they are structured	✔	✔		✔	✔	✔			

LATER	Narrative						Poetry		
	Unit 1 Friend or Foe (Author study)	Unit 2 The Book (Traditional stories)	Unit 3 Oranges... (Other Cultures)	Unit 4 ...One End Street (Classic literature)	Unit 5 Magik Circus (Film narrative)	Unit 6 News and adverts (Media scripts)	Unit 1 Rosen/ Causley (Poetic voice)	Unit 2 Rosen/ Causley (Narrative)	Unit 3 Rosen/ Causley (Perform-ance)
Distinguish between everyday use of words and their subject-specific use									
Explore how authors use language for comic and dramatic effects	✔	✔	✔	✔	✔	✔	✔	✔	
8. Engaging with and responding to texts									
Reflect on reading habits and preferences and plan personal reading goals	✔		✔	✔					
Compare the usefulness of techniques such as visualisation, prediction, empathy in exploring the meaning of texts	✔	✔	✔	✔	✔			✔	
Compare how a common theme is presented in poetry, prose and other genres		✔				✔			
9. Creating and shaping texts									
Reflect independently and critically on own writing and edit and improve it	✔	✔	✔	✔	✔	✔	✔	✔	✔
Experiment with different narrative forms and styles to write their own stories	✔	✔	✔	✔	✔			✔	
Adapt non-narrative forms and styles to write fiction or factual texts, including poems							✔	✔	✔
Vary pace and develop viewpoint through the use of direct and reported speech, portrayal of action, selection of detail	✔	✔	✔	✔	✔				
Create multi-layered texts, including use of hyperlinks, linked with web pages									
10. Text structure and organisation									
Experiment with the order of sections and paragraphs to achieve different effects				✔		✔			
Change the order of material within a paragraph, moving the topic sentence									
11. Sentence structure and punctuation									
Adapt sentence construction to different text types, purposes and readers		✔	✔	✔	✔	✔			
Punctuate sentences accurately, including use of speech marks and apostrophes	✔	✔	✔	✔	✔	✔	✔		
12. Presentation									
Adapt handwriting for specific purposes, e.g. printing, use of italics		✔							
Use a range of ICT programs to present texts, making informed choices of which electronic tools to use for different purposes		✔			✔		✔		

Curriculum Correlation – Wales

The National Curriculum for Wales, English correlation chart

Wales Key Stage 2 Programme of Study	Unit 1 *Friend or Foe* (Author study)	Unit 2 *The Book* (Traditional stories)	Unit 3 *Oranges…* (Other Cultures)	Unit 4 *…One End Street* (Classic literature)	Unit 5 *Magik Circus* (Film narrative)	Unit 6 *News and adverts* (Media scripts)	Unit 1 Rosen/ Causley (Poetic voice)	Unit 2 Rosen/ Causley (Narrative)	Unit 3 Rosen/ Causley (Perform-ance)
Skills Pupils should be given opportunities to:									
1. listen and view attentively, responding to a wide range of communication	✔	✔	✔	✔	✔	✔	✔	✔	✔
2. identify key points and follow up ideas through question and comment, developing response to others in order to learn through talk	✔	✔	✔	✔	✔	✔	✔	✔	✔
3. communicate clearly and confidently, expressing opinions, adapting talk to audience and purpose, using appropriate gesture, intonation and register in order to engage the listener	✔	✔	✔	✔	✔	✔	✔	✔	✔
4. develop their awareness of the social conventions of conversation and discussion	✔	✔	✔	✔	✔	✔	✔	✔	✔
5. develop their ability to use a range of sentence structures and vocabulary with precision, including terminology that allows them to discuss their work	✔	✔	✔	✔	✔	✔	✔	✔	✔
6. develop their understanding of when it is necessary to use standard English, and use formal and informal language appropriately				✔		✔	✔	✔	✔
7. evaluate their own and others' talk and drama activities and develop understanding of how to improve, considering how speakers adapt their vocabulary, tone, pace and style to suit a range of situations.	✔	✔	✔	✔	✔	✔	✔	✔	✔
Range Pupils should be given opportunities to develop their oral skills through:									
1. seeing and hearing different people talking, including people with different dialects	✔			✔		✔	✔	✔	✔
2. experiencing and responding to a variety of stimuli and ideas: visual, audio and written	✔	✔	✔	✔	✔	✔	✔	✔	✔
3. communicating for a range of purposes, *e.g. presenting information, expressing opinions, explaining ideas, questioning, conveying feelings, persuading*	✔	✔	✔	✔	✔	✔	✔	✔	✔
4. speaking and listening individually, in pairs, in groups and as members of a class	✔	✔	✔	✔	✔	✔	✔	✔	✔
5. using a variety of methods to present ideas, including ICT, *e.g. drama approaches, discussion and debate*	✔	✔	✔	✔	✔	✔	✔	✔	✔

Curriculum Correlation – Wales

The National Curriculum for Wales, English correlation chart

Wales Key Stage 2 Programme of Study	Unit 1 *Friend or Foe* (Author study)	Unit 2 *The Book* (Traditional stories)	Unit 3 *Oranges...* (Other Cultures)	Unit 4 *...One End Street* (Classic literature)	Unit 5 *Magik Circus* (Film narrative)	Unit 6 *News and adverts* (Media scripts)	Unit 1 Rosen/Causley (Poetic voice)	Unit 2 Rosen/Causley (Narrative)	Unit 3 Rosen/Causley (Perform-ance)
6. presenting, talking and performing for a variety of audiences	✔	✔	✔	✔	✔	✔	✔	✔	✔
7. increasing their confidence in language use by drawing on their knowledge of English, Welsh and other languages				✔	✔	✔			
8. engaging in activities that focus on words, their derivation, meanings, choice and impact.		✔	✔	✔	✔	✔	✔	✔	✔
Reading Pupils should be given opportunities to:									
1. develop phonic, graphic and grammatical knowledge, word recognition and contextual understanding within a balanced and coherent programme	✔	✔	✔	✔		✔	✔	✔	✔
2. develop their ability to read with fluency, accuracy, understanding and enjoyment	✔	✔	✔	✔		✔	✔	✔	✔
3. read in different ways for different purposes, including:	✔	✔	✔	✔	✔	✔	✔	✔	✔
• skimming, scanning and detailed reading	✔		✔	✔					
• using prediction, inference and deduction	✔	✔	✔	✔	✔				
• distinguishing between fact and opinion, bias and objectivity in what they read/view						✔			
4. recognise and understand the characteristics of different genres in terms of language, structure and presentation	✔	✔	✔	✔	✔	✔	✔	✔	✔
5. consider what they read / view, responding orally and in writing to the ideas, vocabulary, style, presentation and organisation of image and language, and be able to select evidence to support their views	✔	✔	✔	✔	✔	✔	✔	✔	✔
6a. use a range of appropriate information retrieval strategies including ICT, *e.g. the alphabet, indexes and catalogues*	✔		✔	✔					
6b. retrieve and collate information and ideas from a range of sources including printed, visual, audio, media, ICT and drama in performance	✔		✔	✔		✔			
7. use the knowledge gained from reading to develop their understanding of the structure, vocabulary, grammar and punctuation of English, and of how these clarify meaning	✔	✔	✔	✔		✔			

The National Curriculum for Wales, English correlation chart

Wales Key Stage 2 Programme of Study	Unit 1 Friend or Foe (Author study)	Unit 2 The Book (Traditional stories)	Unit 3 Oranges... (Other Cultures)	Unit 4 ...One End Street (Classic literature)	Unit 5 Magik Circus (Film narrative)	Unit 6 News and adverts (Media scripts)	Unit 1 Rosen/Causley (Poetic voice)	Unit 2 Rosen/Causley (Narrative)	Unit 3 Rosen/Causley (Performance)
8. consider how texts change when they are adapted for different media and audiences.		✔			✔		✔	✔	✔
Range Pupils should be given opportunities to develop their reading / viewing skills through:									
1. becoming enthusiastic and reflective readers	✔	✔	✔	✔	✔	✔	✔	✔	✔
2. reading individually and collaboratively	✔	✔	✔	✔	✔	✔	✔	✔	✔
3. experiencing and responding to a wide range of texts that include:	✔	✔	✔	✔	✔	✔	✔	✔	✔
• information, reference and other non-literary texts, including print, media, moving image and computer-based materials	✔		✔	✔	✔	✔			
• poetry, prose and drama, both traditional and contemporary	✔	✔	✔	✔	✔		✔	✔	✔
• texts with a Welsh dimension and texts from other cultures		✔	✔		✔				
4. reading / viewing extracts and complete texts:	✔	✔	✔	✔	✔	✔	✔	✔	✔
• with challenging subject matter that broadens perspectives and extends thinking, *e.g. environmental issues, sustainability, animal rights, healthy eating*	✔		✔			✔			
• with a variety of structural and organisational features	✔	✔	✔	✔	✔	✔	✔	✔	✔
• that show quality and variety in language use	✔	✔	✔	✔	✔	✔	✔	✔	✔
• that reflect the diversity of society in the twenty-first century			✔				✔	✔	✔
• that reflect individual pupils' personal choice of reading matter.	✔			✔					
Writing Pupils should be given opportunities to communicate in writing and to:									
1. use the characteristic features of literary and non-literary texts in their own writing, adapting their style to suit the audience and purpose	✔	✔	✔	✔	✔	✔	✔	✔	✔
2. use a range of sentence structures, linking them coherently and developing the ability to use paragraphs effectively	✔	✔	✔	✔	✔	✔			
3. use punctuation to clarify meaning including full stop, exclamation and question marks, comma, apostrophe, bullet points, speech marks	✔	✔	✔	✔	✔	✔			

The National Curriculum for Wales, English correlation chart

Wales Key Stage 2 Programme of Study	Unit 1 *Friend or Foe* (Author study)	Unit 2 *The Book* (Traditional stories)	Unit 3 *Oranges...* (Other Cultures)	Unit 4 *...One End Street* (Classic literature)	Unit 5 *Magik Circus* (Film narrative)	Unit 6 *News and adverts* (Media scripts)	Unit 1 *Rosen/ Causley* (Poetic voice)	Unit 2 *Rosen/ Causley* (Narrative)	Unit 3 *Rosen/ Causley* (Performance)
4. choose and use appropriate vocabulary	✔	✔	✔	✔	✔	✔	✔	✔	✔
5. use the standard forms of English: nouns, pronouns, adjectives, adverbs, prepositions, connectives and verb tenses	✔	✔		✔	✔	✔			
6. develop and use a variety of strategies to enable them to spell correctly				✔	✔		✔		
7. use appropriate vocabulary and terminology to consider and evaluate their own work and that of others	✔	✔	✔	✔	✔	✔	✔	✔	✔
8. draft and improve their work, using ICT as appropriate, to:	✔	✔	✔	✔	✔	✔	✔	✔	✔
• plan	✔	✔	✔	✔	✔	✔	✔	✔	✔
• draft	✔	✔	✔	✔	✔	✔	✔	✔	✔
• revise	✔	✔	✔	✔	✔	✔	✔	✔	✔
• proofread	✔		✔	✔	✔			✔	
• prepare a final copy		✔		✔	✔		✔	✔	✔
9. present writing appropriately:	✔	✔	✔	✔	✔	✔	✔	✔	✔
• developing legible handwriting		✔		✔					
• using appropriate features of layout and presentation, including ICT.		✔		✔	✔	✔	✔	✔	✔
Range Pupils should be given opportunities to develop their writing skills through:									
1. writing for a range of purposes, *e.g. to entertain, report, inform, instruct, explain, persuade, recount, describe, imagine and to generate ideas*	✔	✔	✔	✔	✔	✔	✔	✔	✔
2. writing for a range of real or imagined audiences	✔	✔	✔	✔	✔	✔	✔	✔	✔
3. writing in a range of forms	✔	✔	✔	✔	✔	✔	✔	✔	✔
4. writing in response to a wide range of stimuli: visual, audio and written.	✔	✔	✔	✔	✔	✔	✔	✔	✔

Curriculum Correlation – NI

The Northern Ireland Curriculum, Language and Literacy correlation chart

Teachers should enable pupils to develop knowledge, understanding and skills in:	Unit 1 Friend or Foe (Author study)	Unit 2 The Book (Traditional stories)	Unit 3 Oranges… (Other Cultures)	Unit 4 …One End Street (Classic literature)	Unit 5 Magik Circus (Film narrative)	Unit 6 News and adverts (Media scripts)	Unit 1 Rosen/ Causley (Poetic voice)	Unit 2 Rosen/ Causley (Narrative)	Unit 3 Rosen/ Causley (Perform-ance)
Talking and Listening Pupils should be enabled to:									
listen and respond to a range of fiction, poetry, drama and media texts through the use of traditional and digital resources	✔	✔	✔	✔	✔	✔	✔	✔	✔
tell, retell and interpret stories based on memories, personal experiences, literature, imagination and the content of the curriculum	✔	✔	✔	✔	✔		✔	✔	✔
participate in group and class discussions for a variety of curricular purposes	✔	✔	✔	✔	✔	✔	✔	✔	✔
know, understand and use the conventions of group discussion	✔	✔	✔	✔	✔	✔	✔	✔	✔
share, respond to and evaluate ideas, arguments and points of view and use evidence or reason to justify opinions, actions or proposals	✔	✔	✔	✔	✔	✔	✔	✔	✔
formulate, give and respond to guidance, directions and instructions	✔	✔	✔	✔	✔	✔	✔	✔	✔
participate in a range of drama activities across the curriculum	✔	✔	✔	✔	✔	✔	✔	✔	✔
improvise a scene based on experience, imagination, literature, media and/or curricular topics	✔	✔	✔	✔	✔	✔	✔	✔	
describe and talk about real experiences and imaginary situations and about people, places, events and artefacts	✔	✔	✔	✔	✔	✔	✔	✔	✔
prepare and give a short oral presentation to a familiar group, showing an awareness of audience and including the use of multimedia presentations	✔	✔	✔		✔	✔	✔	✔	✔
identify and ask appropriate questions to seek information, views and feelings	✔	✔	✔	✔	✔	✔	✔		
talk with people in a variety of formal and informal situations	✔	✔	✔	✔	✔	✔	✔		✔
use appropriate quality of speech and voice, speaking audibly and varying register, according to the purpose and audience	✔	✔	✔	✔	✔	✔	✔	✔	✔
read aloud, inflecting appropriately, to express thoughts and feelings and emphasise the meaning of what they have read	✔	✔	✔	✔	✔	✔	✔	✔	✔
recognise and discuss features of spoken language, including formal and informal language, dialect and colloquial speech.	✔	✔	✔	✔	✔	✔	✔	✔	✔
Reading Pupils should be enabled to:									

Curriculum Correlation – NI

The Northern Ireland Curriculum, Language and Literacy correlation chart

Teachers should enable pupils to develop knowledge, understanding and skills in:	Unit 1 *Friend or Foe* (Author study)	Unit 2 *The Book* (Traditional stories)	Unit 3 *Oranges...* (Other Cultures)	Unit 4 *...One End Street* (Classic literature)	Unit 5 *Magik Circus* (Film narrative)	Unit 6 *News and adverts* (Media scripts)	Unit 1 Rosen/ Causley (Poetic voice)	Unit 2 Rosen/ Causley (Narrative)	Unit 3 Rosen/ Causley (Performance)
participate in modelled, shared, paired and guided reading experiences	✔	✔	✔	✔	✔		✔	✔	✔
read, explore, understand and make use of a wide range of traditional and digital texts	✔	✔	✔	✔	✔		✔	✔	✔
engage in sustained, independent and silent reading for enjoyment and information	✔			✔					
extend the range of their reading and develop their own preferences	✔	✔		✔			✔	✔	✔
use traditional and digital sources to locate, select, evaluate and communicate information relevant for a particular task	✔			✔		✔			
represent their understanding of texts in a range of ways, including visual, oral, dramatic and digital	✔	✔	✔	✔	✔	✔	✔	✔	✔
consider, interpret and discuss texts, exploring the ways in which language can be manipulated in order to affect the reader or engage attention	✔	✔	✔	✔	✔	✔	✔	✔	✔
begin to be aware of how different media present information, ideas and events in different ways	✔	✔			✔	✔	✔	✔	✔
justify their responses logically, by inference, deduction and/or reference to evidence within the text	✔	✔	✔	✔	✔	✔	✔	✔	✔
reconsider their initial response to texts in the light of insight and information which emerge subsequently from their reading				✔				✔	
read aloud to the class or teacher from prepared texts, including those composed by themselves, using inflection to assist meaning	✔	✔	✔	✔		✔	✔	✔	✔
use a range of cross-checking strategies to read unfamiliar words in texts	✔		✔	✔					
use a variety of reading skills for different reading purposes.	✔	✔	✔	✔			✔	✔	✔
Writing Pupils should be enabled to:									
participate in modelled, shared, guided and independent writing, including composing onscreen	✔	✔	✔	✔	✔	✔	✔	✔	✔
discuss various features of layout in texts and apply these, as appropriate, within their own writing	✔	✔			✔	✔	✔	✔	✔
experiment with rhymes, rhythms, verse structure and all kinds of word play and dialect				✔			✔	✔	✔

Curriculum Correlation – NI

The Northern Ireland Curriculum, Language and Literacy correlation chart

Teachers should enable pupils to develop knowledge, understanding and skills in:	Unit 1 Friend or Foe (Author study)	Unit 2 The Book (Traditional stories)	Unit 3 Oranges… (Other Cultures)	Unit 4 …One End Street (Classic literature)	Unit 5 Magik Circus (Film narrative)	Unit 6 News and adverts (Media scripts)	Unit 1 Rosen/ Causley (Poetic voice)	Unit 2 Rosen/ Causley (Narrative)	Unit 3 Rosen/ Causley (Perform- ance)
write for a variety of purposes and audiences, selecting, planning and using appropriate style and form	✔	✔	✔	✔	✔	✔	✔	✔	✔
use the skills of planning, revising and redrafting to improve their writing, including that which they have composed digitally	✔	✔	✔	✔	✔	✔	✔	✔	✔
express thoughts, feelings and opinions in imaginative and factual writing	✔	✔	✔	✔	✔	✔	✔	✔	✔
use a variety of stylistic features to create mood and effect	✔	✔	✔	✔	✔	✔	✔	✔	✔
begin to formulate their own personal style	✔	✔	✔	✔	✔	✔	✔	✔	✔
create, organise, refine and present ideas using traditional and digital means, combining text, sound or graphics	✔	✔			✔	✔		✔	
understand the differences between spoken and written language	✔	✔	✔	✔	✔	✔		✔	✔
use a variety of skills to spell words correctly			✔		✔		✔		
develop increasing competence in the use of grammar and punctuation to create clarity of meaning	✔	✔	✔	✔	✔	✔		✔	
develop a swift and legible style of handwriting.									

Curriculum Correlation – Scotland

The Curriculum for Excellence, Literacy and English correlation chart

SECOND	Unit 1 *Friend or Foe* (Author study)	Unit 2 *The Book* (Traditional stories)	Unit 3 *Oranges…* (Other Cultures)	Unit 4 *…One End Street* (Classic literature)	Unit 5 *Magik Circus* (Film narrative)	Unit 6 *News and adverts* (Media scripts)	Unit 1 Rosen / Causley (Poetic voice)	Unit 2 Rosen / Causley (Narrative)	Unit 3 Rosen / Causley (Performance)
Experiences and Outcomes The development of literacy skills plays an important role in all learning.									
I develop and extend my literacy skills when I have opportunities to:									
– communicate, collaborate and build relationships	✔	✔	✔	✔	✔	✔	✔	✔	✔
– reflect on and explain my literacy and thinking skills, using feedback to help me improve and sensitively provide useful feedback for others	✔	✔	✔	✔	✔	✔	✔	✔	✔
– engage with and create a wide range of texts in different media, taking advantage of the opportunities offered by ICT	✔	✔	✔	✔	✔	✔	✔	✔	✔
– develop my understanding of what is special, vibrant and valuable about my own and other cultures and their languages		✔	✔	✔					
– explore the richness and diversity of language, how it can affect me, and the wide range of ways in which I and others can be creative	✔	✔	✔	✔	✔	✔	✔	✔	✔
– extend and enrich my vocabulary through listening, talking, watching and reading.	✔	✔	✔	✔	✔	✔	✔	✔	✔
In developing my English language skills:									
– I engage with a wide range of texts and am developing an appreciation of the richness and breadth of Scotland's literary and linguistic heritage	✔	✔	✔	✔	✔	✔	✔	✔	✔
– I enjoy exploring and discussing word patterns and text structures.	✔	✔	✔	✔	✔	✔	✔	✔	✔
Listening and talking Enjoyment and choice – within a motivating and challenging environment, developing an awareness of the relevance of texts in my life									
I regularly select and listen to or watch texts which I enjoy and find interesting, and I can explain why I prefer certain sources.	✔	✔		✔	✔		✔	✔	✔
I regularly select subject, purpose, format and resources to create texts of my choice. *LIT 1-01a / LIT 2-01a*				✔		✔		✔	✔
Tools for listening and talking – to help me when interacting or presenting within and beyond my place of learning									

Curriculum Correlation – Scotland

The Curriculum for Excellence, Literacy and English correlation chart

SECOND	Unit 1 Friend or Foe (Author study)	Unit 2 The Book (Traditional stories)	Unit 3 Oranges... (Other Cultures)	Unit 4 ...One End Street (Classic literature)	Unit 5 Magik Circus (Film narrative)	Unit 6 News and adverts (Media scripts)	Unit 1 Rosen / Causley (Poetic voice)	Unit 2 Rosen / Causley (Narrative)	Unit 3 Rosen / Causley (Performance)
When I engage with others, I can respond in ways appropriate to my role, show that I value others' contributions and use these to build on thinking. *LIT 2-02a*	✔	✔	✔	✔	✔	✔	✔	✔	✔
I can recognise how the features of spoken language can help in communication, and I can use what I learn.	✔	✔	✔	✔	✔	✔	✔	✔	✔
I can recognise different features of my own and others' spoken language. *ENG 2-03a*	✔			✔	✔	✔	✔		
Finding and using information – when listening to, watching and talking about texts with increasingly complex ideas, structures and specialist vocabulary									
As I listen or watch, I can identify and discuss the purpose, main ideas and supporting detail contained within the text, and use this information for different purposes. *LIT 2-04a*	✔	✔	✔	✔	✔	✔	✔	✔	✔
As I listen or watch, I can make notes, organise these under suitable headings and use these to understand ideas and information and create new texts, using my own words as appropriate. *LIT 2-05a*									
I can select ideas and relevant information, organise these in an appropriate way for my purpose and use suitable vocabulary for my audience. *LIT 2-06a*	✔	✔	✔	✔	✔	✔	✔	✔	✔
Understanding, analysing and evaluating – investigating and/or appreciating texts with increasingly complex ideas, structures and specialist vocabulary for different purposes									
I can show my understanding of what I listen to or watch by responding to literal, inferential, evaluative and other types of questions, and by asking different kinds of questions of my own. *LIT 2-07a*	✔	✔	✔	✔	✔	✔	✔	✔	✔
To help me develop an informed view, I can distinguish fact from opinion, and I am learning to recognise when my sources try to influence me and how useful these are. *LIT 2-08a*									

The Curriculum for Excellence, Literacy and English correlation chart

SECOND	Unit 1 Friend or Foe (Author study)	Unit 2 The Book (Traditional stories)	Unit 3 Oranges... (Other Cultures)	Unit 4 ...One End Street (Classic literature)	Unit 5 Magik Circus (Film narrative)	Unit 6 News and adverts (Media scripts)	Unit 1 Rosen / Causley (Poetic voice)	Unit 2 Rosen / Causley (Narrative)	Unit 3 Rosen / Causley (Perform-ance)
Creating texts – applying the elements others use to create different types of short and extended texts with increasingly complex ideas, structures and vocabulary									
When listening and talking with others for different purposes, I can:	✔	✔	✔	✔	✔	✔	✔	✔	✔
– share information, experiences and opinions	✔	✔	✔	✔	✔	✔	✔	✔	✔
– explain processes and ideas	✔	✔	✔	✔	✔	✔	✔	✔	✔
– identify issues raised and summarise main points or findings	✔	✔	✔	✔	✔	✔	✔	✔	✔
– clarify points by asking questions or by asking others to say more. LIT 2-09a	✔	✔	✔	✔	✔	✔	✔	✔	✔
I am developing confidence when engaging with others within and beyond my place of learning. I can communicate in a clear, expressive way and I am learning to select and organise resources independently.	✔	✔	✔	✔	✔	✔	✔	✔	✔
Reading **Enjoyment and choice** – within a motivating and challenging environment, developing an awareness of the relevance of texts in my life									
I regularly select and read, listen to or watch texts which I enjoy and find interesting, and I can explain why I prefer certain texts and authors. *LIT 1-11a / LIT 2-11a*	✔	✔		✔	✔		✔		
Tools for reading – to help me use texts with increasingly complex or unfamiliar ideas, structures and vocabulary within and beyond my place of learning									
Through developing my knowledge of context clues, punctuation, grammar and layout, I can read unfamiliar texts with increasing fluency, understanding and expression.	✔	✔	✔	✔		✔			
I can select and use a range of strategies and resources before I read, and as I read, to make meaning clear and give reasons for my selection. *LIT 2-13a*						✔			
Finding and using information – when reading and using fiction and non-fiction texts with increasingly complex ideas, structures and specialist vocabulary									

Curriculum Correlation – Scotland

The Curriculum for Excellence, Literacy and English correlation chart

SECOND	Unit 1 Friend or Foe (Author study)	Unit 2 The Book (Traditional stories)	Unit 3 Oranges… (Other Cultures)	Unit 4 …One End Street (Classic literature)	Unit 5 Magik Circus (Film narrative)	Unit 6 News and adverts (Media scripts)	Unit 1 Rosen / Causley (Poetic voice)	Unit 2 Rosen / Causley (Narrative)	Unit 3 Rosen / Causley (Performance)
Using what I know about the features of different types of texts, I can find, select and **sort** information from a variety of sources and use this for different purposes. *LIT 2-14a*	✔			✔	✔	✔			
I can make notes, organise them under suitable headings and use them to understand information, develop my thinking, explore problems and create new texts, using my own words as appropriate. *LIT 2-15a*									
Understanding, analysing and evaluating – investigating and/or appreciating fiction and non-fiction texts with increasingly complex ideas, structures and specialist vocabulary for different purposes									
To show my understanding across different areas of learning, I can identify and consider the purpose and main ideas of a text and use supporting detail. *LIT 2-16a*	✔	✔	✔	✔	✔	✔	✔	✔	✔
To show my understanding, I can respond to literal, inferential and evaluative questions and other close reading tasks and can create different kinds of questions of my own. *ENG 2-17a*	✔	✔	✔	✔	✔	✔	✔	✔	✔
To help me develop an informed view, I can identify and explain the difference between fact and opinion, recognise when I am being influenced, and have assessed how useful and believable my sources are. *LIT 2-18a*									
I can:									
– discuss structure, characterisation and/or setting	✔	✔	✔	✔	✔	✔	✔	✔	✔
– recognise the relevance of the author's theme and how this relates to my own and others' experiences	✔	✔	✔	✔	✔	✔	✔	✔	✔
– discuss the author's style and other features appropriate to genre. *ENG 2-19a*	✔	✔	✔	✔	✔	✔	✔	✔	✔
Writing **Enjoyment and choice** – within a motivating and challenging environment, developing an awareness of the relevance of texts in my life									

Curriculum Correlation – Scotland

The Curriculum for Excellence, Literacy and English correlation chart

SECOND	Unit 1 *Friend or Foe* (Author study)	Unit 2 *The Book* (Traditional stories)	Unit 3 *Oranges...* (Other Cultures)	Unit 4 *...One End Street* (Classic literature)	Unit 5 *Magik Circus* (Film narrative)	Unit 6 *News and adverts* (Media scripts)	Unit 1 *Rosen / Causley* (Poetic voice)	Unit 2 *Rosen / Causley* (Narrative)	Unit 3 *Rosen / Causley* (Performance)
I enjoy creating texts of my choice and I regularly select subject, purpose, format and resources to suit the needs of my audience. **LIT 1-20a / LIT 2-20a**	✔	✔	✔	✔	✔	✔	✔	✔	✔
Tools for writing – using knowledge of technical aspects to help my writing communicate effectively within and beyond my place of learning									
I can spell most of the words I need to communicate, using spelling rules, specialist vocabulary, self-correction techniques and a range of resources. **LIT 2-21a**				✔	✔		✔		
In both short and extended texts, I can use appropriate punctuation, vary my sentence structures and divide my work into paragraphs in a way that makes sense to my reader. **LIT 2-22a**	✔	✔	✔	✔		✔			
Throughout the writing process, I can check that my writing makes sense and meets its purpose. **LIT 2-23a**	✔	✔	✔	✔	✔	✔	✔	✔	✔
I consider the impact that layout and presentation will have and can combine lettering, graphics and other features to engage my reader. **LIT 2-24a**		✔	✔	✔	✔			✔	
Organising and using information – considering texts to help create short and extended texts for different purposes									
I can use my notes and other types of writing to help me understand information and ideas, explore problems, make decisions, generate and develop ideas or create new text.	✔	✔	✔	✔	✔	✔	✔	✔	✔
I recognise the need to acknowledge my sources and can do this appropriately. **LIT 2-25a**									
By considering the type of text I am creating, I can select ideas and relevant information, organise these in an appropriate way for my purpose and use suitable vocabulary for my audience. **LIT 2-26a**	✔	✔	✔	✔	✔	✔	✔	✔	✔
Creating texts – applying the elements which authors use to create different types of short and extended texts with increasingly complex ideas, structures and vocabulary									

Curriculum Correlation – Scotland

The Curriculum for Excellence, Literacy and English correlation chart

SECOND	Unit 1 Friend or Foe (Author study)	Unit 2 The Book (Traditional stories)	Unit 3 Oranges… (Other Cultures)	Unit 4 …One End Street (Classic literature)	Unit 5 Magik Circus (Film narrative)	Unit 6 News and adverts (Media scripts)	Unit 1 Rosen / Causley (Poetic voice)	Unit 2 Rosen / Causley (Narrative)	Unit 3 Rosen / Causley (Perform-ance)
I am learning to use language and style in a way which engages and/or influences my reader. *ENG 2-27a*	✔	✔	✔	✔	✔	✔	✔	✔	✔
I can convey information, describe events, explain processes or combine ideas in different ways. *LIT 2-28a*	✔	✔	✔	✔	✔	✔	✔	✔	✔
I can persuade, argue, explore issues or express an opinion using relevant supporting detail and/or evidence. *LIT 2-29a*					✔	✔			
As I write for different purposes and readers, I can describe and share my experiences, expressing what they made me think about and how they made me feel. *ENG 2-30a*							✔	✔	
Having explored the elements which authors use in different genres, I can use what I learn to create stories, poems and plays with an interesting and appropriate structure, interesting characters and/or settings which come to life. *ENG 2-31a*	✔	✔	✔	✔	✔		✔	✔	✔

FRIEND OR FOE – novel (Author study)

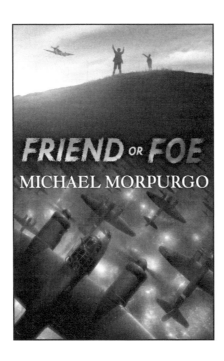

Medium term plan (4 weeks)	
Phase	**Learning Outcomes**
Phase 1: Introducing the author (5 days)	• Children can identify distinctive features of an author's style. • Children can find evidence about where and when a story is set, and make inferences about the author's point of view.
Phase 2: Responding to the story (6 days)	• Children can identify how an author creates excitement and can empathise with a character facing a dilemma. • Children can write a new scene for the story, emulating the author's style.
Phase 3: Finding out about the author (4 days)	• Children can work collaboratively to research an author's life and work. • Children can present their findings to an audience.
Phase 4: Writing a short story (5 days)	• Children can use drama strategies to plan a short story based on the stimulus of a photograph. • Children can write their story using some of the techniques of a significant author. • Children can engage the reader by using appropriate dialogue, language and structural features.

Narrative Unit 1

FRIEND OR FOE

Big picture

The children read stories by Michael Morpurgo, including *Friend or Foe*. They explore story structure, characterisation and the dilemmas faced by particular characters. They write a new scene for the story.

The children work on a collaborative group task to find out more about the author, investigate aspects of his style, read other books that he has written, find out about his popularity and watch an interview with the author. Each child then plans and writes a complete short story inspired by themes and settings from *Friend or Foe*.

Prior learning

This unit assumes that the children can already:

- participate in group discussion: offering reasons for their opinions, summarising ideas, reaching agreement and presenting ideas
- talk about books by a favourite author, explaining why they enjoy them and how and why the books were written
- plan, tell and write complete stories with a clear sequence of events, showing how one event leads to another.

Key aspects of learning

Communication: Express creative ideas and opinions through speaking and writing.

Creative thinking: Write a new scene for the story based on an imaginative response to the text; write a short story.

Empathy: Identify and explore issues faced by characters.

Enquiry: Research the historical background to the story; research biographical information about the author.

Social skills: Work collaboratively; listen to others; support other members of the group; discuss issues and resolve problems.

Progression in narrative

In this unit the children will:

- map out texts showing development and structure; explore aspects of an author's style by comparing themes, settings and characters in different stories; review different ways to build and present a character and discuss response to different characters
- experiment with different story openings; plan and write a complete short story with an interesting opening; organise ideas into paragraphs; use language to create a dramatic effect; use a range of connectives to introduce scenes and link events.

Cross-curricular links

Citizenship: Relationships, people who help us, rules, dilemmas.
History: Children's experience of the Second World War.
ICT: The children could use ICT to make a book of their stories.

Reading time

2 hours 10 mins

PHASE 1: INTRODUCING THE AUTHOR (5 DAYS)

Session 1   *INTERACTIVE TEACHING PROGRAMME ON DISK*

We are learning to ...	Resources
• tell a story using notes • use evidence to explore the features of an author's style • understand and map the story structure (PNS Strands 1.1, 7.1, 7.3) **Assessment Focuses** AF (R): 4	ITP: 1.1, 1.2, 1.3 PCM: 1.1

Shared teaching

- Before the session, assemble a selection of books by Michael Morpurgo. Include some titles for younger readers that some of the children may have read before, e.g. *The Butterfly Lion, Farm Boy, Why the Whales Came*, etc.
- Share the learning objectives. Explain that the children are going to learn more about the author Michael Morpurgo and his books.
- Display the Michael Morpurgo books. *Have you read any of these? Do you know of any other books by Michael Morpurgo?* Take feedback, encouraging the children to express their views about any of the books they have read, or to say which ones look appealing and why.
- Show and read '*Mackerel and Chips*' (ITP 1.1), with the children following on screen. *What did you like about the story? How would you feel if you were Leah? Who do you think the soldier was? Was there anything that puzzled you?*
- Explain that *Mackerel and Chips* is set in the Isles of Scilly. Show 'Map of the UK' (ITP 1.2) and click on the 'Isles of Scilly' and 'Winkleigh' for information. *Has anyone been to these places? Why do you think Michael Morpurgo set* Mackerel and Chips *in the Isles of Scilly?*

- Show 'Comparing stories' (ITP 1.3). Talk Partners discuss what they know about *Mackerel and Chips*.
- Take feedback and complete the first three boxes on ITP 1.3 about *Mackerel and Chips*.

Independent and Guided

- The children make notes about the structure of *Mackerel and Chips*, then retell the story in their own words.

  ⊙⊙⊙ Use 'Story plan 1' (PCM 1.1) to make brief notes on the structure of the story, then use the notes to retell the story orally. (T+)

  ⊙⊙ Use PCM 1.1 to make brief notes on the story structure, then retell the story in pairs.

  ⊙ Use PCM 1.1 to make brief notes about the story structure, then retell the story as a group. (TA+)

Plenary

- Take feedback and add suggestions to ITP 1.3. Save the annotations for use in future sessions. Explain that the children will use the table to compare *Mackerel and Chips* with other books by Michael Morpurgo.
- Recap the learning objectives.
- Select some of the children to retell the story to the class. *What was the main problem in the story? How was it resolved?* Draw out the idea that Leah has to solve a problem that an adult would normally solve. This is often a feature of Michael Morpurgo's books and it adds to the excitement of the story. *Can you think of any other stories by Michael Morpurgo with this feature?*

Assessment pointers

S&L: oral retellings will show how well the children can recount ideas.
AF4 (R): completed PCMs and the children's retelling of the story show how far they understand story structure.

We are learning to ...	Resources
• explore characters using evidence from the text • make inferences about what a character is thinking and feeling (PNS Strands 7.1, 7.2) **Assessment Focuses** AF (R): 2, 3	*Friend or Foe* PCM: 1.2

Shared teaching

• Share the learning objectives. Introduce *Friend or Foe*, looking together at the front cover and discussing the title. *Do you know what a 'foe' is?* If necessary, demonstrate how to check the meaning of an unfamiliar word using 'Glossary' (AR 1.2).

• Explain that *Friend or Foe* is set during the Second World War. *Who do you think the 'foe' is?* (the Germans) Allow the children Think Time to recall what they already know about the Second World War. Take feedback.

• Read Chapter 1 with the children following in their books. *What have we learned about the main character?* Talk Partners look for details, e.g. his name, where he lives, family information, friends, etc.

• Take feedback and use suggestions to complete a Role on the Wall for David. Encourage the children to refer to the text. *Where did we learn David's name?* (page 3) *How do we know that it is wartime? How do we know where David is going? How did we learn these things about the character?* (by gradually picking up clues as we read)

• Explain that the author's style is to show and not to tell. Rather than introducing David and the setting directly, he gives us this information gradually. *Why do you think he does this?* (to create mystery)

• *Is there anything you would like to find out?* (E.g. *I wonder how David's father died?*) Add the children's questions to the Learning Wall to refer back to as you read.

Independent and Guided

• The children look for 'clues' about where the story is set and think about how the Second World War has affected the characters' lives.

  ◌◌◌ Reread Chapter 1, making notes on the setting and effects of war on 'Clues bookmark' (PCM 1.2).

  ◌◌ As above. (TA+)

  ◌ As above, referring to the effect on the characters lives only. (T+)

Plenary

• Recap the learning objectives and take feedback. *What did you learn about where* Friend or Foe *is set?* (wartime London) *What clues told you this?*

• Set up a whole-class Hot-Seating activity to explore the effects the war had on David. Encourage one child to take the role of David. *How has your life changed as a result of the war? How do you feel as the train leaves Paddington Station?* Encourage the other children to ask further questions.

Assessment pointers

S&L: hot-seating will show how well the children can sustain roles to explore issues.

AF2, 3 (R): oral responses and the hot-seating activity will show how far the children are able to retrieve and deduce facts about the background to the book.

We are learning to ...	Resources
• use empathy to make inferences about characters • make predictions about the story (PNS Strands 7.2, 8.2) **Assessment Focuses** AF (R): 3	*Friend or Foe* ITP: (1.2) PCM: 1.3, 1.4

Shared teaching

• Share the learning objectives.

• Recall 'Map of the UK' (ITP 1.2). *Where did* Friend or Foe *start? Why did the children have to be evacuated? Where were they going?* Identify London and Devon on the map and click to reveal the information. Look at Devon in more detail and click to reveal the information for Exeter and Dartmoor. *What differences do you think David and Tucky will notice when they get to Devon? Do you think they will like it there?* Emphasise the differences between living in a city and living in the countryside.

• Read Chapter 2 to the end of page 25 in *Friend or Foe*. Explore how David and Tucky might be feeling at this moment. Remind the children that the characters have left their homes for the first time and that they don't know where they are going or if they will ever see their parents again. *How would you feel?*

• Use Role Play to explore the village hall scene. Divide the class into two groups, evacuees and hosts, ensuring there are two more evacuees than hosts.

• Invite the hosts to choose their evacuees and take them to the back of the room. Pause the action mid-way to focus on how different characters are feeling. *How does it feel to be waiting to be chosen? How do you feel about having a child you've never met come to stay with you?*

• Continue the role play until there are only two evacuees left. Think-Pair-Share their roles. *Can you imagine the scene in the village hall? Does it help to imagine what different people were thinking and feeling?*

• Tell the children that they are going to pretend to be Michael Morpurgo and write the next part of the story. *What do you think will happen next? Will David and Tucky be collected? Will they go back to London?*

• Talk Partners make predictions for what might happen next in the story.

Independent and Guided

• The children work in pairs to predict how the story will continue, using what they already know about the book.

  ◌◌◌ Discuss the statements on 'What next?' (PCM 1.3), then work independently to continue the story.

  ◌◌ As above. (T)

  ◌ Use 'The last two' (PCM 1.4) to write David and Tucky's thought bubbles for what they think will happen next. (TA+)

Plenary

• Recap the learning objectives and share predictions about what will happen to David and Tucky. *Did you use what you already knew about the story to make your predictions? Whose prediction do you think will be closest to what happens in the book?*

Assessment pointers

S&L: role plays will show how well the children can respond to issues and empathise with the characters.

AF3 (R): the children's role play and written predictions will show how far they can retrieve information from the text and make inferences and deductions about what will happen next.

We are learning to ...	Resources
• explore characters using evidence from the text • make inferences about the author's point of view (PNS Strands 7.1, 7.2) **Assessment Focuses** AF (R): 6	*Friend or Foe* *Author reading* (film) ITP: 1.4

Shared teaching

• Recap the problem from Session 3: there was no one to take David and Tucky.
• Continue reading from page 26 to the end of Chapter 2 in *Friend or Foe. What has happened to David and Tucky? Is this what you predicted would happen?*
• (Addtitionally you could watch an extract read from Chapter 2 by Michael Morpurgo in *Author reading*.)
• Share the learning objectives. *How does Michael Morpurgo think children should be treated by adults?* Allow Think Time before taking answers.
• Take feedback and discuss the fact that the characters presented in a good light treat the children well, involving them rather than just telling them what to do. Discuss whether this reflects the author's own point of view.
• Focus on the children's first impressions of Mr Reynolds. *Is there anything that makes you feel that he is going to be a good or a bad character?* Encourage the children to look for evidence that supports their opinion.
• Show 'Mr Reynolds and Miss Evers' (ITP 1.4). *Who does each statement best describe?* Invite individual children to answer this question for each statement. Check whether the rest of the class

agree. Encourage the children to refer back to the text to support their answers.

Independent and Guided

• The children write a short extract from David's diary to show his first thoughts about Mr Reynolds. They should Include plenty of detail, recalling events and commenting on their thoughts and feelings in the role of David. Support the children with an identified need. (T+/TA+)

Plenary

• Share some examples of the children's completed diary entries. Encourage individuals to explain where the ideas for their diary entries are drawn from. Praise examples where the children make inferences based on what they have read.
• Recap the learning objectives. *Which character does the author want you to sympathise with?* (Mr Reynolds) *How can you tell?* (He describes Miss Evers as an angry character; she makes Mr Reynolds choose between the boys.) *Why do you think that is?* (So that you see Mr Reynolds as someone who will stand up for the boys and can be trusted.) *What does this tell you about Michael Morpurgo's own views?*
• Discuss how Michael Morpurgo thinks adults should treat children. Explain that the children will look for further evidence of his views as they continue reading.

Assessment pointers

AF6 (R): oral feedback about the author's point of view shows how well the children are able to identify and comment on author viewpoints.

We are learning to ...	Resources
• make inferences about what a character is thinking and feeling (PNS Strands 7.2) **Assessment Focuses** AF (R): 2	*Friend or Foe* PCM: 1.5

Shared teaching

• Share the learning objectives.
• Recap the end of Chapter 2 of *Friend or Foe*, at which point David and Tucky are on their way to Mr Reynolds's farm. *What do you think it will be like? How would you feel if you were in their place?*
• Read Chapter 3 as far as page 42 to the paragraph ending ' ... further down the bed.'
• Set up a whole-class Hot-Seating activity to explore David's thoughts and feelings, with one child taking the role of David and the other children asking questions, e.g. *What were the first few days on the farm like? What is the best thing about the farm? Is there anything you don't like?*
• Draw attention to the contrast between the fear and danger at the beginning of the book and the positive things that the children have now identified.
• Discuss how David and Tucky are feeling about going to a new school. Talk Partners predict what the new school will be like. *What will the teachers be like? What about the other children? How will it be different from their old school?* Take feedback.
• Read to the end of the chapter. *Did the new school match your predictions?*

Independent and Guided

• The children explore David and Tucky's feelings about their new school.
  ⬤⬤⬤ Use Thought Tracking to map David and Tucky's first day at school, making notes of the key points in the story and how they think the characters feel at each point. (T+)
  ⬤⬤ Use 'The first day at school' (PCM 1.5) to explore David and Tucky's feelings on their first day at the village school.
  ⬤ As above. (TA+)

Plenary

• Recap the learning objectives and take feedback, encouraging the children to use evidence from the book to back up their views of how the boys felt about their new school. *What do you think was the best, worst or most surprising thing? What were they used to? Do you think they were pleased or disappointed not to be going to the same school as the other evacuees? How do you think they settled in? How can you tell?*

Assessment pointers

S&L: hot-seating will show how far the children can sustain roles to explore ideas.
AF2 (R): responses to questioning and completed PCMs show how far the children can retrieve information about the new school.

Session 6

We are learning to ...	Resources
• understand how the author uses dialogue to show us what different characters are like • understand and use punctuation for speech accurately (PNS Strands 7.2, 11.2) **Assessment Focuses** AF (R): 3, 6	*Friend or Foe* PCM: 1.6

Shared teaching

• Share the learning objectives. Recap the final paragraph of Chapter 3 of *Friend or Foe. I wonder how the boys' peace is shattered?* The children Think-Pair-Share predictions.
• Read Chapter 4 as far as the last line of page 58, ending ' … to wish he'd never told anyone.' *Did anything puzzle you about this part of the story? What do you want to find out?* Talk Partners make a note of their questions on sticky notes and keep these for use in Session 7, e.g. *What happened to the plane? What will the soldiers find up on the moor?*
• Explain that the children are going to look at how different characters speak to one another. Divide the class into groups of five to reread the conversation from page 52 to page 54. Each member of a group takes a role: David, Tucky, Ann, Mr Reynolds and a narrator. Encourage the children to think about how the characters would say their lines (tone, accent, etc). Check the children's understanding of punctuation for speech. *How will you know when to start and stop reading your part?*
• Bring the class back together and focus on the way the adults talked to the boys. *Do you think they believed them straight away? What sort of tone did the adults use? What does this tell you about the characters?*
• Draw out the idea that when the adults talk directly to the boys, they listen carefully and ask questions in a gentle way. Michael Morpurgo is using dialogue to show us that the adults are good characters and the boys can trust them.

Independent and Guided

• The children explore the officer's thoughts, based on what he says and how he speaks.
  Read the dialogue on 'The officer' (PCM 1.6), highlighting the officer's and Mr Reynolds's words in different colours. Answer the questions.
  As above. (TA+)
  In a group, discuss what the officer might be thinking and answer the questions on PCM 1.6. (T+)

Plenary

• Take feedback on the children's ideas about the character of the officer. *How does his attitude compare with Mr Reynolds's treatment of the boys? How would you feel if an adult ignored you like this?*
• Recap the learning objectives. *Which character do you think represents the author's own point of view? How can you tell?* (The officer is described as having a mean face.)

Assessment pointers

S&L: oral readings will show how far the children can interpret the text through speech.
AF3 (R): written answers and oral feedback from the independent task show how far the children can make deductions about characters.
AF6 (R): responses to questioning show how far the children are able to infer the author's point of view.

Session 7

We are learning to ...	Resources
• identify how an author creates a sense of danger and excitement (PNS Strands 7.5) **Assessment Focuses** AF (R): 5	*Friend or Foe* ITP: 1.5, 1.6

Shared teaching

• Share the learning objective. Encourage the children to share their questions from Session 6, and take predictions for what the answers might be.
• Continue reading Chapter 4 of *Friend or Foe* from page 60 to page 64. *How do you think the boys felt at the end of the search and when they were teased at school?* Talk Partners look back through the chapter for evidence and also use their imagination.
• Take feedback. Draw attention to the contrast between the Reynolds's reaction and the reaction of everyone else. (For evidence of the Reynolds's belief in the boys' honesty, see pages 61 and 63.)
• Read to the end of the chapter. *Do you think David will get out of the water? What will Tucky do? What would you do?*
• Explore how Michael Morpurgo describes the scene where David falls into the water. *Which words and phrases on page 67 describe the water?* E.g. 'foaming furiously', 'too fast', 'whipped round the rocks', 'roar of the water', 'gap yawned wide', 'frothing and swirling'.
• Show 'Describing the river' (ITP 1.5) and invite suggestions for where to place the words (under 'How the water moved', 'What the water sounded like', or 'What the water looked like').
• Explain that the author builds up the sense of danger by making the water seem like a living thing, like a dangerous animal.

• Look at how the author describes the action in a dramatic way. Ask a volunteer to read 'Friend or Foe' (ITP 1.6) aloud, paying attention to punctuation. Challenge them to pause only at full stops and commas. *Why does Michael Morpurgo use long sentences?* (to increase the pace of the action) *Why does he want you to be out of breath?* (to make you feel how David does)

Independent and Guided

• The children look back through pages 68 to 69 of *Friend or Foe* and choose three phrases that add to the drama of the description. They write a note about each one to explain why they think the phrases are effective.
  Work independently.
  In pairs. (T)
  In groups. (TA)

Plenary

• Share the children's phrases. Encourage the children to explain their choices. Add to the Learning Wall.
• Recap the learning objective and discuss the effect of the author's use of language. Draw out the idea that he 'paints a picture' with words so that the reader can imagine the action.

Assessment pointers

AF5 (R): the children's lists, annotations and oral feedback shows how far they understand an author's use of language.

We are learning to ...	Resources
• use evidence from the text to explore key events and ideas • use empathy to explore characters and story (PNS Strands 7.1, 8.2) **Assessment Focuses** AF (R): 2, 3	*Friend or Foe* PCM: 1.7, 1.8

Shared teaching (1)

• Share the learning objectives.
• Remind the children that at the end of Chapter 4, David thought he was drowning. Explain that in the next chapter, the children will discover the main problem in the story.
• Read Chapter 5 of *Friend or Foe* as far as ' ... it was a duty to make sure they were captured' on page 76. *What is the main problem?* Relate this back to the title of the book. Explain that in castles, guards used to call out 'Friend or foe?' to approaching strangers. But in this story the difference between friends and enemies is not so clear.
• The children Think-Pair-Share the reasons for and against helping the airmen. *What do you think David should do: help the German airmen or tell the British soldiers?* Encourage them to refer back to the text to support their views.
• Organise a Conscience Alley activity to explore David's dilemma. Divide the class into two groups: one for helping the airmen the other against. Give each group time to develop their ideas, referring to the story, e.g. David's thoughts (pages 41 and 56) and Tucky's thoughts (pages 75, 76 and 79). Then one child takes on the role of David while the other children give reasons for and against helping the German airmen. At the end of the activity, ask the child in role what they have decided to do. *Do you agree?* Encourage the children to explain their point of view by referring to the text.

Independent and Guided

• The children explore David's dilemma in more detail.

🖊️ Imagine you are David's mum and David has written to you asking for advice. Use 'Dear Mum' (PCM 1.7) to write a letter to David saying what he should do and what the consequences will be.

🖊️ Use 'Dear diary' (PCM 1.8) to write an entry for David's diary, explaining what he has decided to do and why. (TA+)

💬 In a group, discuss David's decision and what might happen next as a consequence of his decision. (T+)

Shared teaching (2)

• The children share their written responses to David's decision.
• Read to the end of Chapter 5. *Did you find David's decision surprising? Do you agree with his decision? Do you think the plane saw them?*

Plenary

• Recap the main problem in the story and David's decision to help the German airmen. *Why do you think Michael Morpurgo chose this outcome? What is he trying to tell us?* (E.g. that it is not so easy to label people as either a 'friend' or a 'foe'.)
• Recap the learning objectives and share predictions about what will happen next.

Assessment pointers

S&L: drama activity will show how well the children can create and sustain roles to explore issues.
AF2, 3 (R): the children's oral contributions to the drama activity show how far they can select and use ideas from the text.

We are learning to ...	Resources
• use and reflect on drama techniques to explore characters and story • use empathy to explore characters and story • plan and write a new scene for a story (PNS Strands 4.1, 8.2, 9.2) **Assessment Focuses** AF (W): 1, 6	*Friend or Foe* ITP: 1.7

Shared teaching (1)

• Share the learning objectives. Recap the children's predictions about what will happen next. *What would happen to David and Tucky if they were caught helping the Germans?*
• Read Chapter 6 of *Friend or Foe. How does David feel about the decision he has made?* Talk Partners look for evidence in the text of David's ongoing doubts and growing discomfort (pages 94–96).
• *Why do you think David has kept the German airmen a secret?* Encourage the children to think about how people felt about the Germans in wartime Britain.
• Explain that they are going to write a new scene for *Friend or Foe* where David tells Mr Reynolds the truth. *How do you think Mr Reynolds would react if he found out David was helping the German airmen?*
• Show 'Planning a new scene' (ITP 1.7). Use Modelled Writing to plan a new scene, taking suggestions for notes to go under each heading.

Independent and Guided (1)

• Groups use Improvisation to create a new scene where David tells Mr Reynolds about the airmen, using their knowledge of the characters so far. Each group shares out the roles of David, Tucky, Mr Reynolds, the two airmen and the officer. Encourage the children to think about what the characters will say, their facial expressions and body language. Support the children with an identified need. (T/TA)

Shared teaching (2)

• Invite groups to share their improvisations. As they do, Freeze Frame the action and ask the different characters to explain what they are thinking and feeling.
• Use Modelled Writing to demonstrate how to take dialogue from their improvisations and turn this into written speech, recapping the conventions of reported speech.

Independent and Guided (2)

• The children write two to three paragraphs for the new scene from their improvisations, including dialogue and the thoughts and feelings of each character. Support the children with an identified need. (T+/TA+)

Plenary

• Ask the children to share their new scenes. Invite the other children to give feedback. *Did the characters talk and act in a way that fits with the rest of the story so far?*
• Recap the learning objectives. Reflect on what the children have learned from writing the new scene. *How did you make use of what you knew already about each of the characters? Did it help you to understand the characters better?*

Assessment pointers

S&L: improvisation will show how far the children understand the characters and can use this knowledge to create new scenarios.
AF1, 6 (W): written scenes show how far the children can use imaginative ideas; their use of dialogue and accuracy in punctuation.

We are learning to ...	Resources
• find evidence about a character's point of view • use evidence to say how a character changes (PNS Strands 7.1) **Assessment Focuses** AF (R): 2, 3	*Friend or Foe* ITP: 1.8 PCM: 1.9

Shared teaching (1)

• Share the learning objectives.
• Read Chapter 7 of *Friend or Foe* to the bottom of page 106. *Is there anything that puzzles you about this chapter so far? Why does David decide to let the German airman go?*
• Show 'What the German airman says' (ITP 1.8). Click to reveal what the airman says. *What do you think the airman means? Do you agree that they are no longer enemies?* Add notes to ITP 1.8. Encourage the children to make deductions from the text.
• The children Think-Pair-Share how the airman's view compares with David's. Take feedback and discuss the different views. Encourage the children to support their ideas with reference to the text.
• Read the rest of the chapter. *Were you surprised that the other German lied for David?*
• Discuss David's point of view at the end of the chapter. *Have David's views stayed the same? How have David's views changed as a result of meeting the airmen? How do we know this?*

Independent and Guided

• The children read and order the quotes on 'David's views' (PCM 1.9) according to the story. Then discuss what this tells them about David's viewpoint and how it has changed.

In pairs, the children put the quotes in order and consider why David's views have changed.

As above. (TA)

As above with the children working as a group. (T)

Shared teaching (2)

• Take feedback. *Why do you think David's views have changed?*
• Talk Partners discuss any questions that they would like to ask David, e.g. *Why did you go back the second time? Were you nervous?*
• Hold a whole-class Hot-Seating activity. Encourage a confident child to take on the role of David. The class then ask their questions with the child answering in role.

Plenary

• Discuss how looking at what David says and hot-seating have helped to understand his changing viewpoint.
• Recap the learning objectives. *Do you still have any unanswered questions?* Write these on the Learning Wall to refer back to in Session 11, e.g. *What will happen to the two airmen? Will Mr Reynolds continue to be suspicious? Will the boys tell the truth about what they have done? Will anyone find out?*

Assessment pointers

S&L: hot-seating will show how far the children can sustain roles to explore ideas.
AF2, 3 (R): independent activity shows how far the children can retrieve information and make inferences about different characters' points of view.

We are learning to ...	Resources
• explore the author's viewpoint through the characters (PNS Strands 7.2) **Assessment Focuses** AF (R): 2, 6	*Friend or Foe* PCM: 1.10

Shared teaching (1)

• Share the learning objective.
• Look at the unanswered questions on the Learning Wall that the children raised at the end of Session 10. Remind the children that although one of the airmen has given himself up, the other man is still on the moor and that David and Tucky are still afraid that someone will find out about what they have done.
• Read Chapter 8 to page 118, '"I hope not."' *What would Mr Reynolds and Ann do if they knew the truth?* Talk Partners make notes on what they think would happen.
• Read the end of the book. Ask the children to look back at their predictions. *Were you right about the Reynolds's reaction? Why do you think David and Tucky kept coming back to visit Mr and Mrs Reynolds once the war was over?* Take feedback, encouraging the children to raise, and attempt to answer, further questions.
• Discuss the children's thoughts on the book. *Did you enjoy it? Who are your favourite characters? What have you learnt from the book? What do you think the author is trying to tell us?*

Independent and Guided

• In groups, the children explore whether the German airmen are friends or foes by looking at how they are described in Chapters 5 to 8. Each child from the group works on a different chapter and then feeds back

to the rest of the group. They use 'Friend or foe?' (PCM 1.10) to record evidence. Support the children with an identified need. (T/TA)

Shared teaching (2)

• Share descriptions of the German airmen. *Do you think they are friends or foes? Why is it hard to decide?* Draw out the idea that the German airmen start off as foes but become friends.
• Talk Partners discuss whether there are any characters in the story that start off as friends but become foes, e.g. the school children when they think Tucky lied.
• Take feedback. *Do the characters change back to friends again? What do you think Michael Morpurgo is trying to tell us about war?* (E.g. war is complex; easy to hate people you don't know; one good turn deserves another regardless of whether someone is the enemy, etc.)

Plenary

• Recap the learning objective.
• Discuss the overall effect of the book. Remind the children that David's attitude towards war and the German airmen changed during the book. *Has your attitude changed? Would you have helped the German airmen?*

Assessment pointers

AF2, 6 (R): the children's oral feedback shows their response to the book as a whole and how far they are able to relate this to the author's own viewpoint.

Session 12

We are learning to ...	Resources
• use evidence to explore the features of an author's style • discuss preferences and choose more books by the same author • survey the popularity of an author (PNS Strands 7.1, 8.1) **Assessment Focuses** AF (R): 2, 4	ITP: (1.3) PCM: 1.11

Shared teaching (1)

• Remind the children of *Mackerel and Chips. What can you remember about this story? Who were the main characters? What were the main events?*
• Recall annotated 'Comparing stories' (ITP 1.3). Recap the key themes in *Mackerel and Chips. How do these compare with* Friend or Foe*?* Complete ITP 1.3 for *Friend or Foe*.
• Discuss how the two stories are different, e.g. *Mackerel and Chips* is set in the present day and has a young girl as a main character. She is helped by a ghost from the war. *Friend or Foe* tells the story of two male evacuees in wartime Britain who discover two German airmen.
• *Are there any similarities between* Mackerel and Chips *and* Friend or Foe*?* Talk Partners discuss the common features, e.g. the main characters think they have seen something but aren't believed by adults, the main characters are away from home, etc.
• Take feedback. Draw out the idea that both stories involve a child who is faced with a problem that an adult helps them to solve.
• Make a list of common features to add to the Learning Wall. Explain that the children are going to look at other books by Michael Morpurgo to see if they share any of these features.

Independent and Guided (1)

• In groups, the children look for common features in other books by Michael Morpurgo. Using 'Book tasters' (PCM 1.11), or a selection of other books, each group focuses on one of the following features: setting, characters, themes. Envoys then share their findings with the other groups. Support the children with an identified need. (T+/TA+)

Shared teaching (2)

• Take feedback. Use suggestions to complete ITP 1.3. *What other features did you find? Why do you think these books have similar themes, characters and settings?*
• *Do you enjoy books by Michael Morpurgo? What do you like about them? Which ones would you like to read next?*

Independent and Guided (2)

• The children write a list of five books by Michael Morpurgo and conduct a short survey to find out who has read the books and what they liked about them. Each child should ask at least four classmates to complete their survey. Support the children with an identified need. (T/TA)

Plenary

• Take feedback. *What is the most popular book? Why do you think that is?*
• Recap the learning objectives. *What sort of person do you think Michael Morpurgo is?* Explain that the children are going to find out more about him in Session 13.

Assessment pointers

AF2 (R): response to questioning and identification of common features show how far the children can retrieve information from the text.
AF4 (R): paired discussion and oral feedback show how far the children can compare stories and identify common themes.

Session 13

We are learning to ...	Resources
• use and explore different question types • work with a group to plan and research key facts about an author • discuss research about an author • take different roles within research groups (PNS Strands 1.3, 3.1, 3.2, 8.1) **Assessment Focuses** AF (R): 2	*Interview with Michael Morpurgo* (film) ITP: 1.9 PCM: 1.12

Shared teaching (1)

• Share the learning objectives. Explain that today, the children are going to find out more information about Michael Morpurgo. *What do we know about Michael Morpurgo already? How do we know this?*
• Talk Partners discuss what they would ask Michael Morpurgo about *Friend or Foe*. Take feedback and use suggestions to create a 'questions list'.
• Watch *Interview with Michael Morpurgo: Part 1*, asking the children to listen out for the answers to the questions on the 'question list' and to take notes. *Have all of your questions been answered now? What else would you like to know about the author?* Help the children focus and refine their questions by asking: *I wonder what makes a children's author popular and successful?* Add new questions to the 'questions list'. *Can you organise the questions into topics?*
• *How are you going to find the answers to your questions? Where could you look for information?* (Internet, books, etc.)
• Explain that the children will be working in research groups to find information about Michael Morpurgo. Show 'Research groups' (ITP 1.9). *Are there any you would like to add or change?*

Independent and Guided

• In pairs, the children choose a topic from the shared teaching and use 'Michael Morpurgo' (PCM 1.12) to plan and record their research. The children should only fill in one topic. When they have completed this, join pairs together to share information and complete the second topic on PCM 1.12. Support the children with an identified need. (T+/TA+)

Shared teaching (2)

• Take feedback. Ask the children to share their most interesting facts. *I wonder what else we could learn about the author.*
• Watch *Interview with Michael Morpurgo: Part 2. Was your research correct? Did you learn anything new?*

Plenary

• Recap the learning objectives. *How did your research help you? How well do you think you worked in your research groups? What can you do with this information? How does it tell you more about Michael Morpurgo's books?*
• Discuss how what they have learnt about Michael Morpurgo relates to his books, e.g. he lives in Devon and many of his books are set there.

Assessment pointers

• S&L: pair and group work shows how far the children can adopt group roles and share information.
• AF2 (R): research and role on the wall will show how far the children can retrieve information from the text.

We are learning to ...	Resources
• work in groups to plan presentations of research • understand how the author uses real events as ideas for stories (PNS Strands 3.1, 7.2) **Assessment Focuses** AF (R): 2, 3	*Interview with Michael Morpurgo* (film) ITP: 1.10, 1.11, 1.12 PCM: (1.12), 1.13

Shared teaching (1)

• Remind the children of their research in Session 13. *What did you learn about Michael Morpurgo?* The children play Just a Minute to recall as many facts about Michael Morpurgo as possible.
• Share the learning objectives. Explain that they are now going to look at how authors use real events in their stories.
• Show 'Nuggets of truth' (ITP 1.10) and discuss what Michael Morpurgo means by 'nuggets of truth'. Read the extracts while the children follow. *Can you find the 'nugget of truth' in 'Story'?* Draw out the idea that this extract uses the author's memories of boarding school. Discuss how a vivid memory can make the writing vivid too. A feature of Michael Morpurgo's writing is that he makes situations realistic, helping readers to imagine the characters' experiences.
• Talk Partners try to remember other examples of 'nuggets of truth' that Michael Morpurgo gave in his interview, e.g. he said that Ann in *Friend or Foe* was based on his aunt. Rewatch *Interview with Michael Morpurgo: Part 1* if necessary. Take feedback.

Independent and Guided (1)

• In the same research groups as Session 13, the children find references to Michael Morpurgo's life in *Friend or Foe* and record them on 'Nuggets of truth' (PCM 1.13). They use completed 'Michael Morpurgo' (PCM 1.12) and their notes on the interview to help them.

Support the children with an identified need. (T/TA)

Shared teaching (2)

• Explain that the children are going to use the information that they have gathered today and in Session 13, to produce a presentation on what they have learnt about Michael Morpurgo and how these facts are reflected in *Friend or Foe*. Remind the children that a presentation is like a story and will need a beginning, middle and an end.
• Show 'Model presentation' (ITP 1.11) and use Modelled Writing to show how to organise information into a presentation using the children's suggestions. *Can anyone give me a fact about Michael Morpurgo? Where would we put this? How would we end the presentation?*
• Show 'Presentations' (ITP 1.12). *What makes a good presentation? Are there any you would like to add or change?*

Independent and Guided (2)

• In their research groups, the children plan their presentations using ITP 1.12 to help them. They should include as much of the information that they have gathered as possible and think about who will present each part. Support the children with an identified need. (T+/TA+)

Plenary

• Recap the learning objectives. Discuss how well the children have worked in their groups to plan their presentations. *Has everyone got a role? Was it easy to decide what to include? Did you have any problems? How did you solve these?*

Assessment pointers

S&L: group work will show how well the children can adopt group roles, drawing ideas together and promoting effective planning.
AF2, 3 (R): group work will show how far the children can retrieve and interpret information from texts.

We are learning to ...	Resources
• work in groups to make presentations about an author (PNS Strands 3.1) **Assessment Focuses** AF (R): 2, 3	ITP: (1.12), 1.13

Shared teaching (1)

• Share the learning objective. Explain that the children will have time to complete their presentations and then each group will present to the class.
• Take one group's presentation plan as an example. Recap the success criteria on 'Presentations' (ITP 1.12). *Does this presentation cover all of the points? What is good about the presentation? What could you improve? How could you do this?*
• Remind the children that their audience will be members of their class, or another class, and that the purpose of the presentation is to share facts on Michael Morpurgo and to show how these are reflected in *Friend or Foe*.
• Show 'Tips for presenting' (ITP 1.13). *How are you going to make your presentation interesting?* Encourage the children to generate two more tips to add to the list.

Independent and Guided

• In the same research groups, the children review their plans for their presentations using the success criteria on ITP 1.12. They make improvements to their plans to finalise the content, making sure they include information from all members of their group. The children then rehearse their own part of the presentation for the rest of their group. The children should offer constructive criticism on how to improve the

content and style of their presentations. Support the children with an identified need. (T/TA)

Shared teaching (2)

• Each research group performs their presentation to the rest of the class. After each presentation, allow time for the children to ask questions and to give Two Stars and a Wish as feedback.
• Once all the groups have finished, refer to the success criteria on ITP 1.12 and allow the children a few minutes to evaluate their own presentations. *What went well? What would you change if you were doing it again?* Take feedback from each group in turn, encouraging the others to make constructive comments.

Plenary

• Recap the learning objective. Discuss what the children have learnt about Michael Morpurgo from each other's presentations. Ask each child to give one new fact they have learnt about Michael Morpurgo.
• Explore how this information has helped the children to understand the key features of Michael Morpurgo's books and to identify these in *Friend or Foe*.
• Ask the children to reflect on all that they have done in the last few weeks to answer the question: *What is it that makes Michael Morpurgo a 'significant children's author'?* Encourage them to draw on their own reading and research.

Assessment pointers

S&L: presentations will show how well the children can talk in extended turns to convey ideas.
AF2, 3 (R): presentations will show how far the children are able to retrieve and interpret information from texts.

Session 16

We are learning to ...	Resources
• understand and map the story structure • plan and write a story inspired by a significant author's work (PNS Strands 7.3, 9.2) **Assessment Focuses** AF (W): 3	ITP: (1.3), 1.14, 1.15 PCM: 1.14

Shared teaching

• Share the learning objectives.
• Recap the common features of Michael Morpurgo's books, e.g they usually involve children having to face a problem, an adult helps them, people aren't what they seem, etc. Refer to the completed 'Comparing stories' (ITP 1.3) if necessary.
• Remind the children that *Friend or Foe* was written about the experiences of children in wartime Britain. Show 'Evacuees' (ITP 1.14). Elicit speculation about the evacuees in the photos. *Who might they be? Where might they have come from? What could have happened to them?*
• Agree on a back story, e.g. the evacuees are a brother and sister who are being evacuated from London. Their father died in the war and their mother has to go to work.
• Ask the children to imagine that they are the children in the photo. Their teacher has just put them on a train out of London. They are surrounded by strangers.
• In pairs, the children Role Play a discussion between siblings in this situation. *How do they feel? What do they say to each other?*
• Pause the drama. Now ask them to imagine that they have fallen asleep on the train. When they wake up, they realise that the train has stopped. There is no one else left on the train and they aren't sure where they are. They step off the train onto the platform, and see a stranger walking towards them.
• The pairs prepare Freeze Frames of their reaction to the stranger. *Who are they? How do you feel?*
• Show 'Story plan' (ITP 1.15). Use Modelled Writing to show how to make brief planning notes under each heading, using the scenario from the drama activities.
• Talk Partners discuss ideas for what might happen next in the story.

Independent and Guided

• The children complete their own story plan, filling in the chart on 'Story plan 2' (PCM 1.14).
• 000 Independently complete PCM 1.14.
• 00 As above. (TA+)
• ◉ In a group, discuss and agree a story plan together. (T+)

Plenary

• Share ideas for stories, and ask the children for feedback. *What do you like about the ideas? What do you think could be improved? Has anybody used features from any of Michael Morpurgo's books? Which ones? Are there any other features you could include?*
• Recap the learning objectives.

Assessment pointers

S&L: role plays will show how well the children can explore and develop ideas through drama.
AF3 (W): written plans show how far the children can plan and organise a complete story.

Session 17

We are learning to ...	Resources
• write effective story openings • use 'show not tell' style (PNS Strands 9.2, 9.4) **Assessment Focuses** AF (W): 1	ITP: 1.16, 1.17 PCM: (1.14)

Shared teaching

• Share the learning objectives. Explain that today, the children are going to write the opening for their stories.
• Talk Partners discuss what makes a good story opening. Encourage them to refer to *Friend or Foe* or other Michael Morpurgo books. *What makes his opening so interesting? How does the author capture the reader's attention?* Refer back to the work done in Session 2 if necessary. Take feedback.
• Show 'Story openings' (ITP 1.16). Read the success criteria. *Are there any you would like to change or add?*
• Read 'Model opening' (ITP 1.17). *Do you think this is a good story opening?* Encourage the children to refer back to the success criteria. *How could we make this opening more like a Michael Morpurgo story?* (E.g. reveal details about the characters gradually by dropping in clues.)
• Use Think Alouds to demonstrate how to compose sentences orally before adding to and altering the model text on ITP 1.17, e.g. *I'll never forget evacuation day, 10th October 1940, the day I met my guardian angel. But I'd better start at the beginning.*
• Use Modelled Writing to show how to 'show not tell' in the style of Michael Morpurgo. Point out that you haven't used any names yet.

These could be mentioned by a character, rather than just given by the narrator, e.g. *'Look after Frank, Meg. Don't let go of his hand,'* Mum *called as she waved goodbye.*

Independent and Guided

• The children refer to their completed 'Story plan 2' (PCM 1.14) to write the opening to their story, ending with the evacuees falling asleep on the train.
• 000 Write the story opening. (TA+)
• 00 As above.
• ◉ Write the story opening, referring to the group plan and saying each sentence aloud before writing it down. (T+)

Plenary

• Recap the learning objectives. Ask two or three confident children to read their story openings to the class. Invite the others to offer feedback, referring to the success criteria. Praise examples of 'showing not telling' information in ways that grab the reader's attention.

Assessment pointers

S&L: responses to the other children's work will show how well the children can express opinions sensitively.
AF1 (W): peer assessment of story openings and improvements made to fulfil the success criteria, show how far the children can write imaginative and effective story openings.

We are learning to ...	Resources
• understand how to use direct speech effectively • understand and use punctuation for speech accurately (PNS Strands 9.4, 11.2) **Assessment Focuses** AF (W): 6	*Friend or Foe* PCM: (1.14), 1.15

Shared teaching (1)

• Share the learning objectives.
• Talk Partners develop ideas about who they think the stranger is. Encourage them to use ideas from Michael Morpurgo's stories to shape their character, e.g. *Are they a friend or a foe?*
• Take feedback and discuss ideas.

Independent and Guided (1)

• The children complete 'The stranger' (PCM 1.15), describing the stranger's identity, appearance and behaviour. Support the children with an identified need. (T/TA)

Shared teaching (2)

• Take feedback. Ask one child to describe their stranger in detail. Invite this child to take on the role of the stranger. Ask two more children to take on the roles of the evacuees.
• Role Play their first meeting, focusing on what they might say to one another. Make a note of key dialogue.
• Reinforce the idea that the way that you say something often shows how you are feeling. Michael Morpurgo uses a variety of verbs in his writing to describe how things are said. *Why do you think he does this? Can you find any of the words and phrases that he uses to describe dialogue in* Friend or Foe?

• Make a list of words and phrases that the children could use instead of 'said' in their writing, e.g. sighed, groaned, agreed reluctantly, miserably, replied happily, joked.
• Recap how to put this into written speech. *What words and phrases could we use? How do we punctuate speech?*
• Remind the children that they stopped writing their stories just before the evacuees woke up. Now they have to introduce the main problem in the story (the evacuees are alone and lost on a deserted platform) and write their first dialogue between the evacuees and the stranger.
• Take feedback and use Modelled Writing to demonstrate how to introduce the problem in an interesting and exciting way. *How could you make it dramatic? What words would help the reader imagine what is happening?*

Independent and Guided (2)

• The children continue writing their stories, referring to their 'Story plan 2' (PCM 1.14). They then check what they have written, particularly the punctuation for direct speech. Support the children with an identified need. (T+/TA+)

Plenary

• Share some examples of the children's writing. Praise examples where the children use a range of verbs and adverbs to show how the characters are feeling when they speak.
• Recap the learning objectives.

Assessment pointers

S&L: role plays will show how well the children can convey ideas about characters through speech and gesture.
AF6 (W): written paragraphs show how far the children can write with technical accuracy, particularly regarding direct speech.

We are learning to ...	Resources
• use varied words and sentences to add drama to writing • understand and use punctuation for speech accurately (PNS Strands 9.4, 11.2) **Assessment Focuses** AF (W): 5, 7	ITP: (1.15), 1.18 PCM: (1.14)

Shared teaching (1)

• Share the learning objectives.
• Display 'Story paragraphs for improvement' (ITP 1.18). Explain to the children that these paragraphs don't give much of a sense of drama and don't paint a picture with words, the way Michael Morpurgo does.
• Read through the paragraphs and use Modelled Writing to show how to make changes to make the writing more dramatic and vivid on ITP 1.18.
• Remind the children that Michael Morpurgo uses events from his own life in his stories to make them more believable. Talk Partners discuss experiences in their own lives which could help to make this part of the story more believable. *Have you ever been away from your parents? Have you ever been lost? How did you feel? What did you do?*
• Take feedback and add ideas from the children's experiences to the model text on ITP 1.18.
• Use Modelled Writing to demonstrate improvements such as varying the length of sentences and adding descriptions, direct speech and questions that draw the reader in. *Would this work better as a short sentence, to make it more dramatic? How could we improve the dialogue? How can we show that this story is set during the war?*

Independent and Guided (1)

• The children look back at their work so far and make improvements based on the issues addressed in the shared teaching. Support the children with an identified need. (T+/TA+)

Shared teaching (2)

• Take feedback. *What changes have you made? How do you think this has improved your story?*
• Refer to annotated 'Story plan' (ITP 1.15). Explain that the children are now going to write how the problem is solved.
• Talk Partners discuss how the problems are solved in *Mackerel and Chips* and *Friend or Foe*.
• Take feedback. Discuss the different roles characters play in solving the problem. *Do the characters need to make difficult decisions? Could you do something similar in your story?*

Independent and Guided (2)

• The children continue their stories and write a solution to the problem, referring back to their 'Story plan 2' (PCM 1.14). They then Think-Pair-Share their stories so far and offer and receive feedback on content and style. Support the children with an identified need. (T+/TA+)

Plenary

• Ask one or two of the children to share how they solved the problem. *How did you make it dramatic? Did you use any events from your own life? Did you use any of the ideas from Michael Morpurgo's stories?*
• Recap the learning objectives.

Assessment pointers

AF5, 7 (W): the children's stories show how far they can vary sentences and use effective vocabulary for dramatic effect.

We are learning to ...	Resources
• evaluate, edit and improve our writing • write imaginative endings (PNS Strands 9.1, 9.2) **Assessment Focuses** AF (W): 1, 3	ITP: 1.19, 1.20 PCM: (1.14), 1.16

Shared teaching (1)

• Share the learning objectives and explain that the children will now finish their stories. *What makes a good ending for a story? How does Michael Morpurgo write his story endings?* Draw out the idea of leaving a question 'hanging in the air' at the end to give the reader something to think about when they close the book.
• Show 'Story endings' (ITP 1.19). Read the success criteria and encourage the children to add to the list.
• Use Modelled Writing to demonstrate adding a final paragraph to the story. Draw the children's attention to points about sentence construction and vocabulary choices as you write.
• Remind the children of the technique of leaving a question for the reader to think about at the end of the story, in the style of Michael Morpurgo.

Independent and Guided (1)

• The children complete the final part of their stories, referring to their 'Story plan 2' (PCM 1.14) and the success criteria on ITP 1.19. Support the children with an identified need. (T+/TA+)

Shared teaching (2)

• Show 'Model ending' (ITP 1.20) and demonstrate evaluating the text against the success criteria. Praise the things that the author has done well and encourage the children to offer suggestions for how to make improvements.
• Talk Partners swap stories and offer feedback using the success criteria on ITP 1.19 to help them give constructive criticism. *Did your partner leave the reader something to think about? How could they improve their ending?*

Independent and Guided (2)

• The children revise their stories using their partner's feedback to make improvements and 'Marking ladder' (PCM 1.16) to check their work. Support the children with an identified need. (T+/TA+)

Plenary

• Discuss ideas for displaying final stories, e.g. wall display, short story collection, readings for another class, recorded extracts, etc.
• Recap the learning objectives. *What did you like about your ending? What changes did you make?*
• Review the unit as a whole. *What have you learnt about Michael Morpurgo and his writing? What techniques did you enjoy using? Do you want to read more of his books?*

Assessment pointers

S&L: pair work will show how sensitively the children can give and respond to opinions.
AF1, 3 (W): self-assessment and written evidence from completed stories show how far the children can plan and write an imaginative story with a clear structure.

Story plan 1

Add notes to describe the events in *Mackerel and Chips*.

Ending

Resolution

Problem

Build-up

Opening

Clues bookmark

Cut out the bookmark and use it to record clues as you read.

✂

Clues bookmark

Your name: _____

Book title: *Friend or Foe* _____

Chapter: 1 _____

Puzzle: *How can you tell* _____
where the story is set? _____

Page   **Clue**

____:_____

____:_____

____:_____

____:_____

____:_____

____:_____

____:_____

Chapter: 1 _____

Puzzle: *How can you tell* _____
the war has affected the _____
characters' lives? _____

Page   **Clue**

____:_____

____:_____

____:_____

____:_____

____:_____

____:_____

Are there any more puzzles
you would like to discuss?

_____

_____

_____

✂

Fold

What next?

1. Discuss the statements about what might happen to David and Tucky.

David and Tucky have
to live in the village hall.

Someone comes to
collect David and Tucky.

Miss Roberts looks after
David and Tucky.

David and Tucky run
away.

David and Tucky are
sent home.

David and Tucky are
separated.

2. Use one of the statements or your own idea to continue the story.

_____

_____

_____

_____

_____

_____

_____

_____

_____

_____

_____

_____

The last two

Write what David and Tucky think will happen next.

Tucky thinks …

David thinks …

The first day at school

Use pages 42 to 46 of *Friend or Foe* to help you complete the table.

	How they get to school	The school	The children at the school	The teacher	How David and Tucky are treated
What information are you given?	They walk three miles.		There are only 20–30 children. They are boys and girls.		The teacher is welcoming. The children are cautious at first, then friendly.
What are David and Tucky's feelings?	It's a long way.				
How do you know how they feel?	'It seemed more like ten miles'. (page 42)			'He spoke clearly and kindly'. (page 45) 'I hope you'll be very happy whilst you're with us'. (page 45)	

Literacy Evolve Year 5 © Pearson Education 2009

The officer

1. Highlight the officer's words in one colour and Mr Reynolds's words in another.

> ## Extract from *Friend or Foe*
> ### Michael Morpurgo
>
> 'Twas out of the bedroom window, sir,' he was saying, 'so it must be in this area here somewhere, almost for certain.'
>
> 'But Reynolds,' the officer took off his cap and shook it, 'there's two observation posts between here and there. Surely if there had been a plane someone else would have spotted it?'
>
> 'Not if they were following the searchlight, sir. The boys say the searchlight was sweeping over the village itself at the time.'
>
> The officer turned to face the boys. He had a mean face with a thin moustache that barely covered his top lip. 'You say they're evacuees, Reynolds?'
>
> 'That's right, sir. And fine lads they are too, sir. Been with us for three months now. If they say they saw it, then you can be sure they did, sir.'
>
> 'Quite so, Reynolds,' said the officer, but he did not sound convinced.

2. Answer the questions.

a. Do you think the officer believes the boys? Why or why not?

_____

_____

_____

b. Why do you think the officer doesn't speak to David or Tucky at all?

_____

_____

_____

c. What sort of man do you think the officer is? How can you tell?

_____

_____

_____

Dear Mum

Imagine you are David's mum. Write a response to David's letter.

Dear Mum,

I'm really enjoying living on the farm. Mr Reynolds and Ann are very nice, but I wish you could be here too. Last week Tucky and me saw a German bomber crash-land in the moors. We went out to try and find it, but I fell in the river and almost drowned. One of the German airmen jumped in to save me. He even built a fire to help me get dry.

I don't know what I should do. He's a German after all, and the Germans are our enemies. I thought that I should tell Mr Reynolds about him but Tucky said that I owed the pilot for saving my life. He said it wouldn't be right to tell on him after he had helped me.

Now the airmen want me to take them food and blankets. That means I'd have to steal from Mr Reynolds and that doesn't seem right either. What do you think I should do?

David

Dear David,

_____

_____

_____

_____

_____

_____

_____

_____

_____

_____

_____

_____

 Literacy evolve

Dear diary

Continue David's diary about his dilemma and what he plans to do.

Tuesday 4th June

Today was a very strange and confusing day. I almost drowned while Tucky and me were out looking for the German plane we saw crash-land. But I was saved by a German pilot. He pulled me out of the river and got all of the water out of me. He even built a fire to help get me dry. Oh, wait. Ann is calling me. I'll write more later.

_____

_____

_____

_____

_____

_____

_____

_____

_____

_____

_____

_____

_____

_____

David's views

Order David's thoughts and discuss how his view has changed.

'I've paid you back, haven't I?'

'He can hardly walk, Ann; he's tired out and coughing; he should see a doctor.'

'We only did it 'cos you helped us. That's all. We're still enemies.'

David was tempted to catch his eye, to thank him, but he dared not take the risk.

'Jip found him, Mr Reynolds. He's a German bomber pilot – Luftwaffe.'

'We have done enough. There won't be any more.'

'I could make you come too.'

David had thought it all out as they came across the fields, and the story came out now convincingly.

Friend or foe?

Write how the German airmen are described in *Friend or Foe*.

Friend	Foe
'There was nothing threatening or frightening about them ...' (page 73)	'Perhaps these were the men who had shot down his father ...' (page 73)

Book tasters

Read the book tasters and look for common features.

The Butterfly Lion

Bertie makes a friend for life when he rescues a white lion cub from the African veld. But when Bertie is sent to boarding school, the cub is sold to a circus and they are separated. But Bertie promises never to forget his friend. He knows they will see each other again …

The Wreck of the Zanzibar

Life is hard on the Scilly Isles in 1907. Laura's twin brother disappears and then a violent storm ruins everything. But the storm also wrecks the Zanzibar on the island's rocks, bringing hope with it. Follow the story through Laura's diary entries, as the dramatic events unfold in this thrilling story.

Kensuke's Kingdom

An accident at sea leaves Michael stranded on a desert island. His parents are gone and he has no idea how to survive on his own. Losing all hope, Michael curls up on the floor to die. But when he wakes, there is a plate of food beside him. It looks like he is not alone …

War Horse

In 1914, a young farm horse, Joey, is sold to the army. He leaves his home and his young master behind, and is thrust into the horror of the First World War. The horse's courage impresses the soldiers, but Joey misses his life on the farm. Will he ever make it home to see his master again?

Michael Morpurgo

Choose a topic. Plan and record your research in Topic 1. Then share information with another pair and complete Topic 2.

I want to find out …   I'm going to find out by …   I found out …

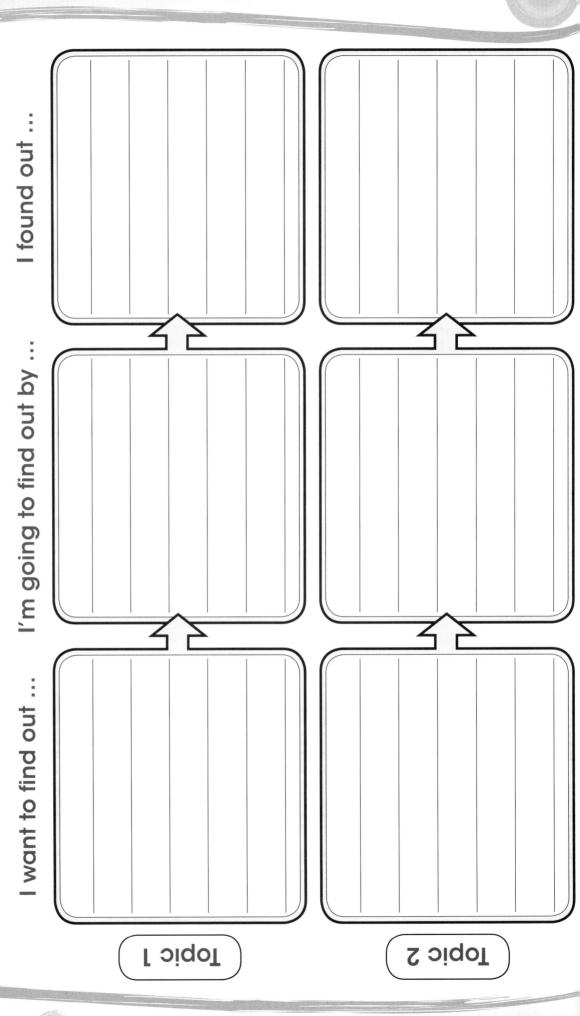

Topic 1

Topic 2

Nuggets of truth

Find links between *Friend or Foe* and Michael Morpurgo.

Friend or Foe	Michael Morpurgo

Friend or Foe is set on the Moors in Devon.

Michael Morpurgo lives on a farm in Devon.

Story plan 2

Add notes to plan your story.

Ending

Resolution

Problem

Opening

The stranger

Write a character profile to describe the stranger.

Name: _____

_____

Age: _____

_____

Lives: _____

_____

Looks like: _____

_____

_____

Acts like: _____

_____

_____

_____

Friend or foe? _____

_____

Marking ladder

Use the marking ladder to check your work.

Teacher's comments

My comments

- I have introduced details about the characters gradually.
- My dialogue shows how the characters are feeling.
- I have used description to create a picture for the reader.
- I have used different verbs to make my story more interesting.
- I have included a solution for the problem.
- I have used events from my own experience in my story.
- My ending gives the reader something to think about.

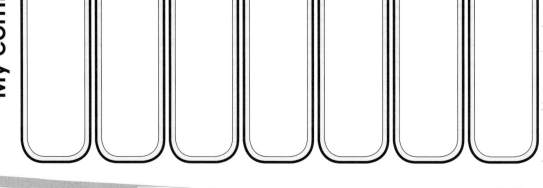

Narrative Unit 2

THE BOOK – film (Traditional stories)

Medium term plan (4 weeks)	
Phase	**Learning Outcomes**
Phase 1: Reading; familiarisation with text type (4 days)	• Children can identify features of the traditional tale genre. • Children can compare different versions of a story written in different forms. • Children can perform a poem using dramatic conventions.
Phase 2: Analysing and comparing features of a legend (6 days)	• Children can infer a narrator's viewpoint. • Children can understand a character using direct evidence and inference. • Children can retell a story from a different character's perspective.
Phase 3: Comparing texts: analysing film (2 days)	• Children can identify and understand the effects of different film shots and techniques. • Children can discuss similarities and differences between written and visual texts.
Phase 4: Planning, oral storytelling and writing legends (8 days)	• Children can create a legend-style story for oral storytelling. • Children can perform an oral storytelling using expression, dynamics and powerful and patterned language. • Children can plan and carry out the filming of an oral storytelling. • Children can rehearse, appraise and improve a performance. • Children can write a legend-style story using appropriate language and style.

Narrative Unit 2

THE BOOK

Big picture

The children read a selection of traditional stories from different cultures and times and identify features of the genre. They explore the language and structure used in different versions of traditional tales. The children then read *The Book*, using drama strategies to explore and empathise with characters. They then rewrite aspects of the story in the forms of a diary and a legend. Then they compare the written version with the film *The Book*. The children go on to apply their learning about the different impacts of written, oral and visual texts by creating a story which they tell orally then write as a legend text.

Prior learning

This unit assumes that children can already:
- identify distinctive features of a genre
- read and respond to stories, discussing setting, mood, characters and structure
- use drama strategies to explore characters
- select powerful language for particular effects.

Key aspects of learning

Communication: Express ideas through speaking, listening and writing; retell a story orally and listen to others telling theirs.

Creative thinking: Use imagination to create a legend-style story for an oral telling; use powerful language to capture the listener's interest.

Empathy: Explore different characters' points of view; write a diary in role from the perspective of a character.

Social skills: Work collaboratively to prepare a performance; provide and respond to constructive peer appraisal.

Enquiry: Pose open questions to explore a mystery object.

Progression in narrative

In this unit the children will:
- write for a range of purposes
- rewrite or retell a story in different narrative forms
- write a legend using varied sentences and powerful language to create mystery and tension.

Cross-curricular links

Art and Design: Create a book of the finished legends.

Geography: Investigate where in the world the legends in the unit come from.

History: Explore the role of legends in different cultures.

ICT: Develop the oral storytellings into other formats e.g. recording them as voiceover narrations to accompany illustrations; preparing a 'storytape'.

Viewing time

8 minutes 40 seconds approx.

PHASE 1: READING; FAMILIARISATION WITH TEXT TYPE (4 DAYS)

Session 1

We are learning to ...	Resources
• compare the structure and features of traditional stories (myths, legends, tales) (PNS Strands 7.3)	ITP: 2.1 PCM: 2.1, 2.2, 2.3
Assessment Focuses	
AF (R): 4, 7	

Shared teaching

- Share the learning objective and explain that this is a narrative unit about traditional stories, fairy tales, myths and legends. Introduce the 'Big Picture' for the unit.
- Write the headings: Traditional tales, Legends, Myths and Fairy tales. *What do you know about these genres? Have you come across myths and traditional tales while working in other curriculum areas? Can you remember any myths or legends you read in previous years?*
- The children Think-Pair-Share examples of each genre, and identify their typical features. Take feedback and scribe responses under each heading.
- Show 'Traditional stories' (ITP 2.1). Click and read about different types of traditional stories. *How far do the descriptions match your examples of each genre? What would you add to the description of each genre?*
- Explain to the children that the differences between each of these types of traditional tale are often blurred. The genres share many things in common, e.g. themes exploring good and evil, the use of imagery, similar story structures, etc. Explain that many of these stories were first told 'orally' (passed on by word of mouth) and were later written down. Some stories have been written in many different versions over the years.

Independent and Guided

- Place a selection of stories in brown envelopes and explain to the children that you have a mystery envelope for each group which contains a selection of stories. From the information on ITP 2.1 and their own ideas, they have to identify the features of each story and decide which genre each story best fits into. Give the children time to read through each story and make a group decision. Emphasise that the aim is to look closely at the structure and discuss the language of the texts rather than to identify the 'right' genre.

  (◎◎◎) Read 'Sir Gawain and the Green Knight' (PCM 2.1), 'The Cherokee Little People' (PCM 2.2) and 'Theseus and the Minotaur' (PCM 2.3).

  (◎◎) As above. (T+)

  (◎) Read PCM 2.1 and PCM 2.2. (TA+)

Plenary

- Ask members of the higher and middle ability groups to summarise *Theseus and the Minotaur*.
- Take feedback from all groups. *What genres do you think the stories belong to?* Remind the children that all of these genres share some similar features.
- Recap the learning objective.

Assessment pointers

- S&L: group work will show how far the children can engage with others, draw ideas together and promote discussion.
- AF4, 7 (R): response to questions and group discussions show how far the children are able to respond to the language and structure of texts and relate them to cultural traditions.

We are learning to ...	Resources
• compare different versions of the same story and explain the similarities and differences • identify how an author creates a sense of danger and excitement (PNS Strands 7.5, 8.3) **Assessment Focuses** AF (R): 4, 5, 7	ITP: (2.1), 2.2, 2.3, 2.4, 2.5 PCM: 2.4, 2.5, 2.6

Shared teaching

• Discuss what the children learnt about different genres in Session 1. Recall 'Traditional stories' (ITP 2.1) if necessary.
• Share the learning objectives.
• Show and read 'The Children of Hamelin' (ITP 2.2). *Is this a familiar story? Do you know another name for this story? Who do you think this story is written for?* (children) *When do you think this story was written?* (quite recently; it's a modern version) *Do you think this story is a legend?*
• Show 'Pictures of the Pied Piper' (ITP 2.3). *Which illustration is older? Which is more recent? What tells you this?*
• Explain that the story of the Pied Riper has appeared in many versions over hundreds of years. The oldest written record dates from 1450, which is nearly 600 years ago. The first version was apparently written by a historian, Heinrich von Herford, and is set in Hamelin in the year 1284. but the story has been embellished over the years.
• Explain that the children are now going to look at a different version and show 'The Pied Piper of Hamelin' (ITP 2.4). *Do you think this is a modern version? How is this version different from* The Children of Hamelin? *Which version do you think is the most effective?*

• Explain that the children are going to take a closer look at the authors' use of language. Show 'The rats' (ITP 2.5) and read the two quotations. *Which gives the most vivid picture of the rats? Which gives you the strongest sense of the townspeople's fear?*
• Explain that 'Extract 2' on ITP 2.5 is a stanza from the most famous version of the story from Robert Browning's poem, *The Pied Piper of Hamelin*. Explain that they will read more of the poem in Session 3.

Independent and Guided

• In groups, the children complete 'Comparing versions' (PCM 2.6). They should allocate roles within their groups, e.g. a leader, a scribe, etc.
• **ooo** Compare 'The rats are leaving 1' (PCM 2.4) and 'The rats are leaving 2' (PCM 2.5) and complete PCM 2.6.
• **oo** As above. (TA+)
• **o** Compare the two extracts on PCM 2.5 and complete PCM 2.6. (T+)

Plenary

• Recap the learning objectives.
• Encourage the groups to give feedback. *What similarities or differences did you find? What striking language did you find particularly effective?*
• Talk Partners discuss their preferences. *Which version do you prefer?*
• Take feedback and discuss the preferences as a class with a show of hands.

Assessment pointers

• S&L: group or pair work will show how far the children can adopt group roles, drawing ideas together and promoting effective discussion.
• AF4, 5, 7 (R): response to questions and group work shows how far the children can comment on the structure, organisation and language of texts, relating them to historical contexts.

We are learning to ...	Resources
• use drama techniques and empathy to explore stories and say how useful these techniques are • perform a poem making use of dramatic conventions (PNS Strands 4.2, 8.2) **Assessment Focuses** AF (R): 3	ITP: 2.6, 2.7 PCM: (2.4)

Shared teaching

• The children work in pairs to play Just a Minute, recapping as much of the Pied Piper story as they can remember.
• Share the learning objectives.
• Show and read 'The Pied Piper of Hamelin' (ITP 2.6). Explain any unfamiliar language. *What part of the story is this? How do you think the townspeople felt when the children disappeared?*
• Set up a whole-class Hot-Seating activity. Choose three children to be townspeople and put them in the 'hot seat'. Encourage the class to ask questions based on the extract and their knowledge of the whole story, e.g. *How frightening were the rats? What did you think of the Pied Piper when you first saw him? Who did you think he was? Why didn't the council pay him? What was the town like without any children?*
• Continue the hot-seating activity and choose a child to be the Pied Piper in the 'hot seat'. Encourage the children to ask questions to find out more about him, e.g. *Who are you? Where did you come from? Why did you go to the town?*
• Discuss the drama activity. *Has this helped you to understand the legend better? Did it help you understand the characters any better?*
• Explain that in the rest of this session, the children are going to perform parts of the poem.

• Show 'The Pied Piper of Hamelin' (ITP 2.7). Choose four of the children to read the extract from Robert Browning's poem. Demonstrate how to divide up the lines so that each child reads some. *How shall we divide up the lines? Which lines should be read loudly or softly?* Annotate the ITP to indicate who reads which line and how the lines are read.
• The four children read the stanzas according to the annotations. Encourage the class to offer positive feedback about the performance.

Independent and Guided

• In groups the children work on performances of lines from the poem using different colours to mark the script. Groups should allocate different roles, e.g. a director, readers, etc.
• **ooo** Print out and perform ITP 2.6.
• **oo** Perform 'The rats are leaving 1' (PCM 2.4). (TA+)
• **o** Print out and perform the second stanza from ITP 2.7. (T)

Plenary

• Each group performs their lines from the poem. While each group is performing ask the rest of the class to try to visualise the action.
• Recap the learning objectives and as a class, reflect on whether the hot-seating technique, the performances and the visualisation helped the children to gain a better understanding of the poem.

Assessment pointers

• S&L: hot-seating will show how far the children can sustain roles to explore ideas.
• AF3 (R): hot-seating and group work show how far the children can make inferences and interpret characters' emotions and motives.

We are learning to ...	Resources
• make notes using evidence to support our ideas • explore how authors use language for comic and dramatic effects (PNS Strands 7.1, 7.5) **Assessment Focuses** AF (R): 4, 5, 7	ITP: (2.2), 2.8, 2.9

Shared teaching (1)

• Recap what the children have learnt so far and remind them of the legends they read in previous sessions.
• Share the learning objectives and explain that they are now going to read another short legend.
• Show and read 'The Legend of Randwick' (ITP 2.8). *What do you think of this legend?* Explain that the children are going to learn how to make notes on texts to help them explore the texts at a deeper level.
• Focus on ITP 2.8. *What do we know about where the story is set?* Highlight all phrases related to setting in a specific colour. Include details of where and when the story is set. Annotate the ITP accordingly.
• Now focus on characters. *What do we learn about Tom and Dick? What kind of characters are they?* (E.g. strong farm lads, practical jokers, a little silly.) Highlight the relevant text using a different colour and add the children's comments in the margins.
• Now focus on the language. Ask the children to highlight the powerful verbs in a third colour, e.g. 'grinning', 'bobbed', 'goggling', 'grabbed', 'shouting', 'yelling', 'screaming', etc. *What picture do we get of Ma Heggerty and the boys running away? How is it funny?*

• Remind the children that the story is written in the past tense and highlight some past tense verbs in a fourth colour.

Independent and Guided

• Print out copies of 'The Children of Hamelin' (ITP 2.2) for the children. They work in groups to make notes on the text using different colours to highlight information about settings, character and powerful verbs. Encourage the children to add their own thoughts in the margins. Support the children with an identified need. (T/TA)

Shared teaching (2)

• Take feedback. *What are your favourite words and phrases from* The Children of Hamelin? *What makes these words and phrases effective?*
• The children Mind Map the ingredients they would need to write effective legends. Allow Think Time before taking feedback.
• Show 'Writing a legend' (ITP 2.9) and discuss ideas. *Is there anything you would like to add or change?* Add the children's suggestions and save for use in later sessions.

Plenary

• Recap the learning objectives. *What have you learnt about the language and features of legends? Which legend did you enjoy most?*

Assessment pointers

• AF4, 5, 7 (R): annotations to the texts show how far the children can identify and comment on the structure, organisation and language of texts and how far they can recognise different features of the genre.

PHASE 2: ANALYSING AND COMPARING FEATURES OF A LEGEND (6 DAYS)

We are learning to ...	Resources
• make notes on a text to help us understand the narrator's viewpoint • understand a character from what is known and what can be inferred (PNS Strands 7.1, 7.2) **Assessment Focuses** AF (R): 2, 3, 7	ITP: 2.10 PCM: 2.7, 2.8

Shared teaching

• Share the learning objectives and explain that so far in this unit, the children have read myths and legends with fairly traditional structures. In this session, they are going to read a modern story about a different kind of legend: a legend about ghosts, that has been passed down by word of mouth through generations and may or may not have been based on truth.
• Show 'The Book' (ITP 2.10) and read to the end of Screen 2.
• Talk Partners play Just a Minute to explain to each other what has happened in the story so far.
• Take feedback. *Where is the story set? What is the old legend that has been passed down over the years? What do you think might happen next? How does Zoe feel about the library? How does Abbie feel about the library?*
• Explain that the children are now going to think about how the author is telling the story. *What is the author's viewpoint? What is the author's view of Zoe? What does he tell us about her?*
• Remind the class of what they learnt about making notes around the text in the Session 4. *What have you learnt about Zoe?* Add the

children's suggestions to ITP 2.10, e.g. she is imaginative; she is spooked by the library; she is fascinated by the old legend.
• Discuss what the author has told us about Abbie. *What kind of person is she? What kind of things does she like?* Again, annotate ITP 2.10.
• Explain that this method of making notes on the text will help them to look at a text more closely. Sometimes they will also need to make notes on a separate piece of paper to draw their thoughts together. Talk Partners discuss how to make useful notes, e.g. use headings to group thoughts together, don't write in full sentences, use details from the text, etc.

Independent and Guided

• The children make notes on what they have learnt so far about Zoe and Abbie. If necessary, print out the first two screens of ITP 2.10 for the children to work from.
  ⦿⦿⦿ Complete 'Making notes 1' (PCM 2.7). (T+)
  ⦿⦿ Complete 'Making notes 2' (PCM 2.8).
  ⦿ As above. (TA+)

Plenary

• Recap the learning objectives. Ask the children to share examples of their notes and summarise what they have learnt about the characters. *What notes have you written? What headings have you used? Why have you grouped notes under certain headings?*

Assessment pointers

• AF2, 3, 7 (R): group discussions and notes show how far the children can make inferences about characters and draw evidence from the text when making their notes.

Session 6

We are learning to ...	Resources
• retell a story in role • use and explore different question types • use drama and role play to empathise with characters (PNS Strands 1.1, 1.3, 4.1)	ITP: (2.10), 2.11
Assessment Focuses AF (R): 3	

Shared teaching

• Wrap a 'mystery object' in brown paper before the session. This could be an unusual but useful object, something intriguing, or something funny.
• Tell the children that someone has left a mystery parcel on your chair and you're very curious about it. Encourage the children to suggest questions you could ask about the parcel, e.g. *What is it? What's in it?*
• Open the parcel and encourage the children to suggest more questions you could ask, e.g. *How can I use it? What shall I do with it? Who sent it to me? Why did they send it to me? Where did they get it?*
• Share the learning objectives and explain that in this session, the children are going to think about different types of questions and the impact different questions have.
• Show 'Question types' (ITP 2.11). *Which of these question types did we use when discussing the mystery object?*
• Explain that there are closed questions, which have specific answers, and open questions which invite people to explore things. Drag the questions under the correct headings. Encourage the children to suggest more examples that could be added to the lists.
• Remind the children of the story of 'The Book' (ITP 2.10). Set up a whole-class Hot-Seating activity and invite the children to take the

place of Zoe and Abbie in the 'hot seat'. Encourage the class to ask the characters questions using a wide range of question types.
• Explain that they are now going to explore the story from different points of view. *Whose point of view might we use?* (E.g. Zoe, Abbie, Mr Beeson, someone using the library.) Remind the children that stories told from a character's viewpoint will use the first person.

Independent and Guided

• The children rehearse an oral retelling of the story so far from the viewpoint of one of the characters in *The Book*. Remind the children to stay 'in character' throughout and to share the retelling between all group members. Each group then performs their story for another group, who listen and identify the character. Groups take it in turn to question each other about their characters, answering questions in character. Support the children with an identified need. (T+/TA+)

Plenary

• Recap the learning objectives. *Which questions were most effective? Which were hard or easy to answer? Did retelling the story as a character help your understanding of the text?*

Assessment pointers

• S&L: oral retellings will show how well the children can recount ideas.
• AF 3 (R): group work, the children's questions and oral retellings will show how far the children are able to make inferences about characters based on the text.

Session 7

We are learning to ...	Resources
• use drama techniques to explore the meaning of the text • make predictions about the story (PNS Strands 4.1, 8.2)	ITP: (2.10)
Assessment Focuses AF (R): 3	

Shared teaching (1)

• Recall 'The Book' (ITP 2.10) and remind the children of what has happened in the story so far. *What have you learnt about the characters?*
• Share the learning objectives and explain that the children are going to use drama techniques to explore the story more deeply and then predict what might happen next.
• Return to ITP 2.10 and continue reading the story until the end of Screen 3. Explain any unknown vocabulary. *Does the author give you any more information about the characters? Are you puzzled by anything?*
• Gather the children around in a circle and place a book in the centre of the circle. Ask the children to focus on the book. *What might it be about?* Share thoughts around the circle. Then ask a child to enter the circle in the character of Zoe and open the book as they feel she would have done.
• Create a Freeze Frame of Zoe opening the book. Use Thought Tracking to explore what she might be thinking as she does so.

Independent and Guided

• The children work in pairs and use Improvisation to explore what they think will happen next in the story. The children then Mind Map their predictions. Support the children with an identified need. (T+/TA+)

Shared teaching (2)

• Take feedback and discuss the children's predictions. *What do you think will happen next? What in the story made you think that?*
• Recall ITP 2.10 and read the rest of *The Book*. *Were you surprised by what happened? Do you think the ending is effective? How does the ending differ from your predictions?*

Plenary

• Recap the learning objectives.
• Reflect on the techniques used to explore the story in the previous two sessions, i.e. drama, empathy with characters, prediction, visualisation. *Which techniques do you think were the most effective in helping you to understand the story and characters?*

Assessment pointers

• S&L: improvisations will show how well the children can create and sustain roles to explore and develop ideas.
• AF 3 (R): improvisations, responses to questioning and predictions show how far the children are able to make inferences based on the text.

We are learning to ...	Resources
• explore how an author uses language, sentence structure and punctuation to create dramatic effects and tension • punctuate sentences accurately and effectively (PNS Strands 7.5, 11.2) **Assessment Focuses** AF (R): 5; AF (W): 6	ITP: (2.10), 2.12 PCM: 2.9, 2.10

Shared teaching (1)

- Share the learning objectives and explain that the children are going to focus on style, punctuation and how the author builds tension in the writing.
- Give the children copies of 'Correcting text' (PCM 2.9).
- Read the first few sentences and then ask for a volunteer to read out the rest. Choose an able, fluent reader. When the reader gets to the second paragraph, where the text is no longer punctuated, wait to see what happens and look to see who notices in the class. If the reader naturally adds their own punctuation by continuing to read fluently, stop them and ask them what they have noticed about the text.
- Discuss the missing punctuation. *How does it feel to read a text without punctuation? Is it hard to read without punctuation? What is punctuation for?* (E.g. to guide the reader, indicate pauses and expression, etc.)
- Encourage the children to give examples of the punctuation that is missing from PCM 2.9, e.g. full stops, commas, speech marks, apostrophes, question marks, exclamation marks. Scribe a list.
- *Can you explain the purpose of each type of punctuation?* If some children are unsure, hold a brief punctuation revision session.

Independent and Guided

- The children work in pairs to punctuate texts, adding the full range of punctuation, and reading aloud to hear where the punctuation goes.
- Complete PCM 2.9.
- As above. (T)
- Punctuate 'What's missing?' (PCM 2.10). (TA+)

Shared teaching (2)

- Show 'Style and punctuation' (ITP 2.12). *What punctuation did you add?* Click to reveal the punctuation. *Did you add all of the missing punctuation?*
- Recall 'The Book' (ITP 2.10). *How has the author used punctuation to create tension and suspense?* (E.g. the use of ellipses.) *What other techniques has the author used to create tension?* (E.g. the use of vocabulary like 'heart raced.') *What words and phrases are used? What images does the writing create?* Allow Think Time before discussing as a class.

Plenary

- Recap the learning objectives. *What have you learnt about using punctuation and creating tension, mystery and suspense? How might you create tension in your own writing?*
- Take feedback and add to the Learning Wall for future sessions.

Assessment pointers

- AF5 (R): response to questioning and annotated PCMs show how far the children can identify and explain how the author uses language and punctuation to create tension.
- AF6 (W): annotated PCMs show how well the children understand and can use punctuation effectively.

We are learning to ...	Resources
• use empathy to make inferences about characters • plan and write diary entries • punctuate sentences accurately and effectively (PNS Strands 7.2, 9.2, 11.2) **Assessment Focuses** AF (W): 1, 3, 5, 6	ITP: 2.13 PCM: (2.7, 2.8), 2.11

Shared teaching

- Remind the children of the work they did in Session 6 (oral retellings of the story from a character's point of view) and in Session 5 (the notes they made about the characters). Make sure the children have a copy of their notes or PCM 2.7 or PCM 2.8 from Session 5.
- Share the learning objectives and explain that the children will write two diary entries for Zoe: one for the evening before her visit to the library and one for the evening after, describing her trip.
- Discuss the key features of diary entries. *What do you need to think about when writing from a character's point of view? What information do you need to include to make it seem like a real diary?* (E.g. write in the first person, include her thoughts and feelings, write the date, etc.)
- Explain that as the first diary entry will be written the night before the library trip, it will anticipate what is going to happen. Talk Partners discuss how Zoe might feel about going on the trip. *Is she excited about the trip? What do you think she is looking forward to most? Do you think Abbie is going to enjoy the trip?*
- Take feedback and discuss as a class.
- Discuss ideas for writing the second diary entry, when Zoe has

returned from the library trip. *What did Zoe learn about the library? How does Zoe feel now? What happened after Abbie disappeared?*

- Remind the children of the work they did on punctuation and creating tension in Session 8.
- Talk Partners discuss what they think the success criteria might be for writing a diary entry.
- Show 'Writing a diary' (ITP 2.13) and add any further suggestions to the success criteria.

Independent and Guided

- The children work independently to write two entries for Zoe's diary. Encourage the children to refer to ITP 2.13.
- Write Zoe's diary entries for the night before the library trip and the night after.
- As above. (TA)
- As above using 'Zoe's diary' (PCM 2.11). (T+)

Plenary

- The children self-assess their diary entries against the success criteria. The children then share one thing they would like to improve.
- Recap the learning objectives.

Assessment pointers

- AF1, 3, 5, 6 (W): self-assessment against the success criteria and written pieces show how far the children can punctuate, organise and write imaginative texts and vary sentence structures.

We are learning to ...	Resources
• plan and write an old legend • adapt sentences for different types of text and readers • understand and use punctuation for speech accurately (PNS Strands 9.2, 11.1, 11.2) **Assessment Focuses** AF (W): 1, 2, 5, 6	ITP: (2.1, 2.9), 2.14

Shared teaching

• Share the learning objectives and recap how diary entries are written. *What effect does writing in the first person have? Is the writing personal or informal?*
• Ask the children to imagine a time in the future, fifty to one hundred years after the incident involving Zoe and Abbie. *How would the writing of the legend be different from that of the diary entries?* (E.g. written in the third person, more formal, using language typical of legends and retellings, etc.)
• Recall 'Traditional stories' (ITP 2.1) and click on 'Legends'. *Which of these features might you include in a legend about the library?*
• Show Screen 1 of 'Zoe's diary' (ITP 2.14). Explain that the children are going to rewrite the text as a short legend. *Which parts of this text might appear in the legend?* (E.g. the personal views won't be included; the history of the old library will be included but written in a different way.) Highlight the parts of the text that would be included in the legend but written in a different style.
• Talk Partners discuss how the legend might begin.
• Take feedback and scribe suggestions. Focus on the description of

the library. *How might these sentences be rewritten in the style of a legend?* Scribe responses.
• Show Screen 3 of ITP 2.14. Highlight language and features typical of legends, e.g. use of time connectives, set in a particular time and place in history, use of more formal language, etc.
• Explain that the children are going to continue writing the legend. Show 'Writing a legend' (ITP 2.9). Discuss and add to the success criteria. Save annotations for later sessions.

Independent and Guided

• The children rewrite their diary entries as a legend. Encourage them to find specific sentences that can be rewritten in the style of a legend. Support the children with an identified need. (T/TA)

Plenary

• Recap the learning objectives.
• Ask the children to share examples of specific sentences from their diary entries that they have rewritten in the style of a legend.

Assessment pointers

• AF1, 2, 5, 6 (W): the children's legends show how far they are able to adapt content, language and sentence structures for audience and punctuate correctly.

PHASE 3: COMPARING TEXTS: ANALYSING FILM (2 DAYS)

We are learning to ...	Resources
• use evidence to evaluate a visual presentation • identify how and why different shots and techniques are used in films • explore how a film maker uses film techniques to create tension (PNS Strands 7.1, 7.3, 7.5) **Assessment Focuses** AF (R): 4, 5	*The Book* (film) ITP: 2.15, 2.16

Shared teaching (1)

• Explain that so far in this unit, the children have read the modern story of *The Book*, rewritten the story in the form of diary entries and rewritten it again in the form of a legend. Today they are going to watch the film on which the modern story is based.
• Watch the whole of *The Book*. Talk Partners discuss the film and agree on three differences that really stood out between the film and the story. Take feedback and discuss as a class.
• Show 'Film shots' (ITP 2.15) and talk through the different shots.
• Share the learning objectives and explain that in this session, the children are going to study the effects that the different shots have on the viewer and how these effects add to the overall impact of the film.
• Watch *The Book* from the beginning to Marker 1 and ask the children to note as many different types of camera shots used as they can. Show the clip twice to give the children time to add any detail. Share responses.
• Show 'Stills from *The Book*' (ITP 2.16). Examine each image and discuss the effects. *What effect does this shot have and why is it used here? What do you think this tells us? What do you think will happen next?* Add notes to ITP 2.16

• Remind the children of the work they did on making notes in Session 5. Explain that they are going to watch another short clip from the film and make notes on how the film director uses film techniques to create tension.

Independent and Guided

• Show *The Book* from Marker 1 to Marker 2. The children work in groups to make notes about how the director uses film techniques to create tension in the film. Support the children with an identified need. (T+/TA+)

Shared teaching (2)

• Encourage the groups to give feedback. Pause to highlight the children's ideas where necessary. *How did the different shots make you feel? How do you think the story is going to continue?* Add more notes to ITP 2.16.
• Continue to watch from Marker 2 to Marker 3. *What happened? Where did the key come from? What is the key for? How do you think the story will continue?* Explain that they will find out in Session 12.

Plenary

• Recap the learning objectives. *How are different shots and techniques used in films? What was the most exciting or frightening part of the film so far? How did the director create this feeling?*

Assessment pointers

• AF 4, 5 (R): group work and notes show how far the children are able to identify and comment on the use of different techniques and shots in a film.

We are learning to ...	Resources
• compare the similarities and differences between a text and a film (PNS Strands 7.3) **Assessment Focuses** AF (R): 2, 4, 5	*The Book* (film) ITP: (2.10) PCM: 2.12, 2.13

Shared teaching (1)

• The children play Just a Minute to recap the story of *The Book* so far.
• Share the learning objective and recall '*The Book*' (ITP 2.10) and explain that the text is based on the film but there may be some differences. Read to the end of Screen 3. *What differences and similarities are there? Why do you think the author decided to write the opening this way?* Take feedback and scribe ideas.
• Recap that the film was stopped at the point when Zoe was lying on the floor with a key. *What puzzles you about this? I wonder what's going to happen next.*
• Watch *The Book* from Marker 3 to 4. *What different film techniques were used?* (E.g. special effects, music, shorter camera shots, etc.) *How did this make you feel? How would you show this in a narrative?*
• Recall ITP 2.10 and read to the end of Screen 5. *Where and how does the author create tension?* (E.g. the use of ellipses: 'A hooded monk turning … '; and short sentences: 'Then she saw him yet again. The monk. Coming towards them. Coming for them … '.)
• Focus on how tension is created in the film and remind the children of the work they did in Session 11.
• Encourage the children to offer a few suggestions about how the film and the narrative are similar and different. Explain that they are going to explore this more in groups.

Independent and Guided

• The children work in groups to compare the similarities and differences between the film and the written version, focusing on Markers 3 to 4 of the film and Screens 3 to 5 of ITP 2.10.
  oo Complete 'Making comparisons 1' (PCM 2.12). If time, they extend their notes to incorporate the opening section of the film and text. (T)
  oo Complete 'Making comparisons 2' (PCM 2.13).
  o As above. (TA+)

Shared teaching (2)

• Take feedback and note down key differences and similarities. Encourage the children to support their ideas by referring to the film or text. *How do you think the film is going to continue? Will the text end differently?*
• Watch the film from Marker 4 to the end and read from Screen 6 to the end on ITP 2.10. *Did the film or the text end how you expected it to? What was surprising? Does anything still puzzle you? Why do you think the author ends the text this way? Which ending do you prefer?*

Plenary

• Recap the learning objective. The children Think-Pair-Share which version they think was most effective and why. Take feedback.

Assessment pointers

• S&L: group work will show how well the children can adopt group roles and express relevant ideas.
• AF2, 4, 5 (R): response to questions, group work and completed PCMs show how far the children can identify and compare the structures of the story and film and the use of language features and film techniques.

PHASE 4: PLANNING, ORAL STORYTELLING AND WRITING LEGENDS (8 DAYS)

We are learning to ...	Resources
• use and explore different question types • understand and map the story structure • use storyboards or a planner to create a structure (PNS Strands 1.3, 7.3, 9.2) **Assessment Focuses** AF (W): 3	ITP: (2.1, 2.2, 2.11), 2.17 PCM: 2.14

Shared teaching

• Before the session, collect a box of different objects such as old hats, an ornament, a stone, an artificial flower, a bag, etc. to be used in a group drama activity.
• Recap what the children have learnt in previous sessions, e.g. that written, oral and visual texts all create different effects and have a different impact.
• Share the learning objectives and explain that in the last phase of this unit, the children are going to write their own legends in groups. The legends will be written for a tourist guide about an old building. The children will use drama to create their legends and prepare an oral storytelling before writing the story down.
• Explain that first they are going to review the structure of legends. Study the relevant notes on the Learning Wall and recall 'Traditional stories' (ITP 2.1) again. Remind the children that most legends have a brave character who usually goes on a journey or quest to solve a problem.
• Reread '*The Children of Hamelin*' (ITP 2.2).
• Show 'Legend plan' (ITP 2.17). Use Modelled Writing to map the structure of *The Children of Hamelin*.
• Explain to the children that they are now going to use drama to explore

ideas for writing their own legends. Recall 'Question types' (ITP 2.11) and remind the children that they can use different questions to help them explore their ideas.
• Seat the children in a circle, open the box of props and explain that the props will be used to prompt ideas. Pull out an object and encourage the children to ask questions, e.g. *Where was it found? What has it got to do with the legend of the old building? Who did it belong to?*
• Explain that the children will now work in groups, with the goal of creating a legend plan like the one on ITP 2.17.

Independent and Guided

• The children work in groups to explore and plan their legends. Each group chooses a prop from the box and asks questions about it. They create answers to the questions and use this information to create an Improvisation of a legend. They then complete 'Legend plan' (PCM 2.14). Support the children with an identified need. (T/TA)

Plenary

• Recap the learning objectives.
• Ask groups to self-assess their legend plans. *Have you got a clear structure for your story in place?*
• Take feedback and discuss ideas. *Are there any problems you need help with?*

Assessment pointers

• S&L: improvisations will show how far the children can create and sustain roles to explore ideas.
• AF3 (W): group work shows how effectively the children used drama and discussion to create a purposeful structure for their legends.

We are learning to ...	Resources
• make notes to support oral stories • use different techniques in our notes (PNS Strands 1.1, 12.1) **Assessment Focuses** AF (W): 3	ITP: 2.18 PCM: (2.14)

Shared teaching

• Share the learning objectives and explain that groups are going to write notes to use as prompts during an oral telling of their legends.

• Use Modelled Writing to show how to make notes to support oral storytelling. Use Think Alouds to model explaining ideas, e.g. *If I were making notes to help me tell the story of* Goldilocks and the Three Bears, *would I write out 'Once upon a time ... ' in my notes?* Agree that it is unnecessary to write all phrases in detail. Only key words are necessary, to prompt their memory.

• Show 'Notes on Goldilocks' (ITP 2.18). *What would I need to add to these notes to support my oral storytelling? Should I remind myself of particular words and phrases? What powerful adjectives and verbs might I use?* Take suggestions from the class and annotate ITP 2.18.

• *How should I say each section? When should I talk loudly? When should I talk quietly? How can I remind myself?* Use Modelled Writing to add performance directions, and to show the children how to use different techniques to highlight parts of the notes, e.g. highlight directions to speak quietly and softly. Save the annotations.

• Now model how the notes can be used to orally tell the story of *Goldilocks and the Three Bears,* filling out the detail. *Was this oral story interesting to listen to and to watch?*

• The children Think-Pair-Share how to improve the oral storytelling.

What actions and gestures could I use? When could I address the audience directly? Could I use questions such as 'What do you think happened next?' Should I repeat any words and phrases for effect?

• Take feedback from the class and annotate the notes on ITP 2.18, using different techniques and different colours for actions and gestures or the use of questions.

• Ask for volunteers to tell parts of the story based on the notes.

Independent and Guided

• Working in the same groups as in Session 13, the children write notes for an oral storytelling of their legends using their completed 'Legend plan' (PCM 2.14). Encourage the children to use different techniques to add directions and memory prompts for specific words and phrases in their notes. They then practise their oral storytelling, allocating different sections to each group member. Support the children with an identified need. (T/TA+)

Plenary

• Recap the learning objectives.

• Encourage the groups to share things they have changed or added to their notes after practising their oral stories. *What mark up or notes did you use, such as colour scheme, highlighting, performance directions? Did the changes or additions help your oral storytelling? Did you find adding the notes easy or difficult? What technique do you think worked the best?*

Assessment pointers

• S&L: group work will show how well the children can adopt group rules, drawing ideas together and promoting effective planning.

• AF3 (W): annotated story plans show how far the children can write effective notes and make use of different annotation techniques.

We are learning to ...	Resources
• tell a story using notes • apply knowledge of film techniques to improve oral performances • use ICT to present a visual text (PNS Strands 1.1, 12.2) **Assessment Focuses** AF (W): 2	ITP: (2.15), 2.19

Shared teaching

• Collect examples of the children's storytelling notes from Session 14 and display so the class can see them.

• Share the learning objectives and explain that in this session, the children will perform their oral stories, ready to evaluate the performances in Session 16.

• Show 'Oral storytellings' (ITP 2.19) and discuss the success criteria. *Is there anything you would like to add or change?* Allow Think Time before taking responses.

• Focus on the examples of the children's storytelling notes. Talk Partners use ITP 2.19 to think of Two Stars and a Wish about each example.

• Take feedback and model how to give positive and constructive feedback, e.g. *These notes are good because they have shared out the roles, but they could think about how each person should say the lines and add this to the notes.*

• Explain that the children are now going to look again at their own storytellings. *If the performances were filmed, is there anything you could add to the notes?* (E.g. film directions, instructions for different shots, etc.)

• Recall 'Film shots' (ITP 2.15). *What film shots could you use in your*

storytellings? Encourage the children to explain their choices. *Why would a close-up work well here? How would it make the audience feel?*

Independent and Guided

• In their groups, the children edit their notes, adding any final notes or film directions if they wish. The children then practise their storytellings and discuss ways to improve their performances. When the children are ready, film the oral storytellings and save them for evaluation in Session 16. (Alternatively if you do not wish to film the storytellings, split the performances so that some groups perform and are evaluated today and the rest are performed in Session 16. (See Session 16 notes for evaluation guidance.) Support the children with an identified need. (T/TA)

Plenary

• Recap the learning objectives.

• Discuss the storytellings. *What have you learnt during the preparation and filming of your performances? Were your notes helpful? What would you do differently next time?*

Assessment pointers

• S&L: group work and storytelling will show how far the children can talk in purposeful and imaginative ways.

• AF2 (W): group work and edits to the storytelling notes show how far the children can use success criteria to write texts appropriate to task.

Session 16

We are learning to ...	Resources
• evaluate writing using success criteria	PCM: (2.12, 2.13), 2.15
• use a variety of sentence structures and direct and reported speech to make writing more interesting (PNS Strands 9.1, 9.4)	
Assessment Focuses	
AF (W): 5, 6, 7	

Shared teaching

• Remind the children that they will focus on evaluating the performances filmed yesterday and also on understanding how the oral storytelling task will help them to write their legends.

• Hand out 'Marking ladder' (PCM 2.15). Explain that the children will watch and evaluate each performance in turn, including their own. Remind them that the purpose of evaluation is to help us all reflect and improve on what we do. Evaluation needs to be fair and constructive. Also remind the children that this is not a competition.

• The children watch each performance and evaluate it using the marking ladder.

• Take feedback. *What was the effect of watching the storytellings on film rather than as live performances? How did the use of camera angles and the different film shots enhance the stories?*

• Ask the children how the experience of planning and performing oral storytellings might help them when they begin to write their legends down. *How could you recreate the actions and gestures in written words? What will need to be different when you change your oral stories into written legends?* Remind the children of the work that they did in Session 12 and encourage them to refer to completed 'Making comparisons 1' (PCM 2.12) and 'Making comparisons 2' (PCM 2.13).

• Focus on specific features of the performances. *How would you write the direct speech? How would you show the different intonation and excitement in the storytelling?* Ask the children to share specific examples from their oral storytellings and use Modelled Writing to change them into written form.

Independent and Guided

• The children work independently to practise writing parts of their oral storytellings, using powerful words and phrases.

[000] Choose three specific points from the storytellings to write down, focusing on using powerful words and correct punctuation.

[00] As above. (T+)

[0] Choose two specific points from the oral storytellings to write down in full sentences, focusing on using powerful words. (TA+)

Plenary

• Recap the learning objectives.

• Ask the children to share their sentences. Encourage the class to offer feedback. *What do you like about this sentence? Are there any points that could be improved? Are there any words we could change? Is there any punctuation we could add?*

Assessment pointers

• S&L: responses to the other children's work will show how well the children can express opinions sensitively.

• AF5, 6, 7 (W): the children's written sentences show how far they can choose effective vocabulary, vary sentences for effect and punctuate accurately.

Session 17

We are learning to...	Resources
• plan and write an old legend	ITP: (2.1, 2.9), 2.20
• adapt sentences for purpose and audience (PNS Strands 9.2, 11.1)	
Assessment Focuses	
AF (W): 1, 2, 4, 6	

Shared teaching

• Share the learning objectives and remind the children that the aim is to write a legend for part of a tourist information leaflet about an old building.

• Study the information on the Learning Wall and remind the children of the features of legends on 'Traditional stories' (ITP 2.1).

• Show 'Legend openings' (ITP 2.20) and discuss the openings. *What is similar about these openings?* (E.g. they introduce the time and place of the setting, some of the characters, and, in the first two examples, the problem that must be solved.)

• Recall 'Writing a legend' (ITP 2.9) and discuss the success criteria. *What could be added to the success criteria which specifically relates to this task? Are there any points you would like to change?* Take suggestions from the children and add them to the success criteria.

• Take one of the oral storytelling plans from Session 16. Use Modelled Writing to demonstrate writing the opening and second paragraph of the legend from the notes, using Think Alouds e.g. *I'm going to start by describing the setting. I'm going to think of a time connective here. I'm going to use powerful adjectives to make the old building sound eerie and mysterious.*

• Now ask the children how the writing could be improved. *What could we do to improve the writing? Could we make sentences shorter or longer? Could we address the reader with direct questions? Should we add speech?*

• Edit your writing using the children's suggestions.

• Explain that the children are now going to write the first part of their legends based on their oral storytellings.

Independent and Guided

• The children work independently to write their legends. Encourage them to write as much as they can during this session, at least several paragraphs, referring to ITP 2.9 to check against the success criteria. Support the children with an identified need. (T+/TA)

Plenary

• Recap the learning objectives. Ask the children to assess their writing against the success criteria on ITP 2.9 and to think of Two Stars and a Wish. They write these on sticky notes. Ask volunteers to share their points for improvement with the class. Add these to the Learning Wall.

• Collect in the children's work and prepare feedback for Session 18.

Assessment pointers

• AF1, 2, 4, 6 (W): written legends show how far the children are able to write imaginative, appropriate texts which are organised into paragraphs and are written with technical accuracy.

Session 18

We are learning to ...	Resources
• evaluate, edit and improve our writing • plan and write an old legend • adapt sentences for purpose and audience • punctuate sentences accurately and effectively (PNS Strands 9.1, 9.2, 11.1, 11.2)	ITP: (2.9)
Assessment Focuses AF (W) 1, 3, 5, 6, 7	

Shared teaching

• Give the children time to read your comments on their legends and to review the Two Stars and a Wish points that they wrote on sticky notes in Session 17.
• Continue the Modelled Writing from Session 17. If the children's stories were filmed, watch the clips again and discuss how they could recreate the suspense and mystery in their writing.
• Use Modelled Writing to compose the next paragraphs of the legend, using Think Alouds. Discuss using ellipses and varied short and long sentences to create tension and remind the children of the work they did in Session 8. As you write, also ask the children for alternative words and phrases to increase the sense of mystery and tension.
• Reread the paragraphs you have written and ask the children to suggest further improvements. *Are there any words and phrases we could repeat? Could we ask any direct questions to the reader?*
• Discuss success criteria for legends. *Can you remember any of the success criteria we thought of for writing legends? What success criteria do you think are the most important?*
• Take feedback and recall 'Writing a legend' (ITP 2.9). *Are there any you would like to add or change?*

• Explain that the children will now edit the writing that they did in Session 17 and also finish their writing. In the final sessions of this unit, they will prepare their legends for publication, using ICT, or another form of presentation.

Independent and Guided

• The children work independently to edit their writing so far, taking into account your feedback, their Two Stars and a Wish and the success criteria. The children then finish writing their legends. Support the children with an identified need. (T+/TA)

Plenary

• Recap the learning objectives.
• Talk Partners swap their legends and assess each other's work according to the success criteria, using Two Stars and a Wish.
• Take feedback. *What did you think about your partner's work? What feedback did they give you?*

Assessment pointers

• S&L: pair work will show how sensitively the children can express and respond to opinions.
• AF1, 3, 5, 6, 7 (W): written legends show how far the children are able to write and organise imaginative texts, with technical accuracy.

Session 19

We are learning to ...	Resources
• evaluate, edit and improve our writing • use different techniques in our notes • use ICT to present a visual text (PNS Strands 9.1, 12.1, 12.2)	PCM: 2.16
Assessment Focuses AF (W) 1, 3, 5, 6, 7	

Shared teaching

• Share the learning objectives and explain that the children will have a chance to make a final edit to their legends. They will then produce their legends for publication using ICT or another form of presentation.
• Discuss how the legends could be presented. Remind the children that the legends were written to be part of a leaflet about an old building. The children may wish to produce their legends as a page of the leaflet, using ICT. Alternatively, they may wish to produce their legends as a handwritten page of the leaflet using different styles of handwriting and adding illustrations. (If you have limited access to ICT in the classroom, encourage the children to opt for a range of alternative solutions.)
• Hand out 'My marking ladder' (PCM 2.16) and discuss the criteria on the marking ladder. Give the children time to reread their legends and explain that they are going to evaluate their legends using the marking ladder.

Independent and Guided

• The children assess their legends by using the marking ladder on PCM 2.16. They highlight each ticked criteria using a different colour and then find examples of each criteria in their legends, highlighting

them in a matching colour. If they can't find examples, the children edit and improve their legends to help meet the criteria. The children who finish editing early can begin work on the final presentation, preparing their legends for publication. Support the children with an identified need. (T+/TA+)

Plenary

• Recap the learning objectives.
• Ask for volunteers to share some aspects of their writing. *Why did you change that? How has it improved your legend?* Encourage the class to add constructive comments.

Assessment pointers

• AF1, 3, 5, 6, 7 (W): written legends show how far the children are able to write and organise imaginative texts, varying sentences for audience and purpose and writing with technical accuracy.

We are learning to ...
- use different techniques in our notes
(PNS Strands 12.1, 12.2)
- Use ICT to present a visual text.

Assessment Focuses

AF (W): 1, 2

Shared teaching

- Ask the children to reflect on what they have learnt about legends in this unit as a whole. Remind them of the legends they read in Sessions 1 to 4. *What did you learn about the typical features of myths and legends? What can you say about settings, character, language?*
- Remind the children of the story of *The Book* in all of its different versions. *Of all the different legends, you read which did you enjoy most? Which narrative form did you think was the most effective?*
- Ask the children if they can remember the different drama techniques used in this unit, e.g. *Hot-Seating and Freeze Frames. Which techniques helped you to understand the texts better?*
- Remind the children of other techniques they used to help them deepen their understanding of texts, e.g. making notes on the text, empathy, prediction, etc. *Which techniques did you find useful? Which techniques might you apply during your own reading?*
- Share the learning objectives.
- Remind the children of the decisions they made in Session 19 about how to publish their legends and ask if they have any further ideas. *What types of handwriting are you going to use? Are you going to add any illustrations?* If some of the children are going to use ICT, discuss the features they could use, e.g. different fonts, shapes, images, etc.

- Talk Partners discuss ideas about developing their work for publication. Take feedback and encourage the class to comment on the ideas.
- Tell the children they are now going to continue working on the publication of their legends.

Independent and Guided

- The children create a final copy of their legends for publication, either using ICT or handwriting with special features. Pause half way through for pairs to share their legends and offer suggestions as to how to improve the presentation of their partner's work, e.g. extra illustrations, different fonts, etc. Support the children with an identified need. (T/TA)

Plenary

- The children talk the class through their 'published' legends, how they chose to present them and what they are most pleased with.
- Encourage the children to comment on their own work. *What do you like best about your legend. Is there anything you would change?*
- Collect the children's work and display it so that the other children can read the legends.
- Recap the learning objectives and evaluate the unit as a whole. *What have you learnt about legends? What are the similarities and differences between film and written legends? What was your favourite legend? How do you think you have most improved? What do you still find hard?*

Assessment pointers

- S&L: pair work will show how sensitively the children can express and respond to opinions.
- AF1, 2 (W): edits in light of feedback and techniques used in the final presentations show how far the children are able to create imaginative texts appropriate to reader and purpose.

Sir Gawain and the Green Knight

Read and identify the features of the story. Then guess what genre it is.

Long, long ago, the brave and noble King Arthur ruled over Camelot. He lived in a majestic castle, surrounded by his loyal and trusted Knights of the Round Table.

One day, just before a great feast, King Arthur and his knights were disturbed by a raucous noise. The heavy wooden hall doors were flung wide open and standing in front of them was the most terrifying man they had ever seen. Towering above even the tallest knight, the fearsome stranger was as tall as a tree and as broad as an ox. He was green from head to toe and held in one hand a holly branch and in the other a giant, monstrous axe.

The Green Knight looked steadily at each Knight of the Round Table.

'Where is your leader?' he asked.

'I am head of this court', Arthur replied gracefully. 'You are welcome here. What can we do to help you?'

The Green Knight lifted his powerful head high and said, 'I have come to offer a challenge to your bravest knight. Whoever dares, can challenge me in a duel. If a knight is brave enough, he may strike me once with this axe. But the challenger must be prepared to take a return blow a year and a day from now'.

Of all the knights, only the brave Sir Gawain was courageous enough to take up the challenge. He rose from his seat and went to stand opposite the Green Knight.

'I accept your challenge,' he said. With that, he swung the axe high in the air and brought it swiftly down, beheading the Green Knight in a single blow.

For a moment, there was a stunned silence. Then, to the amazement of the court, the Green Knight stood up and picked up his head. As he turned to leave he said to Sir Gawain, 'Remember the challenge. I will see you in one year and one day.'

The rest of the story tells of Sir Gawain's adventures as he tries to keep his promise and find the Green Knight but because Sir Gawain shows courage, loyalty and chivalry during these adventures, the Green Knight does not behead him, instead only nicks his neck.

The Cherokee Little People

Read and identify the features of the story. Then guess what genre it is.

There once lived a Cherokee man and woman named Tooni and Polly. They lived together in a little cabin near the mountains.

Every spring Polly and Tooni planted corn. In summer, the corn grew taller and taller in luscious golden cornfields. In autumn, Polly and Tooni gathered the corn and in the long, cold winter they made food from it to keep them alive. So it was, year after year.

One year, the corn grew so tall and there was so much of it that Tooni and Polly couldn't gather it all.

'I will go into town to try to get help,' said Tooni and off he went. Tooni was gone for a very long time. Polly waited anxiously, watching large crows gathering over the corn. Polly knew that if Tooni did not return soon the crows would eat all the corn. She began to cry.

Meanwhile, two Cherokee Little People, Kamama and Kanunu, were playing in a big tree next to the little cabin and they heard Polly crying. They saw the crows circling the corn and, at once, they knew what they must do.

Kamama and Kanunu danced and sang a special song to make Polly go to sleep. Then Kamama and Kanunu and their little friends gathered the corn and put it next to the little cabin.

The next morning, Tooni returned home looking glum. There was nobody to help gather the corn as they were busy in their own cornfields. Suddenly, he saw the empty fields and the corn stacked next to the cabin. He woke Polly.

'Did you gather the corn yourself?' Tooni asked in amazement. 'No,' said Polly, 'I was sleeping. I think I dreamed that the Cherokee Little People did it.'

Then Tooni and Polly saw tiny little footprints on the porch step and at once, they knew that the Little People had gathered the corn.

'We must make gifts,' said Polly. Polly made pairs of small moccasins and Tooni made cornbread and cut it into tiny pieces. They put the gifts under the big tree. When night came, the Little People ate the cornbread, put on the moccasins and danced by the light of the silvery moon.

Theseus and the Minotaur

Read and identify the features of the story. Then guess what genre it is.

After years of war, King Minos of Crete hated the people of Athens. He ordered that seven young men and seven young women from Athens should be sent to Crete every four years. The young men and women would face a terrible fate. They would be fed to the Minotaur.

The Minotaur was a monstrous creature with the head of a bull and the body of a man. It was extremely dangerous, with a ravenous appetite. It lived in a vast labyrinth under the palace in Crete which was full of dark, twisting, winding passages. It was almost impossible to find the way out.

King Aegeus of Athens was really upset about King Minos' order. Nevertheless, he was afraid of King Minos so for some years he sent the young people to Crete. When his son, Theseus, learned what was happening he decided that he would try to kill the Minotaur himself.

In Crete a lavish feast was held for the young Athenians who were about to be sacrificed to the Minotaur. At the feast Theseus met Ariadne, King Minos' daughter. When she saw Theseus, she fell in love with him and decided to help him. Just before Theseus went into the labyrinth, Ariadne sneaked past the guards to give Theseus a ball of silk and a sword.

Theseus began his lonely trek through the maze. As he walked, he unwound the ball of silk behind him so that he would be able to find his way out.

After some time, Theseus came to the Minotaur's lair. The Minotaur was truly ugly, terrifying and ferocious. Theseus was beaten back several times but he was brave and fought hard. He lunged toward the Minotaur one last time, swung his sword high in the air and plunged it deep into the Minotaur's flesh. Finally, the Minotaur lay dead.

Theseus followed the line of silk out of the maze, found Ariadne and married her.

Theseus and Ariadne sailed for Athens. But tragically, Theseus forgot to put up white sails instead of black sails when he neared home. Believing his son was dead, King Aegeus jumped into the sea. To this day, the sea, the Aegean, is named after him.

The rats are leaving 1

Read and compare the poem with other texts.

Extract from *The Pied Piper of Hamelin*
Robert Browning

Into the street the Piper stept,
Smiling first a little smile,
As if he knew what magic slept
In his quiet pipe the while;
Then, like a musical adept,
To blow the pipe his lips he wrinkled,
And green and blue his sharp eyes twinkled,
Like a candle-flame where salt is sprinkled;
And ere three shrill notes the pipe uttered,
You heard as if an army muttered;
And the muttering grew to a grumbling;
And the grumbling grew to a mighty rumbling;
And out of the houses the rats came tumbling.
Great rats, small rats, lean rats, brawny rats,
Brown rats, black rats, grey rats, tawny rats,
Grave old plodders, gay young friskers,
Fathers, mothers, uncles, cousins,
Cocking tails and pricking whiskers,
Families by tens and dozens,
Brothers, sisters, husbands, wives –
Followed the Piper for their lives.
From street to street he piped advancing,
And step for step they followed dancing,
Until they came to the river Weser
Wherein all plunged and perished!

The rats are leaving 2

Read and compare the extracts.

Extract from *The Pied Piper of Hamelin*
The Brothers Grimm

The sun was still below the horizon, when the sound of a pipe wafted through the streets of Hamelin. The pied piper slowly made his way through the houses and behind him flocked the rats. Out they scampered from doors, windows and gutters, rats of every size, all after the piper. And as he played, the stranger marched down to the river and straight into the water, up to his middle. Behind him swarmed the rats and every one was drowned and swept away by the current.

Extract from *The Children of Hamelin*
Pie Corbett

Well, the deal was sealed with a shake of the hand and, no sooner than this was agreed, Brightman pulled out a strange pipe and began to play a melodious tune. The townsfolk were amazed because all the rats began to stream out of the houses and barns, following Brightman as he strode through the streets.

What a sight it was. The tall piper leading the way, followed by a thousand rats squealing and squeaking after him. It looked like a living river streaming out behind him.

Brightman led his strange procession out of the town, across the down and on to where the Weser River flowed. There he paused, before taking off his coat and plunging into the waters. Amazingly, the rats followed, thousands of them swarming into the water till for a moment it seemed to boil with their bodies. But the current there is strong and a few moments later there was silence. The rats had drowned and already their bodies were drifting down the stream to wash up on the banks over the next few miles where they lay rotting for the next few weeks.

Comparing versions

Add notes about the rats leaving Hamelin.

Similarities

Differences

Striking language

Making notes 1

Write about the characters. Add two more headings and notes.

Name: _____

First impressions of this

character: _____

_____

Likes and dislikes: _____

_____

Feelings about the library: _____

_____

_____

_____

_____ : _____

_____ : _____

Name: _____

First impressions of this

character: _____

_____

Likes and dislikes: _____

_____

Feelings about the library: _____

_____

_____

_____

_____ : _____

_____ : _____

Literacy Evolve Year 5 © Pearson Education 2009

Making notes 2

Write about the characters.

(Zoe)

First impressions of this character

How she is feeling

Likes and dislikes

(Abbie)

First impressions of this character

How she is feeling

Likes and dislikes

Correcting text

Read the story and discuss what is missing.

Extract based on *The Book*
Haydn Middleton

The library stood tall and elegant in the centre of the town. Every day students and scholars came to read the priceless old books or to use the new computers. In medieval times a monastery had stood here – so for centuries people had been coming to this place. Most of those people then went away again, although not quite all. For while the monastery was now long gone, some said a monk's spirit still haunted one of the library's upper rooms. Somewhere in the building too a later librarian had gone missing, forever …

Zoe knew nothing of this before visiting the library as part of Mr Beesons class but she felt a chill as she stepped inside Abbie her friend saw her shiver and asked what was wrong.

Nothing Zoe smiled Nothings wrong But the past had never seemed so close or real All the dusty books seemed to be breathing out gently urgently and just to *her*

Zoe could barely concentrate on Mr Beesons dry lecture on how the carved wooden panels on the walls showed dead birds and fruit and how the eyes in one of the painted portraits seemed to follow you around Abbie easily bored didn't even try to listen

… Somewhere in this place there is believed to be a lost room Mr Beeson droned on

A room asked Zoe pricking up her ears How can a room be lost

How indeed Mr Beeson replied One hundred years ago a senior librarian thought he had found its key But then apparently he vanished into thin air

Zoe felt a tug at her sleeve This is so dull Abbie whispered Lets vanish too

What's missing?

Add punctuation to the story.

Extract from The Book
Haydn Middleton

Somewhere in this place there is believed to be a lost room Mr

Beeson droned on

A room asked Zoe pricking up her ears How can a room be lost

How indeed Mr Beeson replied One hundred years ago a senior

librarian thought he had found its key But then apparently he

vanished into thin air

Zoe felt a tug at her sleeve This is so dull Abbie whispered Lets

vanish too

Name: _____   Date: _____

Zoe's diary

Write Zoe's diary for the night before and the evening after her visit to the library.

Sunday 25th March

We're going on our school trip tomorrow.

I think Abbie is going to want to sit with

me on the bus. I'm not _____

_____

_____

_____

_____

_____

Monday 26th March

I can hardly write I am so scared. You

will never believe what happened today.

It was awful. As soon as I walked into

the old building, _____

_____

_____

_____

_____

_____

Literacy Evolve Year 5 © Pearson Education 2009

Making comparisons 1

Compare the similarities and differences between the film and the written version of *The Book*.

	Similarities	Differences
Structure		
Language		
Features		
How tension is created		

Making comparisons 2

Name: _____ Date: _____

Add more similarities and differences between the film and the written version of *The Book*.

	Similarities	Differences
Structure	Both versions tell the story in the same order.	The written version gives background information about the library.
Language	Both versions include dialogue.	The film shows Zoe's feelings through her expression.
Features	Both versions tell the story from Zoe's point of view.	The film uses special effects.
How tension is created	Both versions include the strange figure of the monk.	The film uses music to create tension.

Literacy Evolve Year 5 © Pearson Education 2009

Legend plan

Add notes to plan your legend.

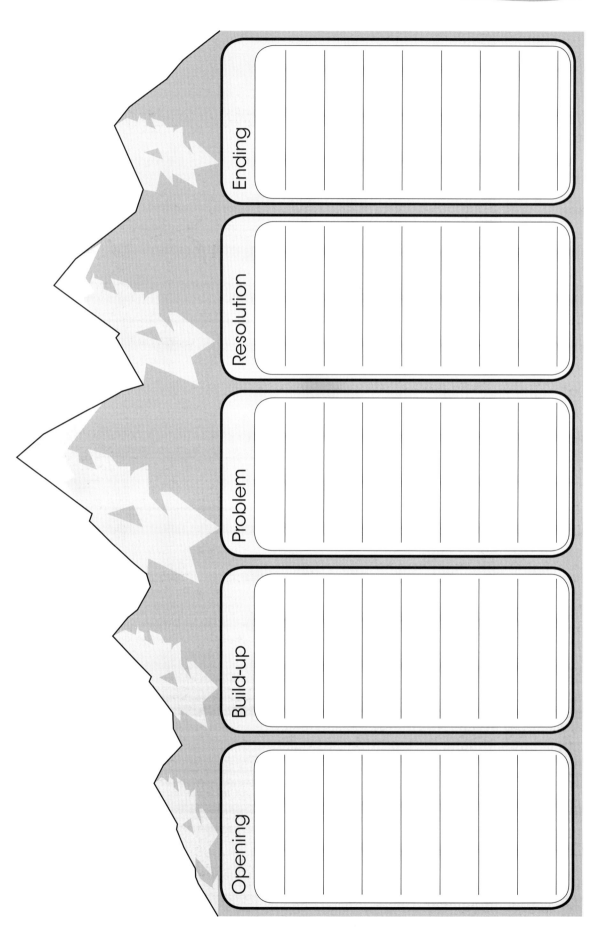

Ending

Resolution

Problem

Build-up

Opening

Marking ladder

Use the marking ladder to check the group stories.

	Group 1	Group 2	Group 3	Group 4	Group 5	Group 6
Each group member takes part.						
Storytellers vary their tone of voice and pitch (loud, soft, etc).						
Storytellers use a range of interesting words and phrases.						
Storytellers use techniques such as asking questions.						
Storytellers use gestures and actions.						
The story is lively and engages the audience.						

Literacy Evolve Year 5 © Pearson Education 2009

My marking ladder

Use the marking ladder to check your work.

My comments		Teacher's comments
	My legend is set in a specific place and time.	
	It is written in the third person.	
	It is clearly organised with an opening, problem, build-up, resolution and ending.	
	I have used time connectives.	
	I have used powerful verbs, adjectives and images.	
	I have used a variety of sentence structures for dramatic effect.	

ORANGES IN NO MAN'S LAND – novel (Other cultures)

Medium term plan (3 weeks)	
Phase	**Learning Outcomes**
Phase 1: Understanding the context of the story (4 days)	• Children can find evidence about the setting of a story and can relate this to background information about the author and the specific historical, political and geographical context of the story. • Children can identify the main character's feelings, using direct evidence (specific reference to the text) and indirect evidence (deduction and inference).
Phase 2: Reading and responding to the story (5 days)	• use drama techniques to explore key events in the story, to understand characters' viewpoints, feelings and changing relationships, and to develop empathy for the characters. • Children can write direct and indirect speech and retell a scene using first-person narrative, from various characters' perspectives. • Children can identify how language is used to create dramatic effects and tension.
Phase 3: Retelling the story (6 days)	• Children can retell the story from the point of view of a different character. • Children can consider the effect of the writing techniques they are using on the intended audience. • Children can draw on role-play experience to write detailed descriptions of a character's thoughts and feelings. • Children can select and incorporate relevant details from the book into their stories. • Children can give and respond to feedback to improve their stories.

ORANGES IN NO MAN'S LAND

Big picture

The children read *Oranges in No Man's Land*. They explore characters, emotions, different points of view, how language is used for effect and the challenges faced by the main character. They rewrite the story from another character's point of view.

Prior learning

This unit assumes that the children can already:
• understand story structure and identify aspects of the plot
• tell a story in the first person
• identify key events from a book to use in a retelling of the story, and invent appropriate details where they are needed
• infer characters' feelings and deduce reasons for characters' behaviour.

Key aspects of learning

Communication: Respond to a text and characters through speaking, listening and writing; use collaborative drama activities to share and explore creative ideas.
Creative thinking: Write a story from a character's point of view, using inference and deduction to work out relevant details from the book, and empathy, imagination and improvisations to invent further details.
Empathy: Understand issues faced by characters; explore characters' feelings through role play and drama.

Enquiry: Ask questions about the factual background to a story: the civil war in Lebanon; the role of the UN; the impact of war on civilians.
Social skills: Work collaboratively on group improvisations; listen to others; support other members of the group; offer constructive criticism.

Progression in narrative

In this unit the children will:
• plan, structure and write a complete short story from the perspective of another character; identify key events to include from the original story; find evidence about a character's point of view and feelings
• write a first-person narrative and use dialogue to build character; use drama techniques to empathise with the character and develop ideas
• organise paragraphs to create mood, tension and convey emotion.

Cross-curricular links

Art and Design: Create artwork based on details described in the book, e.g. the war-torn city; the characters' feelings; Samar's treasures; food.
Citizenship: Link with themes of war; humanitarian aid; making choices; human rights; respect; differences.
Geography: Find out about the setting of the book (Lebanon).
ICT: The unit could be extended to include filming of improvisations.

Reading time

1 hour 35 minutes

PHASE 1: UNDERSTANDING THE CONTEXT OF THE STORY (4 DAYS)

Session 1

We are learning to …	Resources
• find out about the author and the background to a story to help us enjoy it (PNS Strands 8.1)	*Oranges in No Man's Land* ITP: 3.1, 3.2 PCM: 3.1, 3.2, 3.3
Assessment Focuses AF (R): 7	

Shared teaching

• Share the learning objective. Show the cover and title of *Oranges in No Man's Land* by Elizabeth Laird.
• Talk Partners make predictions about the story. *Is this the type of book you would normally choose to read?* The children use 'Bookmark' (PCM 3.1) to record their first impressions.
• Explore the context with some first-hand experience. Divide the room in half. Explain that the children with birthdays in the first half of the year are 'in control' of one side. Those with birthdays in the second half of the year are on the other side. The children sitting in the wrong place are 'refugees' and have to leave all their belongings behind and move to the other side. Explain that the area either side of the dividing line is 'no man's land.' Continue the session with the class divided.
• Explain that *Oranges in No Man's Land* is set in Lebanon 30 years ago during a civil war. Explain that this is when people in the same country start fighting one another. The story is set int the capital city, Beirut, which was divided during the civil war, with people fighting over who would be in control. Many people had to leave their homes.
• Explain that civil wars can mean that people who used to be friends end up on different sides. Talk Partners discuss, dividing the class into two halves. *How does the experience of dividing the class make you feel?*

• Show 'Map of Lebanon' (ITP 3.1). Click on Beirut, Lebanon and Israel to reveal information about these locations.
• Read the Preface to *Oranges* as the children follow in their books. Discuss the author's experiences and where she got her ideas for the story.
• Display 'Glossary' (ITP 3.2). Discuss any new or unfamiliar words. Print ITP 3.2 to start the Learning Wall. Encourage the children to refer to it throughout the unit.

Independent and Guided

• The children work in groups, using 'Information about Lebanon' (PCM 3.2) to answer 'Questions about Lebanon' (PCM 3.3). Each group shares out the questions so that each pair focuses on different information. When they have finished, the children share their answers to complete PCM 3.3. Support the children with an identified need. (T/TA)

Plenary

• Recap the learning objective.
• Take feedback and reflect on what the children have discovered. *Does it make you curious about reading the book? How do you think this information will help us understand the book better?*

Assessment pointers

• AF7 (R): oral explanations of the book title will show how well the children understand the cultural context of the story.

We are learning to ...	Resources
• explore characters using evidence from the text • use and discuss visualisation techniques (PNS Strands 7.1, 8.2) **Assessment Focuses** AF (R): 2, 3	*Oranges in No Man's Land* ITP: 3.3

Shared teaching

• Share the learning objectives. Explain that after the research the children completed about Lebanon in Session 1, they are now ready to start reading *Oranges in No Man's Land*.
• Read Chapters 1 and 2 as the children follow in their books. Ask them to think about who the main character in the story is while you are reading.
• *Who is telling the story?* Show 'The main character' (ITP 3.3). Talk Partners refer to Chapters 1 and 2 and identify information that could be entered under each of the headings on ITP 3.3.
• Take feedback and add suggestions. Encourage the children to explain how they know particular facts, referencing the text. Point out that the author gradually reveals the information rather than including everything in the first few sentences. *What effect does this have?*
• Discuss the headings that cannot be completed (religion, friends, worries and fears). Explain that the children will find out more about Ayesha as they read more of the book.
• The children Think-Pair-Share to reflect on the events in Ayesha's life so far. Refer to pages 3–4. *How do you think Ayesha felt on that 'terrible day'? How did it change her life?*
• Take feedback. *Are there any questions that you would like to ask*

Ayesha? Add suggestions to the Learning Wall and explain that the children will return to these questions as they read more of the story.

Independent and Guided

• The children reread the description of the flat (pages 6–9), then visualise what Ayesha's new home may be like inside.
∞ Work individually to draw a sketch of the flat based on the description in the story.
∞ Work in small groups. Each child sketches one feature of the flat. (TA+)
◉ Guided reading of Chapters 1 and 2. Produce a timeline of events to display on the Learning Wall. Explain that this will be used in Session 3. (T+)

Plenary

• Invite several children to show their drawings. Encourage the other children to talk about something they like in the drawing and how it represents parts of the text. *What question would you like to ask about the drawing?* Draw out contrasts to the children's own homes to help them think more deeply about being a refugee.
• Recap the learning objectives. Reflect on visualisation as a technique to aid comprehension. *Did drawing the flat help you to imagine Ayesha's home in more detail? How would you feel if you had to live in a place like that?*

Assessment pointers

• AF2 (R): responses to questioning show how far the children can select information from the text.
• AF3 (R): independent and guided work will show how well the children are able to interpret information from the text.

We are learning to ...	Resources
• use and reflect on drama techniques to explore characters and story • use empathy to make inferences about characters (PNS Strands 4.1, 7.2) **Assessment Focuses** AF (R): 2, 3	*Oranges in No Man's Land* ITP: (3.2, 3.3), 3.4 PCM: 3.4

Shared teaching

• Share the learning objectives. Recall what has happened to Ayesha so far in *Oranges in No Man's Land*. Invite the children from the lower ability group in Session 2 to explain the timeline they created.
• Ask the children to Think-Pair-Share what it would be like to be a refugee. *Imagine having to leave your home and possessions and find somewhere to live. What basic things would you need? How would you get them?* As the children share ideas, reinforce the fact that the refugees have lost their jobs, as well as their homes and would have very little money.
• Ask the children to recall how Beirut was divided during the civil war (e.g. east and west). *Why would the division make it even more difficult for refugees to get shelter, food, fuel and water?*
• Start reading *Oranges* Chapter 3 and pause at the end of page 15 to allow the children Think Time. *How was Ayesha feeling that morning? Can you predict what might happen at the checkpoint?*
• Continue reading until the end of Chapter 4. Encourage the children to refer to 'Glossary' (ITP 3.2) on the Learning Wall to explain any words they are unsure of.
• Show 'Beirut in the civil war' (ITP 3.4). Look together at the photos. Invite the children to drag the quotations from *Oranges* to label the

photos. *How would it feel to be living in this place?* Encourage the children to empathise with Ayesha and the difficulties she faces.

Independent and Guided

• In groups of three, the children Role Play the scene at the checkpoint (pages 16–18), taking turns to play different roles in the drama, with one child acting as 'observer' to freeze the action. When the action is paused, the children should discuss their thoughts and feelings.
∞∞ Use 'Ayesha at the checkpoint' (PCM 3.4). Make notes about how it feels to act each role.
∞ As above. (TA+)
◉ As above. Reread the scene as a group, before acting the roles. (T+)

Plenary

• Recall annotated 'The main character' (ITP 3.3). *What new facts have we found out about Ayesha?* Add information about her religion. *Do you have any new questions?* Add suggestions to the Learning Wall.
• Set up a Teacher In Role activity. Take on the role of Ayesha and encourage the children to ask questions based on what they have read. If necessary, prompt them with ideas. *How do you feel about the war? What are you worried about at the moment?*
• Recap the learning objectives and reflect on the drama activities. *Did acting out the roles help you to understand Ayesha better?*

Assessment pointers

• S&L: role plays will show how well the children can respond to issues and empathise with characters.
• AF2 (R): suggestions for questions to ask Ayesha show how far the children can select information from the text.
• AF3 (R): responses to questioning and drama work show how well the children can make deductions and inferences about characters.

We are learning to ...

- understand a character from what is known and what can be inferred
- explore how language is used to express feelings (PNS Strands 7.2, 7.5)

Assessment Focuses

AF (R): 2, 3; AF (W): 7

Resources

Oranges in No Man's Land
ITP: (3.3), 3.5, 3.6
PCM: (3.1), 3.5

Shared teaching

- Share the learning objectives. Talk Partners discuss their best friends. *What do you like doing together?* Explain that this session will focus on Ayesha's friend.
- Read Chapter 5 of *Oranges in No Man's Land* until the end of the first sentence on page 28. Encourage the children to think about how Ayesha and Samar learnt to communicate.
- The children Think-Pair-Share about the friendship. *Why was Ayesha worried to begin with? Why do you think they got on so well together?* Draw out what is known and what can be inferred, e.g. both girls were lonely and had left all their friends behind.
- Continue reading to the end of page 33. Talk Partners discuss Ayesha's problem and predict what she might do, adding notes to annotated 'Bookmark' (PCM 3.1).
- Read to the end of Chapter 6. *Were your predictions right? How has the mood of the story changed?* Encourage the children to identify that Ayesha is getting increasingly worried about Granny. Show '*Oranges in No Man's Land*' (ITP 3.5). Discuss how the author uses different words and phrases to indicate how Ayesha is feeling.
- Show 'Ayesha's worries' (ITP 3.6). Click to show what Ayesha says. *Are these the same phrases you highlighted?* Draw the graph to show how

worried Ayesha is. Identify the turning point when Ayesha decides she must take action herself.
- The children Think-Pair-Share about her feelings. *How does Ayesha feel once she has made her decision to go to Dr Leila?* Encourage them to refer back to pages 35–37 of *Oranges* for evidence. Point out that her thoughts are focused on action, not just feeling afraid.

Independent and Guided

- The children use a thesaurus to explore different ways of using language to express feelings.
- **ooo** Use 'Expressing emotion' (PCM 3.5). Work independently to research vocabulary and compose phrases to express degrees of emotion.
- **oo** As above. (T+)
- **o** Enter new information about Ayesha's friends, worries and fears on 'The main character' (ITP 3.3). (TA+)

Plenary

- Recap the learning objectives. Review the story so far and recall annotated ITP 3.3. *What do we know about Ayesha and her family?* Ask the lower ability group to explain the new information they have added. Add any new questions to the list on the Learning Wall.
- Explain that a crucial point in the story has been reached: Ayesha has faced the biggest problem and made a decision. Focus on PCM 3.1 again. *I wonder how Ayesha can make such a dangerous journey? I'm not sure that she is brave enough, what do you think?*

Assessment pointers

- AF2, 3 (R): responses to questioning show how far the children can retrieve and infer information.
- AF7 (W): written outcomes show whether the children can use appropriate and effective vocabulary to express degrees of emotion.

PHASE 2: READING AND RESPONDING TO THE STORY (5 DAYS)

We are learning to ...

- use evidence from the text to explore key events and ideas
- understand the difference between direct and reported speech
- use punctuation for speech accurately (PNS Strands 7.1, 9.4, 11.2)

Assessment Focuses

AF (R): 2, 3; AF (W): 5

Resources

Oranges in No Man's Land
ITP: 3.7
PCM: (3.1), 3.6

Shared teaching

- Share the learning objectives and ask the children to recall what happened in the last part of the story. Write labels on sticky notes summarising the key events to add to the timeline on the Learning Wall, e.g. Granny's medicine has run out and she is very ill; Ayesha decides to cross the Green Line and find Dr Leila.
- Remind the children that at the end of Chapter 6 of *Oranges*, Ayesha was lying in bed, working out how to get Granny's medicine. *What do you think she will do next?* Refer to the predictions that the children made on 'Bookmark' (PCM 3.1). Invite them to share ideas.
- Read Chapter 7. *What will happen next?* Read Chapter 8. *Were your predictions correct?*
- Discuss the action in these chapters. Involve the children in identifying each of the challenges that Ayesha has to overcome. Write labels on sticky notes to add to the Learning Wall to keep track of events, e.g. runs past the first checkpoint, stops at second checkpoint, pretends to be deaf, rescued by Abu Boutros.
- Show 'Reported speech' (ITP 3.7). Recap the difference between direct and reported speech. Look at the first example and click to

see the changes made. Encourage the children to transform the other examples into reported speech. Discuss the changes and what difference they would make to the story. *What makes the direct speech effective in this scene?*

Independent and Guided

- The children write about what happened to Ayesha at the second checkpoint from the point of view of Abu Boutros using reported speech.
- **ooo** Work independently using 'Abu Boutros' (PCM 3.6).
- **oo** Work in small groups to reread the scene. Complete PCM 3.6. (TA+)
- **o** Guided reading of the scene. Work as a group to complete PCM 3.6. (T+)

Plenary

- Recap the learning objectives and select several children to read their accounts of the scene at the second checkpoint. Encourage the children to refer to the text to explain where they found the information they used to write from Abu Boutros' point of view.
- Discuss the effect of using reported speech. *Do you prefer the version using direct or reported speech?* Draw out the idea that it is often effective to use a mixture of direct and reported speech to keep the story moving on.

Assessment pointers

- AF2, 3 (R): responses to questioning about Ayesha's challenges show how well the children can retrieve and interpret information.
- AF5 (W): written outcomes show the children's understanding of the difference between direct and reported speech.

We are learning to ...
- use evidence from the text to explore key events and ideas
- make inferences about the author's point of view (PNS Strands 7.1, 7.2)

Assessment Focuses
AF (R): 3, 6

Resources
Oranges in No Man's Land

ITP: (3.4)

PCM: 3.7

Shared teaching
- Share the learning objective. Talk Partners tell each other the story so far in no more than six sentences. The children take turns to say one sentence each.
- Introduce the next two chapters of Oranges in No Man's Land by saying that Ayesha's emotions go up and down, changing from excitement and happiness to fear and despair. It's a bit like going up and down on a rollercoaster. Encourage the children to look out for examples of the ways in which her emotions change.
- Show 'Beirut in the civil war' (ITP 3.4). Refer to the photo of the Green Line to remind children of the type of environment that Ayesha is passing through.
- Read Chapter 9 and pause to discuss Ayesha's emotional ups and downs.
- Read from pages 61–63, pausing at the end of the second paragraph. If possible, peel one or more oranges to share with the class. As they eat, encourage the children to talk about the way that the taste and smell of a particular food can bring back memories. How does Ayesha feel at this point in the story? Has eating the orange helped you to understand Ayesha's experience?

- Finish reading Chapter 10 and talk about the changing emotions Ayesha felt as she got closer to finding Dr Leila.

Independent and Guided
- The children look for examples of contrasts in Chapters 9 and 10 of Oranges in No Man's Land.

  ∞∞∞ Look at descriptions of people that Ayesha meets. Consider and make notes about whether they are portrayed as typical enemies. (T+)

  ∞∞ Use 'Contrasts' (PCM 3.7). Look for examples of contrasts in the city streets before and during the war.

  ◉ As above. (TA+)

Plenary
- Recap the learning objective and ask the higher ability group to explain what they found out about the people Ayesha meets who are from the 'other side'. Encourage the children to make links with the point of view of the author. Does the author tell us which side is 'good' and which is 'bad'? Are there good people on both sides of the divide? What does this tell you about the author's attitude to the war?
- Encourage the children to suggest examples of contrasts in the streets and buildings. Have you found anything that suggests that the author thought things were better before the war?
- Use sticky notes to add labels to the timeline on the Learning Wall summarising the events that have been read about in this session.

Assessment pointers
- AF3 (R): independent work shows how well the children are able to deduce and interpret specific information from the text.
- AF6 (R): responses to questioning show the children's awareness of, and how well they can comment on, the author's viewpoint.

We are learning to ...
- use and reflect on drama techniques to explore characters and story
- use evidence from the text to explore key events and ideas
- collect evidence about events and historical details (PNS Strands 4.1, 7.1)

Assessment Focuses
AF (R): 2, 3, 6

Resources
Oranges in No Man's Land

ITP: 3.8

PCM: 3.8

Shared teaching
- Share the learning objectives. Remind the children of Ayesha's rollercoaster of emotions in Session 6. How did Ayesha feel when she finally saw Dr Leila? What do you think Ayesha will do next?
- Read Chapter 11 of Oranges in No Man's Land. Is there anything that shows what Dr Leila's attitude to the war is? Encourage them to look for evidence (on page 74 she uses the word 'us'; on page 75 she says 'There weren't any sides, in the good old days'). I wonder whether her auntie feels the same? Ask the children to look out for more evidence of her auntie's attitude in the next chapter.
- Read Chapter 12 until the end of the second paragraph on page 79. Show 'About the UN' (ITP 3.8). Explain that some of the children will be doing research later to find out why Ayesha would be safe in the ambulance.
- Read the rest of Chapter 12.
- Pairs do a Hot-Seating activity with one child taking the role of Ayesha and the other asking her questions. What were some of the good things you experienced at Dr Leila's? Why weren't you used to these things? The children swap roles and ask Ayesha further questions. What do you think of Dr Leila? What do you think of her auntie?

- Ask the children to Think-Pair-Share about the experience of role-playing Ayesha. Does it help you to understand the story better? How?

Independent and Guided
- In groups, the children find out more about a character's attitude or carry out research about the United Nations.

  ∞∞∞ Find evidence in Chapter 12 to show how Dr Leila's auntie's actions and words express her attitude towards Ayesha and the war. (TA+)

  ∞∞ Read 'The United Nations' (PCM 3.8) and use the information to compose captions for ITP 3.8. (T+)

  ◉ Read PCM 3.8 and answer the questions on a separate piece of paper.

Plenary
- Recap the learning objectives. Show ITP 3.8. Discuss the captions that have been added. Why is the UN needed in places like Beirut during the civil war?
- Ask the higher ability group to talk about Dr Leila's auntie and her attitude to Ayesha. Why do you think she hates Ayesha so much? Explain that Muslims and Christians lived on opposite sides of the Green Line dividing Beirut.
- Refer to Dr Leila's final words on page 83. I wonder why she told Ayesha not to hate anybody. Do you think that the author thinks that as well?

Assessment pointers
- S&L: hot-seating will show how far the children can sustain roles to explore ideas.
- AF2, 3 (R): drama activities show how far the children can make references and understand the characters' attitudes.
- AF6 (R): responses to questioning will show the children's awareness of the author's viewpoint.

Session 8

<table>
<tr><td>We are learning to ...
• explore how an author uses language, sentence structure and punctuation to create dramatic effects and tension
• develop viewpoint through action and detail (PNS Strands 7.5, 9.4)
Assessment Focuses
AF (R): 5; AF (W): 5, 7</td><td>Resources
Oranges in No Man's Land
ITP: 3.9
PCM: 3.9</td></tr>
</table>

Shared teaching

• Share the learning objective. Remind the children that Ayesha is about to leave the safety of Dr Leila's house and travel back across the Green Line in an ambulance. Talk Partners discuss how she might be feeling.
• Read Chapters 13, 14 and 15. Encourage the children to look out for the ways that the author helps the reader to imagine this dangerous and difficult journey.
• Discuss the dangers. *What do you think would have happened if the soldiers at the enemy checkpoint had looked in the back of the ambulance? I wonder why Abu Bashir stopped before he got to the checkpoint on Ayesha's side.*
• Show 'Oranges in No Man's Land' (ITP 3.9). Explain that the children are going to take a closer look at the words and phrases the author uses to convey a sense of urgency and danger.
• Ask the children to identify words and phrases that describe the speed of travel, e.g. 'make a dash for it', 'racing furiously', 'wild dash'. Highlight examples.
• Ask the children to Think-Pair-Share other words for 'fast', then write a phrase to describe travelling fast. Share some examples.
• Explain that authors can create effects not only in their choice of

words, but also in the way they construct sentences. Refer to the paragraph on page 87 beginning 'I couldn't believe my eyes'. Ask the children to read it and note the number of sentences. Encourage them to identify examples of simple, compound and complex sentences. *What is the effect of the short, simple sentences?* (E.g. they add emphasis and reinforce an important point; emphasising the empty street raises the tension because it has been deserted so quickly.)

Independent and Guided

• The children write an account of the ambulance journey from the point of view of Abu Bashir, using words and phrases to describe the speed and sense of danger.

∞ Write independently, varying sentence structure and vocabulary to evoke a sense of danger and express Abu Bashir's fears.

∞ Use 'Jumbled sentences' (PCM 3.9). Order the sentences, then use the sentences to write in more detail, expressing danger and urgency. (T+)

◉ Use PCM 3.9. (TA+)

Plenary

• Recap the learning objective. Ask some of the children to share their accounts. Encourage the other children to give feedback on effective words and phrases. *Do they evoke a sense of danger?*
• Encourage the children to make predictions. *We have almost reached the end of the book – I wonder what will happen next?*

Assessment pointers

• AF5 (R): responses to questioning show how far the children can comment on an author's use of language.
• AF5, 7 (W): written outcomes show how well the children can select vocabulary effectively and use a variety of sentence structures.

Session 9

<table>
<tr><td>We are learning to ...
• use evidence to say how a character changes
• say what we think about the story as a whole (PNS Strands 7.1, 8.1)
Assessment Focuses
AF (R): 3</td><td>Resources
Oranges in No Man's Land
ITP: 3.10
PCM: (3.1)</td></tr>
</table>

Shared teaching (1)

• Share the learning objectives. Ask the children to recall the key events of the last few chapters. *Imagine that you are Ayesha. You want to tell Samar all about what happened when you crossed no man's land.* Allow Think Time for Talk Partners to plan what they would say, then share some of the accounts.
• Add summary notes to the timeline of events on the Learning Wall.
• Remind the children that Ayesha had just arrived home at the end of Chapter 15. *What did you predict would happen next?*
• Read Chapters 16, 17 and 18. Involve the children in summarising the key events. Add notes to the Learning Wall. *Did anything surprise you? Were you satisfied with the ending? Are there any questions that are left unanswered?* Ask the children to Think-Pair-Share ideas.

Independent and Guided (1)

• The children reflect on the book as a whole and make notes on 'Bookmark' (PCM 3.1) to describe their thoughts at the end of the story. Support the children with an identified need. (T/TA)

Shared teaching (2)

• Take feedback. Explain that the children will look more closely at one example of how Ayesha changes during the story: her relationship with her brother.

• Show 'Ayesha and Latif' (ITP 3.10). Click each part of the story to show quotes from *Oranges*. *How do you think Ayesha feels about Latif at this particular time?* Encourage the children to read between the lines and make deductions when looking for evidence of changes in their relationship.

Independent and Guided (2)

• The children explore Ayesha's changing attitude to Latif.

∞ In groups, find and discuss other evidence of Ayesha's changing attitude. They then do a Hot-Seating activity with one child in role as Ayesha. (T+)

∞ In pairs, act out the conversation between Ayesha and Latif on pages 106–109 and 111–112. Take turns to play Ayesha, explaining her feelings about Latif.

◉ Reread and act out the conversation between Ayesha and Latif as above. (TA+)

Plenary

• Recap the learning objectives. *Why has Ayesha's attitude to Latif changed? Did you notice any other changes during the story? Does role play help you understand Ayesha better?* Encourage the children to reflect on their experiences of role play while reading the book.
• If possible, provide other books by Elizabeth Laird for the children to read independently.

Assessment pointers

• S&L: drama pieces will show how far the children can sustain roles and scenarios to explore the text.
• AF3 (R): responses and role play activities show how well the children can make inferences about how the character's feelings change.

Session 10

We are learning to ...	Resources
• find evidence about a character's point of view • plan and write from a character's point of view • use storyboards or a planner to create a structure (PNS Strands 7.1, 9.2) **Assessment Focuses** AF (R): 3	*Oranges in No Man's Land* ITP: 3.11 PCM: 3.10, 3.11

Shared teaching

• Share the learning objectives and introduce the final phase of the unit by explaining that the children are going to write their own version of the *Oranges in No Man's Land* story from the point of view of Ayesha's best friend, Samar. Explain that the audience are children who enjoyed reading the original story.

• Talk Partners discuss what they can remember about Samar. Show 'Samar' (ITP 3.11). Encourage the children to identify whether they can complete any of the information about Samar.

• Reread pages 23–27 of *Oranges* as the children follow in their books. Discuss any new information about Samar and add it to ITP 3.11 under the appropriate headings.

• Ask the children to recall further information from other parts of the story. Explain that the author does not give all the details about Samar, so the children will need to imagine what the missing information might be as they retell the story. Begin a list of questions to ask Samar to display on the Learning Wall.

• Ask the children to Think-Pair-Share the missing information and questions that they would like to ask Samar. Add these to the list, e.g. *What happened to her father? How did she end up as a refugee? How did she feel before Ayesha came? How did she get her special*

treasures? What was it like on the day that Ayesha crossed the Green Line? What was it like when she left Ayesha and moved to a new flat?

Independent and Guided

• The children think imaginatively to answer questions and create new information for the beginning of Samar's story.

🔵🔵🔵 Work with a partner to complete 'Questions for Samar' (PCM 3.10), adding imaginative detail.

🔵🔵 Work with a partner to complete PCM 3.10. (TA+)

🔵 Sketch Samar's special treasures described on page 26. Mind Map ideas to explain how she got them. (T+)

Plenary

• Recap the learning objectives. Give each child a copy of 'Planning grid' (PCM 3.11) and display an enlarged copy. Discuss each heading representing the different parts of Samar's story.

• Ask each group for feedback from the independent activities. Encourage the children to listen and make notes of good ideas on PCM 3.11. Explain that they will add to the notes on PCM 3.11 as they plan each section of the story and refer to it when they are writing in later sessions.

Assessment pointers

• AF3 (R): paired work will show how far the children are able to make inferences and deductions from the text and add their own creative and imaginative ideas.

Session 11

We are learning to ...	Resources
• evaluate writing using success criteria • write effective story openings (PNS Strands 9.1, 9.2) **Assessment Focuses** AF (W): 1, 5	ITP: 3.12, 3.13 PCM: (3.10, 3.11)

Shared teaching

• Share the learning objectives. Talk Partners discuss good ways to start a story, relating their ideas to writing Samar's story.

• Refer to 'Planning grid' (PCM 3.11) that the children used to make notes during Session 10. *How do you think Samar's story should start?*

• Show 'Opening for Samar's Story' (ITP 3.12). Read through the opening paragraphs for the story together. Use Modelled Writing to demonstrate how they can be improved to make sure that the opening grabs the reader. *Could you address the reader directly? Could you start by asking a question? Would varying the sentence length help?* Involve the children in making suggestions and demonstrate how to make the changes.

• Use Think Alouds to explain the changes that you are making, e.g. *I think it would be good to start with a question that will hook the reader and make them want to read on. I wonder what Samar would want to say first.*

• Reread the opening paragraphs to check that they make sense. Encourage the children to review the story opening and make comments. *Is all the basic information about Samar included? Does it explain how she came to be a refugee?*

• Show 'Writing openings' (ITP 3.13). Discuss the success criteria for the

story opening. Invite the children to generate more suggestions and add these to ITP 3.13.

Independent and Guided

• The children add notes to PCM 3.11, then write independently to create their own versions of opening paragraphs for Samar's story.

🔵🔵🔵 Write a paragraph to introduce Samar and describe her life before she became a refugee. Incorporate ideas about Samar's life based on completed 'Questions for Samar' (PCM 3.10) and PCM 3.11. Read completed paragraphs to a partner, then make changes if necessary.

🔵🔵 As above. (TA+)

🔵 Write a paragraph to add to the modelled story opening on ITP 3.12. Explain each of the treasures that Samar managed to bring with her. (T+)

Plenary

• Recap the learning objectives. Ask several of the children to read their opening paragraphs to the class. Involve the other children in giving feedback. Demonstrate how to evaluate the story openings against the success criteria on ITP 3.13.

• Allow the children Think Time to evaluate their own writing. *Does your story opening meet the success criteria?* Ask the children to show thumbs up, down or half way to indicate how satisfied they are with their writing. *Is there anything you would like to change or improve?* Allow the children time to make changes to their story openings.

Assessment pointers

• AF1, 5 (W): self and peer assessment shows how well the children can write in an imaginative way, including essential information and varying sentences to interest the reader.

<table>
<tr><td>

We are learning to ...
- perform a scripted scene
- plan and write from a character's point of view
- develop viewpoint though action and detail
  (PNS Strands 4.2, 9.2, 9.4)

Assessment Focuses
AF (W): 1

</td><td>

Resources
Oranges in No Man's Land
ITP: 3.14
PCM: (3.11)

</td></tr>
</table>

Shared teaching

- Share the learning objectives. Refer the children to 'Planning grid' (PCM 3.11). Explain that during this session they will be writing an important part of *Samar's* story: when Samar meets Ayesha and they become friends. Remind the children to make notes on their planning grid of good ideas to include.
- Encourage the children to recall the facts from this part of the story (refer to pages 6 and 23–27 in *Oranges in No Man's Land* if necessary). Record brief sentences on sticky notes to add to the Learning Wall, e.g. Mrs Zainab and Samar saw Ayesha's family on the street and waved for them to come in; Ayesha was scared of Samar at first; Mrs Zainab explained that Samar was deaf and wanted to be friends; Samar took Ayesha to her special place, they shared their treasures and learnt cat's cradle; they found a way to communicate and became best friends.
- In groups of three, the children use Improvisation to act out three scenes: when Ayesha and her family first come to the flat; when Mrs Zainab asks Ayesha to be Samar's friend and they go to Samar's special place for the first time; a week later when the girls are best friends.
- Freeze Frame during each scene and ask the children playing Samar to describe her thoughts and feelings. Encourage reflection. *How*

were you feeling before Ayesha came? Were you worried that Ayesha wouldn't want to be friends? What was the best thing about making a new friend?
- Show 'Writing stories' (ITP 3.14). Discuss success criteria relevant to this part of the story. *Are there any you would like to add or change?* Add suggestions to ITP 3.14.

Independent and Guided

- The children reread their story openings, add notes to PCM 3.11 and then write the next part about meeting Ayesha and making friends with her. Encourage the children to refer to the Learning Wall.
- **∞∞∞** Include detailed descriptions of Samar's thoughts and feelings, drawing on the improvisations.
- **∞∞** Describe the events and some description of Samar's feelings. (T)
- **◉** Include details of the three main events based on the improvisations. (TA+)

Plenary

- Recap the learning objectives. Talk Partners take turns to share their writing so far. Ask the children to provide peer assessment, focusing their responses around the success criteria.
- Share examples of effective words and phrases. Make further suggestions to improve the flow of the stories as appropriate.

Assessment pointers

- S&L: improvisations will show how far the children explore characters and situations through speech, gesture and movement.
- AF1 (W): written outcomes and drama activities show how far the children can describe a character's feelings and incorporate imaginative ideas into a text.

<table>
<tr><td>

We are learning to ...
- use a variety of sentence structures and direct and reported speech to make writing more interesting
- adapt sentence for purpose and audience
  (PNS Strands 9.4, 11.1)

Assessment Focuses
AF (W): 5, 6

</td><td>

Resources
Oranges in No Man's Land
ITP: (3.14), 3.15
PCM: (3.11)

</td></tr>
</table>

Shared teaching

- Share the learning objectives. Look together at 'Planning grid' (PCM 3.11). Introduce the part of the story that the children will be writing during this session: the big day. *What can you remember about Ayesha's big adventure? Can you remember what happened to Samar that day?* Ask Talk Partners to discuss.
- Show 'The big day' (ITP 3.15). Divide the children into groups, allocating each group a different section of *Oranges in No Man's Land* to read.
- Ask for feedback about each section. Encourage the children to explain what happened from Samar's perspective. Add notes to ITP 3.15 to summarise the key events. Remind the children that they will need to use imagination to describe the extra part of the story when Samar's uncle arrives, as details of this don't appear in the original story.
- Use Modelled Writing to show how to expand the notes into complete sentences. Demonstrate with the paragraph beginning 'When Ayesha was gone ... '. Use Think Alouds to model the process, rehearsing a sentence orally before writing, varying sentence structure and using direct and reported speech. Involve the children in checking that you have punctuated the direct speech correctly.
- Recall annotated 'Writing stories' (ITP 3.14). Discuss success criteria

relevant to writing this part of the story. Invite the children to add more suggestions. Remind them to pay particular attention to the punctuation of direct speech during the extended writing session.

Independent and Guided

- The children use planning notes from ITP 3.15, adding ideas to PCM 3.11 before continuing to write Samar's Story.
- **∞∞∞** Vary the sentence structure for effect. (T)
- **∞∞** Include examples of direct and reported speech to add interest and help move the story on.
- **◉** Focus on writing at least one or two complete sentences for each heading on ITP 3.15. (TA)

Plenary

- Recap the learning objectives. Invite several children to read what they have written so far. Encourage the other children to provide feedback about original imaginative ideas and the use of direct and reported speech.
- Allow Think Time for the children to check their writing against the success criteria. *Do you need to make any changes?* Make time available for the children to make any amendments or improvements necessary before the next session.

Assessment pointers

- AF5, 6 (W): self-assessment and written outcomes show how far the children understand how to vary sentence structure for effect and how well they can use punctuation accurately.

Session 14

We are learning to ...	Resources
• write imaginative endings • punctuate sentences accurately and effectively (PNS Strands 9.2, 11.2) **Assessment Focuses** AF (W): 1, 3, 6	ITP: (3.14) PCM: (3.11)

Shared teaching

• Share the learning objectives. Refer to 'Planning grid' (PCM 3.11) and explain that the children will be writing the final part of Samar's Story during this session.

• Act as Teacher in Role and recount the last part of Samar's story, using your imagination to add details as appropriate, e.g. *That evening we finished packing our few belongings. We followed my uncle to a new part of town. It looked so different from the war-damaged buildings I'd got used to. The fighting hadn't reached this far and everything looked normal and calm. It was great to feel safe and to have all that space to ourselves. But I missed Ayesha so much. Eventually I made some new friends at school, but I never forgot her. In a time of danger, hatred and fear she was my special friend.*

• Talk Partners make notes based on Samar's account to PCM 3.11 to refer to during the extended writing. Encourage them to use their imagination to visualise these events. *What questions would you like to ask Samar about the end of her story?* Answer the children's questions to Samar, in role.

• Recall annotated 'Writing stories' (ITP 3.14). Discuss success criteria relevant to writing the final part of Samar's Story. Invite the children to generate more ideas of success criteria for story endings. Add suggestions to ITP 3.14.

Independent and Guided

• The children reread their stories so far and write the ending, developing ideas on PCM 3.11. Encourage the children to use what they know about the characters and setting and to focus on using punctuation accurately.

COO Include original ideas and descriptions of Samar's thoughts and feelings.

CO As above. (TA)

O Work collaboratively to produce a story ending. (T+)

Plenary

• Recap the learning objectives. Invite several children to share their story endings. Encourage the other children to evaluate the endings against the success criteria. Praise examples of original ideas that fit with what is known about the characters and setting from *Oranges in No Man's Land*. Ask questions if there are any points that need clarification. *How have you punctuated the direct speech? Is it clear that this is the end of the story?*

• Allow time for the children to make changes to their own work in response to the examples of story endings they have heard.

• Before Session 15, read the children's completed stories and comment on one or two specific points for each child to work on.

Assessment pointers

• S&L: responses to the other children's work will show how well the children can express opinions sensitively.

• AF1, 3, 6 (W): written outcomes show how well the children can write texts using original ideas, good structure and accurate punctuation.

Session 15

We are learning to ...	Resources
• evaluate, edit and improve our writing • evaluate writing using a marking ladder • punctuate sentences accurately and effectively (PNS Strands 9.1, 11.2) **Assessment Focuses** AF (W): 3, 7	PCM: 3.12

Shared teaching (1)

• Share the learning objectives and explain that the children will be editing and improving their finished stories.

• Distribute the children's stories with any comments you have made. Allow the children Think Time to review your comments and consider any improvements that are needed.

• Use 'Marking ladder' (PCM 3.12) to help the children reflect on how to improve their writing. Discuss each point in turn and the type of changes the children might need to make, e.g. *Can you improve your descriptions of the characters? How could you make the setting clearer? Have you used paragraphs and linking words to make your story flow?* etc.

Independent and Guided (1)

• The children work independently to check and edit their version of Samar's story, then pairs swap stories and make comments on their partner's writing. The children finalise their stories based on their partner's comments and add illustrations if time allows.

COO Use PCM 3.12. Focus on ways to improve their own writing. (T+)

CO As above.

O Focus on points identified from the marking of their work. (TA+)

Shared teaching (2)

• Ask the children to review their own progress as a writer. *What are you most proud of in this piece of writing? What do you think you need to improve?* Encourage the children to Think-Pair-Share ideas before taking feedback. Add a list of suggestions to the Learning Wall.

Independent and Guided (2)

• Small groups read each other's stories. Where possible, organise groups so that they are able to read stories they haven't seen yet.

COO Read as many stories as possible in the time available.

CO As above. (TA)

O As above. Provide reading support as necessary. (T)

Plenary

• Recap the learning objectives. Ask the children to share something they liked about someone else's story and explain why. Encourage them to be specific and to refer to the writing techniques covered throughout the unit.

• Arrange for the finished versions of Samar's Story to be displayed with copies of the original book *Oranges in No Man's Land*, e.g. in the school library. Invite other classes in the school to read the book and the accompanying stories written by the children.

• Ask the children to give feedback on the process of writing a story from another culture. *What did you enjoy most in this unit? What did you learn while reading the story?*

Assessment pointers

• AF3, 7 (W): written outcomes show how well the children can choose appropriate vocabulary and structure and organise texts effectively.

Bookmark

Use the bookmark to record your thoughts as you read *Oranges in No Man's Land.*

Bookmark

Name: _____

Title: *Oranges in No Man's Land*

First impressions: _____

_____
_____
_____
_____

Questions to ask: _____

_____
_____
_____
_____
_____

| Ayesha's problem: _____

_____
_____
_____
_____

I predict she will:_____

_____
_____
_____
_____
_____

Thoughts at the end: _____

_____
_____
_____
_____
_____

Fold

Information about Lebanon

Read the information to find out more about Lebanon.

Lebanon

Lebanon is a small, mountainous country in the Middle East. The people of Lebanon come from lots of different religious groups and this has caused serious problems in the past.

Key facts

Population: approximately four million
Capital: Beirut
Main language: Arabic
Main religions: Islam and Christianity

Beirut

The capital city of Lebanon is Beirut, on the Mediterranean coast. During the civil war it was split into two sections, east and west, with Muslims on one side and Christians on the other. The two sides were separated by the Green Line and the area in the middle was called no man's land. The buildings were all damaged by the constant fighting and it wasn't safe for anyone to live there.

Civil war

In 1975 civil war broke out in Lebanon and lasted until 1990. Different groups of people wanted to take control of the country. They had their own militias to protect them and fight their enemies. The country was divided, with different groups controlling the north and south. During the civil war a great number of people were hurt or killed.

Beirut

Questions about Lebanon

Use 'Information about Lebanon' to answer the questions.

a. Where is Lebanon?

_____

_____

b. What is the capital city of Lebanon?

_____

_____

c. What sea is Beirut near?

_____

_____

d. What groups make up the Lebanese population?

_____

_____

e. When did the civil war in Lebanon start and finish?

_____

_____

f. Why did the civil war start?

_____

_____

g. How was Beirut separated during the civil war?

_____

_____

h. How did the civil war affect Beirut?

_____

_____

Ayesha at the checkpoint

1. **Act out the scene from pages 16 to 18 of** *Oranges in No Man's Land*.

> **Ayesha**
>
> > Granny has sent you to the checkpoint to collect cooking oil when the refugee truck arrives. You are carrying your baby brother. You hardly slept all night because of the noise from the fighting. You are feeling tired and quite scared of the soldiers with their guns.

> **Militiaman**
>
> > You've been up all night fighting in a battle, firing at the enemy on the other side of the Green Line. You are exhausted and you are missing your baby boy back at home. You see a young girl carrying a baby, hanging around by the checkpoint.

> **Observer**
>
> > Watch as Ayesha and the militiaman act out the scene. Choose a place to freeze the action. Ask each person to say what their character is thinking and feeling at that moment. Start the action again.

2. **Pause when the observer tells you to and answer the questions about the characters.**

a. **What were they thinking and feeling?**

_____

_____

b. **Did you learn anything new?**

_____

_____

Expressing emotion

1. Write the words in order on the scale. Add more of your own words.

worried	scared	terrified	uneasy

cautious

petrified

2. Ayesha says that her 'skin was prickling with fear.' Write your own phrases to describe how it feels when you are frightened.

3. Imagine that you are Ayesha. Write some sentences using 'fear' words to explain how you felt as you gradually realised how ill Granny was.

Abu Boutros

Imagine you are Abu Boutros. Write about meeting Ayesha at the checkpoint. Use reported speech to show what you said.

I was walking down the street when I saw soldiers gathered around a little girl. I said _____

_____

_____

_____

_____

I spoke to the girl and _____

_____

_____

_____

_____

Then _____

_____

_____

_____

_____

_____

Literacy Evolve Year 5 © Pearson Education 2009

Contrasts

Find descriptions of Beirut in *Oranges in No Man's Land*.

Before the war	During the war
The Burj (town square) was crowded with people.	The Burj is deserted.

The United Nations

1. Read the information about the United Nations.

The United Nations

The United Nations (UN) was set up after World War Two. Its purpose is to bring all the nations of the world together to work for peace and to help one another. It believes that each person in the world deserves to be treated fairly and have the chance to live a healthy and happy life.

When the UN started there were 51 member states. Now there are 192. Representatives from each country meet regularly at the UN headquarters in New York, USA. They discuss the problems they are facing and try to work out peaceful solutions to disagreements between countries.

When there is fighting between, or within, countries the UN can send a peacekeeping force. This is made up of soldiers from different countries who work together to stop the fighting, protect people caught up in wars and bring them help and aid.

The flag

The UN flag is blue with a white emblem on it. It shows the world being held in two olive branches which represent peace.

Aims

The UN aims to:
- keep peace around the world
- help countries get along and stop them having wars
- help people live free from poverty and disease, with better health and education
- look after the environment
- teach people to respect one another's rights and freedoms.

2. Answer the questions about the United Nations.

a. What is the UN flag like?

b. When was the UN set up?

c. What does the UN aim to do?

d. What is a UN peacekeeping force?

e. Where is the headquarters of the UN?

Jumbled sentences

Order the sentences about Abu Bashir's journey.

We got through the first checkpoint.

I drove the UN ambulance to Dr Leila's house.

We drove through a deserted street just before the fighting started.

I turned the ambulance round and went back home.

Dr Leila phoned and asked for my help.

I put a bandage round Ayesha's head to pretend that she was hurt.

I collected Ayesha from the doctor's house.

I drove through no man's land very quickly.

I agreed to help because the doctor had treated my daughter.

I asked Ayesha to get out of the ambulance before the second checkpoint.

Questions for Samar

Imagine that you are Samar. Answer the questions. Then write and answer one more question you would like to ask her.

What was your life like before the war?

_____
_____

How did you end up as a refugee?

_____
_____

What happened to your father?

_____
_____

How did you get your special treasures?

_____
_____

What was it like in the flat before Ayesha came?

_____
_____

_____
_____

_____
_____

Literacy Evolve Year 5 © Pearson Education 2009

Planning grid

Add notes to plan your own version of Samar's Story.

Introduction (basic facts about me)	→	

My life before the war	→	

Meeting Ayesha	→	

The big day	→	

My new life	→	

Conclusion	→	

Marking ladder

Use the marking ladder to check your work.

My partner's comments

(empty boxes)

My comments

(empty boxes)

- I have described the main characters: what they look like and how they feel.
- I have included details about Beirut during the civil war.
- I have completed each part of the story and made good links between the different parts.
- I have written the whole story from Samar's point of view.
- I have used a variety of sentence structures.
- I have used direct and reported speech effectively.

THE FAMILY FROM ONE END STREET – novel (Classic literature)

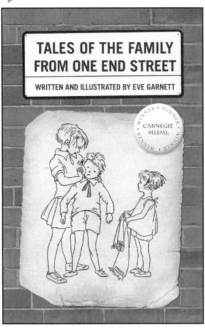

Medium term plan (3 weeks)	
Phase	**Learning Outcomes**
Phase 1: Understanding the context of the story (2 days)	• Children can find evidence about where and when a story is set, and make inferences about the author's point of view.
Phase 2: Reading and responding to the story (7 days)	• Children can empathise with characters and identify techniques used to convey the characters' feelings. • Children can identify historical details in the story, and compare these with their own experiences. • Children can analyse the structure of the story and identify how factual information is used. • Children can use different strategies to engage with stories from a variety of genres.
Phase 3: Writing a new chapter for the story (4 days)	• Children can plan, write and improve a chapter for a classic book, using the author's style, techniques, characters, setting, structural features and appropriate period details. • Children can work collaboratively to evaluate and improve their work.
Phase 4: Comparing other stories (2 days)	• Children can explore their own reading preferences and those of others by selecting other classic texts, researching the views of others, and making comparisons. • Children can use different strategies for understanding unfamiliar language in older texts.

Narrative Unit 4

THE FAMILY FROM ONE END STREET

Big picture
The children read a classic novel, *Tales of the Family from One End Street*. They find out about when and where the story is set and explore how this influences the way people behave and how the plot unfolds. They explore relationships and attitudes, make comparisons with their own experience and look in detail at degrees of formality in dialogue. The children plan and write a new chapter for the book. Then read extracts from some other classic novels.

Prior learning
This unit assumes that children can already:
- make inferences about the author's perspective
- understand story structure and identify aspects of the plot
- plan and write a story with a clear structure
- use direct and reported speech and vary sentence construction to change the pace of the story and add interest or detail.

Key aspects of learning
Communication: Express creative ideas and opinions through speaking and writing; read fiction and non-fiction texts independently.
Creative thinking: Respond imaginatively to the story; generate ideas for a new chapter.
Empathy: Identify with characters and situations in the story; use role play to explore relationships and attitudes in more depth.

Enquiry: Ask questions about the story context; research the background; test predictions about how the characters will relate.
Evaluation: Reflect on own reading preferences and set personal goals to widen reading experience; assess own narrative writing against success criteria and identify ways to improve it.

Progression in narrative
In this unit the children will:
- analyse the structure of complex narrative; look for evidence of the author's perspective; consider the time and place where the story is set and how this affects the characters and plot
- deduce differences in patterns of relationships, customs and attitudes in comparison to their own experience; look at examples of dialogue, degrees of formality and what this shows about relationships
- write in the style of a particular author to create a new chapter; use dialogue to build character; experiment with the order of paragraphs.

Cross-curricular links
Citizenship: Links to citizenship themes of equality in our diverse world.
Geography: Exploration of how the pastimes of the 1930s link with how we spend our time in the present day.
History: Links to exploring what life was like in the past.

Reading time
4 hours 50 minutes

PHASE 1: UNDERSTANDING THE CONTEXT OF THE STORY (2 DAYS)

Session 1

We are learning to ...	Resources
• collect evidence about events and historical details • record impressions in a reading journal (PNS Strands 7.1, 8.1) **Assessment Focuses** AF (R): 2, 7	*Tales of the Family from One End Street* ITP: 4.1, 4.2, 4.3

Shared teaching (1)
- Share the learning objectives.
- Explain that *Tales of the Family from One End Street* was first published in 1937. Look together at the cover. *It's about the adventures of a family who lived in the 1930s. What do you think the story will be like? How will the children's lives differ from yours?* Talk Partners discuss ideas.
- Show 'The Ruggles family' (ITP 4.1) without clicking the hotspots. Encourage the children to look out for information about the characters. Read Chapter 1 with the children following in their books.
- *Were there any words you didn't understand?* Show 'Glossary' (ITP 4.2). Demonstrate how to check meanings of unfamiliar words. Start the Learning Wall with a copy of ITP 4.2.
- Return to ITP 4.1. *What did you learn about the characters?* Take feedback, then click the hotspots to reveal facts about each character.
- *How does this story opening compare with other stories you've read? What are the similarities and differences?*

Independent and Guided (1)
- The children investigate what the Ruggles's house would have been like.

  Use books, or online resources, to research terraced houses in the 1930s, making sketches and notes of the findings. (TA+)

  Reread paragraphs 2 and 3 on page 4 in pairs, looking at the illustrations so far. Discuss how the Ruggles's house might have looked and draw a picture of it.

  Use 'Life in the 1930s' (ITP 4.3) to identify details in the pictures that are similar to and different from modern houses. (T)

Shared teaching (2)
- Take feedback. Display the children's pictures on the Learning Wall. *Can you imagine the setting now?*
- Explain that as they read *Tales of the Family from One End Street* they will be keeping a reading journal to record their thoughts and questions.
- Provide the children with a notebook, or sheets of paper to use as a reading journal.

Independent and Guided (2)
- The children record their first impressions of the book in their reading journals.

  Write independently.

  As above. (T)

  As above. (TA)

Plenary
- Recap the learning objectives. Invite the children to share their first impressions. *What do you think this book will be like? What questions do you have?*

Assessment pointers
- AF2, 7 (R): research work and responses to questioning show how well the children can relate details from the text to the historical context.

<table>
<tr><td>

We are learning to ...
- think about how people speak and what this tells us about them
- explore the author's viewpoint through the characters (PNS Strands 2.2, 7.2)

Assessment Focuses
AF (R): 6, 7

</td><td>

Resources
Tales of the Family from One End Street
ITP: (4.2), 4.4

</td></tr>
</table>

Shared teaching (1)

- *Have you ever tried to do something helpful that turned out wrong?* Ask the children to Think-Pair-Share feelings they had when facing something going wrong. Explain that this is what happens to Lily Rose.
- Share the learning objectives and read Chapter 2 as the children follow in their books. Pause at page 24, '... put the kettle on and get the tea'. *What do you think will happen when Lily Rose has to apologise? How would you be feeling?*
- Continue reading until the end of Chapter 2. Discuss what happened.
- *Did anything puzzle you in this chapter?* Use 'Glossary' (ITP 4.2) to check any unfamiliar words. Discuss differences between the way laundry was done in the 1930s and how it is done now.
- Introduce the idea that there are differences in the way that various characters live and work. *Let's look in more detail at how the characters speak to each other.*

Independent and Guided (1)

- In groups of five, the children Role Play the conversation on pages 25–27, from 'Early today, Mrs Ruggles ...' to '... once a week to be weighed'. One child reads each character and one reads as the narrator. Support the children with an identified need. (T/TA)

Shared teaching (2)

- Ask the children to reflect on the roles that they acted out. *Did you notice differences in the characters' speech? Did you learn anything about the relationships between the characters?* Refer to the respect they show one another.
- Show 'Eve Garnett' (ITP 4.4). Read the information about the author together. *What have you found out about the book and the author? What do you think about the book so far?* Talk Partners discuss ideas.

Independent and Guided (2)

- The children make notes in their reading journals about differences in *Tales of the Family from One End Street.*
- **OOO** Consider how various characters talk, differences between rich and poor people, and differences between then and now. Discuss why these may have been highlighted by the author. (T+)
- **OO** Note differences in how various characters talk, differences between rich and poor people and differences between then and now.
- **O** Note differences between rich and poor people. (TA+)

Plenary

- Recap the learning objectives. Take feedback about the differences that the children have noticed. *I wonder why Eve Garnett chose to write in this way?* Encourage the children to make the link between the information from ITP 4.4 and the way that the story is written.

Assessment pointers

- S&L: role plays will show how well the children can convey ideas about characters through speech and gesture.
- AF6, 7 (R): reading journals and responses to questioning show the children's understanding of the use of different speech patterns in historical and social contexts on the theme of class differences.

PHASE 2: READING AND RESPONDING TO THE STORY (7 DAYS)

<table>
<tr><td>

We are learning to ...
- use drama and role play to empathise with characters
- use empathy to make inferences about characters
- make predictions about the story (PNS Strands 4.1, 7.2, 8.2)

Assessment Focuses
AF (R): 3

</td><td>

Resources
Tales of the Family from One End Street
ITP: (4.1, 4.2)

</td></tr>
</table>

Shared teaching

- Share the learning objectives.
- Explain that this book is like a television series that is divided into episodes. Each chapter has a complete story, involving different members of the family. Show 'The Ruggles family' (ITP 4.1). *What can you remember about Jim and John?* Explain that the next two chapters will focus on their adventures.
- *Have you ever thought that you would like to have an adventure? Where would you go? What would you do?* Talk Partners discuss. Invite the children to share ideas.
- Read Chapter 3 of *Tales of the Family from One End Street* as far as '... upsetting your sleep' on page 44. *Was there anything you didn't understand?* Refer to 'Glossary' (ITP 4.2) if necessary.
- Ask the children to Think-Pair-Share about Jim Ruggles. *Why do you think he wanted to have an adventure? How did he feel about meeting the Gang of the Black Hand? Why do you think he had nightmares?* Encourage the children to imagine Jim's feelings. Remind them to look back at the story for details.
- Arrange a whole-class Hot-Seating activity. Invite a child to take the role of Jim. Model asking questions. *What was it like when the gang accused you of spying? Why was it so hard not to tell John about the*

gang? Encourage the children to ask further questions or take turns in the hot seat.
- Discuss the answers given by Jim in role. Review whether they seem likely. Model referring to evidence from the book. *Would Jim say that? I think he might say ... because on page ... . What do you now know about Jim that you did not know before?* Add to the Learning Wall.
- Refer to page 39 and the Gang of the Black Hand's object of having adventures. *I wonder what adventures the twins will have.*

Independent and Guided

- The children make predictions about the adventures the twins will have in their reading journals.
- **OOO** Work with a partner to discuss and write predictions, explaining at least one idea in more detail with reference to evidence in the text.
- **OO** Share ideas in small groups, selecting one prediction to discuss in more detail and write about. (TA+)
- **O** Talk about adventures as a group, selecting one idea to think through in more detail and write about. (T+)

Plenary

- Recap the learning objectives.
- *Did the hot-seating activity help you to understand more about Jim? Did it help you to predict his adventures? What do you think is going to happen?* Add any new insights to the Learning Wall.

Assessment pointers

- S&L: hot-seating will show how far the children can sustain roles to explore ideas.
- AF3 (R): responses to questioning and written predictions show how well the children can respond imaginatively and make inferences and deductions about a character.

We are learning to ...	Resources
• identify how an author creates a sense of danger and excitement • use empathy to explore characters and story (PNS Strands 7.5, 8.2) **Assessment Focuses** AF (R): 5	*Tales of the Family from One End Street* ITP: (4.2), 4.5 PCM: 4.1, 4.2, 4.3

Shared teaching

• Share the learning objectives.
• Recap Session 3. *Now the twins have joined the Gang of the Black Hand, they need to have an adventure. What did you predict they would do?* Encourage the children to share predictions.
• Continue reading Chapter 3 of *Tales of the Family from One End Street* from page 44 until ' ... they were clear of the docks' on page 57. Refer to 'Glossary' (ITP 4.2) as necessary.
• Talk Partners discuss Jim's plan for an adventure. *When did it start to go wrong? How do you think Jim was feeling at that point?* Encourage the children to draw on what they learnt about Jim in Session 3.
• Reread the paragraph beginning 'But instead of tying up ... ' on pages 52–53. Identify words and phrases that indicate the threatening situation (e.g. 'enormous', 'towered', 'suspended', 'waiting', 'clutch') and show that Jim is getting increasingly worried (e.g. 'Jim's heart gave a great leap').
• Show 'Jim's adventure' (ITP 4.5). Invite the children to highlight words and phrases that show time elapsing between the events. Explain that the author showed how everything happens in quick succession to emphasise how powerless Jim is as events overtake him.
• Invite the children to look for examples of long and short sentences on ITP 4.5. Focus on the final sentence: 'The gulls ... *L'Oiseau-Mouche*!'

Draw attention to the author's use of semi-colons to separate clauses. *How could we break this up?* Encourage pairs to rewrite the sentence as a series of shorter sentences. Share some examples. *Which version is more dramatic? Which conveys a sense of excitement most effectively?*
• Continue to read the book until the end of Chapter 3.

Independent and Guided

• The children identify and note Jim's feelings at different points during his adventure.

  ◉◉◉ Use 'How Jim feels' (PCM 4.1). Use inference and locate words that show Jim's emotions directly. (TA)

  ◉◉ Use 'The lorry ride home' (PCM 4.2). In pairs, use inference and locate words that show Jim's emotions directly.

  ◉ As above. (T+)

Plenary

• *Did the author create a sense of drama successfully in Chapter 3? Did learning about Jim's quickly changing feelings add to the sense of excitement?* Encourage the children to express their own views, referring to particular words, phrases or sentences.
• Recap the learning objectives. Create another moment of excitement by producing a sealed envelope marked 'Telegram' to be read in Session 5, using 'Telegram' (PCM 4.3). Remind the children of the end of Chapter 3 and encourage predictions about John. *What do you think the telegram will say?*

Assessment pointers

• AF5 (R): analysis of the text shows how well the children understand the importance of vocabulary choice and sentence construction to create a sense of excitement.

We are learning to ...	Resources
• collect evidence and details about events and historical details • make predictions about the story (PNS Strands 7.1, 8.2) **Assessment Focuses** AF (R): 6, 7	*Tales of the Family from One End Street* ITP: (4.2, 4.3) PCM: 4.3

Shared teaching

• Share the learning objectives.
• Ask the children to close their eyes and visualise the Ruggles's house. *It is 5pm and Mrs Ruggles is rushing round getting everything ready for tea. Mr Ruggles is slumped in a chair after a hard day at work. Kate has been sent to look for the twins, while Lily Rose washes the other children's hands. There's a knock on the door and a messenger is standing there holding a telegram. Mr and Mrs Ruggles are very worried because telegrams usually bring bad news.*
• Explain that before most people had telephones, telegrams were used to send urgent news. Explain that the messages were always short, because you had to pay for each word separately. Open the sealed envelope containing 'Telegram' (PCM 4.3) and read it out.
• *What will Mrs Ruggles do next? What do you think John has been doing? Who do you think Mr Lawrence is?* Encourage the children to Think-Pair-Share ideas.
• Read Chapter 4 of *Tales of the Family from One End Street* until '(He was not so sure about Mum and Dad.)' on page 76, with the children following in their books. Encourage them to ask questions about anything that puzzles them and use 'Glossary' (ITP 4.2).
• Talk Partners summarise what has happened to John on his adventure,

taking turns to say a sentence each and recall events in the correct order.
• Recall 'Life in the 1930s' (ITP 4.3). Refer to the grand house and car. *The Lawrences have this sort of car and house. How does John feel when he sees where the Lawrence family lives? What impresses him the most?* Encourage the children to look back at pages 71–75 to help them recall John's impressions.

Independent and Guided

• The children reread pages 71–75 and make notes in their reading journals about the differences between the Lawrences and the Ruggles.

  ◉◉◉ Note differences between the rich and poor characters, and how they speak. Pairs discuss John's and their own feelings about these differences.

  ◉◉ Record differences between the homes of the two families. (T+)

  ◉ Draw a picture of Peter's schoolroom or the bathroom. (TA+)

Plenary

• Take feedback on the differences between the two homes. Praise the children referring back to earlier chapters and making their own inferences based on the text.
• Recap the learning objectives.
• Discuss the author's intentions in Chapter 4. *I wonder if Eve Garnett thought it was fair that some families had so much more than others. What do you think?*

Assessment pointers

• AF6, 7 (R): oral feedback shows how far the children are able to make links between the story and the social context and shows their understanding of the author's intentions and viewpoint.

We are learning to ...
• collect evidence about events and historical details
• make inferences about what a character is thinking and feeling
• understand and map the story structure
(PNS Strands 7.1, 7.2, 7.3)

Assessment Focuses
AF (R): 4

Resources
Tales of the Family from One End Street
ITP: (4.2), 4.6
PCM: 4.4

Shared teaching (1)
• Share the learning objectives and recap what has happened to John so far during his adventure. *What do you think Peter's party will be like?*
• Continue reading Chapter 4 of *Tales of the Family from One End Street* from page 76 ('The guests were arriving ... ') until page 88 ('Victims of a snatch and grab raid!'). Encourage the children to ask questions about anything that puzzles them and use 'Glossary' (ITP 4.2).
• Talk Partners discuss the party. *Which part of the party would you have enjoyed most? What do you think John enjoyed most?* Take feedback and share ideas. *How do you think John's parents will react when he gets home?* Record the children's predictions on the Learning Wall.
• Continue reading until the end of Chapter 4. *Did Mr and Mrs Ruggles react as you thought they would?* Refer to the children's predictions on the Learning Wall. *Why didn't Mr Ruggles recognise John straight away? Why do you think Mrs Ruggles stopped being cross when she read the letter?*
• Remind the children of Jim's adventure in Chapter 3. *Did you realise that Jim and John were having their adventures at the same time?* Show 'Adventure timetable' (ITP 4.6). Explain that the children are going to look for clues in the story about what each of the boys was doing at different times.

Independent and Guided
• In groups, the children investigate the timings of the twins' adventures by referring to Chapters 3 and 4. Half the children in each group focus on Jim's adventure and the other half on John's.
  ∞ Complete 'Adventure timetable' (PCM 4.4) for Jim or John.
  ∞ As above. (TA+)
  ◐ As above. (T+)

Shared teaching (2)
• Take feedback and agree timings for Jim and John's adventures. Add suggestions to ITP 4.6.
• Organise a whole-class Hot-Seating activity. Invite two confident children to take the roles of the twins and answer questions about their days. Model asking questions. *What did you do when the hailstorm started? What did you have for lunch? What time did you get back home again?* Encourage the children to ask Jim and John any questions they have.

Plenary
• Recap the learning objectives. Focus on the structure of this part of the story. *The author chose to tell the two boys' stories separately. How else could she have presented them?* (moving from one to the other during the day) Discuss language that might be used in this structure, e.g. 'Meanwhile, Jim ... '.
• *Can you think of any other books, films or television programmes where two stories run alongside each other?*

Assessment pointers
• S&L: hot-seating will show how far the children can sustain roles and recount ideas.
• AF4 (R): responses to questioning show how well the children understand how the text is structured as parallel narratives.

We are learning to ...
• understand how the author uses real events as ideas for stories
• make predictions about the story
(PNS Strands 7.2, 8.2)

Assessment Focuses
AF (R): 2

Resources
Tales of the Family from One End Street
ITP: (4.2), 4.7
PCM: 4.5, 4.6

Shared teaching (1)
• Share the learning objectives.
• Show 'Mr Ruggles's ambition' (ITP 4.7). Explain that this extract is part of the story that doesn't appear in your books. Read the extract together. Explain that later on, Mr Ruggles receives £2 as a reward for handing in some lost property and he decides to use the money to take the family on a day out to the Cart Horse Parade.
• *What do you think the Cart Horse Parade might be?* Explain that it is an actual event and the author used factual information to write about the Ruggles's day out.

Independent and Guided (1)
• The children research aspects of a day out at the Cart Horse Parade in the 1930s.
  ∞ Use 'The Ruggles's day out' (PCM 4.5) and 'Old money' (PCM 4.6) to answer the questions.
  ∞ Read PCM 4.5. Use the Internet to research the history of the Cart Horse Parade. (T+)
  ◐ As a group, use PCM 4.5 and PCM 4.6 to answer the questions. (TA+)

Shared teaching (2)
• Ask groups to share their findings. *What was the Cart Horse Parade? Is £2 enough to take the Ruggles family to the Parade? What might they spend their money on?*
• Read Chapter 5 of *Tales of the Family from One End Street* until ' ... jumped down to greet his relations' on page 113. Encourage them to ask questions and refer to 'Glossary' (ITP 4.2) as necessary.
• Discuss any factual information that the children recognise from their research, e.g. the station name, cost of a comic and time of the parade.
• Read to the end of Chapter 5.

Independent and Guided (2)
• The children write a prediction of what the Ruggles children will do at the play park in their reading journals.
  ∞ Include a description of the play park and what might happen to Pamela and Anthony as well as the Ruggles. (T)
  ∞ Choose one or two of the Ruggles children to write about.
  ◐ Focus on what will happen to Jo Ruggles. (TA)

Plenary
• Recap the learning objectives. *What do you think will happen at the play park?*
• *Why do you think that the author based this episode of the story on factual information rather than making up an imaginary event?* Draw out the idea that using recognisable, familiar facts would have made the story more realistic for the people reading at the time.
• Draw parallels with contemporary authors such as Jacqueline Wilson.

Assessment pointers
• AF2 (R): written outcomes and responses to questioning show how far the children can identify specific information in texts.

We are learning to ...	Resources
• use and reflect on drama techniques to help us explore characters and story • make predictions about the story and say what we learn from this (PNS Strands 4.1, 8.2) **Assessment Focuses** AF (R): 3	*Tales of the Family from One End Street* ITP: 4.8 PCM: 4.7

Shared teaching

• Share the learning objectives.
• Recap where the family were at the end of Chapter 5 of *Tales of the Family from One End Street*. *What do you predict will happen when the children go off to play?* Encourage the children to refer to their reading journals from Session 7 and explain their predictions.
• Show 'Adventure at the park' (ITP 4.8). *What do you know about the different characters in the story?* Click the character names to reveal information and add the children's suggestions. Draw out the idea that, based on the book so far, the Ruggles children are more likely to have an adventure than just play quietly.
• In groups of 4 to 6, the children Role Play what they think will happen in the park. Encourage them to make brief notes, using what they know already about the characters to plan, then agree roles and act out their scenes.
• Ask each group to summarise their predictions for the rest of the class. Praise the children who pick up on clues in the story and incorporate these into their scenes. Look out for imaginative ideas that build on what the children know about specific characters.
• Read Chapter 6 until page 137, ' ... the Grand Parade had begun!'

Independent and Guided

• The children look back over Chapter 6 and make notes about what actually happens to each of the children when they are sent off to play.
• ⦿⦿⦿ Complete 'At the play park' (PCM 4.7).
• ⦿⦿ As above. (TA+)
• ⦿ Focus on Jo and Peg Ruggles on PCM 4.7. (T+)

Plenary

• Recap the learning objectives.
• Compare the children's predictions with what actually happened in the story. *Which do you prefer, your own ideas or those in the story? What questions do you still have about particular characters and events?* Explain that authors don't always include every detail, but leave room for the reader to imagine what might have happened. *Did making predictions help you to understand and enjoy this episode more?*

Assessment pointers

• S&L: role plays will show how far the children understand the characters and can use this knowledge to create new scenarios.
• AF3 (R): role play scenes show how well the children are able to infer details about individual characters and to use this to make detailed predictions about their behaviour and interactions.

We are learning to ...	Resources
• reflect on the story we have read using the notes in our reading journals • use and reflect on visualisation, prediction and empathy techniques (PNS Strands 8.1, 8.2) **Assessment Focuses** AF (R): 6	*Tales of the Family from One End Street* ITP: (4.2, 4.4), 4.9 PCM: 4.8

Shared teaching

• Share the learning objectives.
• Introduce the 'perfect day' theme for the final episode of the story. Show 'Posh tea shop' (ITP 4.9). Ask the children to talk about what they can see in the picture. If appropriate, set up the classroom like a restaurant with music playing in the background and seat children as though they were customers.
• *What would it be like to go to this restaurant? What would you eat and drink? How do you think the Ruggles family would feel at a restaurant like this?* Talk Partners discuss their thoughts.
• Read *Tales of the Family from One End Street* from page 137 until the end of Chapter 6. Encourage the children to ask questions and refer to 'Glossary' (ITP 4.2).
• Cut up several copies of 'Character cards' (PCM 4.8) and give one card to each child. Explain that they have to find someone else who has the same card as them. Ask the children to Role Play what that character would have enjoyed most about their trip to London.
• Take feedback and explain that now they have reached the end of the story, they should look back at their reading journal to remind them of the things they noted as they were reading.
• Talk Partners discuss whether their first impressions of the book were

right and any changes in opinion that they have had. Invite individuals to tell the class about how and why their opinion of the book has changed.
• Recall 'Eve Garnett' (ITP 4.4) and remind the children about the author's reasons for writing the book. *How successful was the author in showing you how different people lived at this time?* Encourage the children to look back at their notes about differences.

Independent and Guided

• The children complete their reading journals by writing about which character they would most like to be and what they will remember about the book.
• ⦿⦿⦿ Refer to evidence in the text to support writing.
• ⦿⦿ As above. (T)
• ⦿ As a group, discuss the characters and memories of the book. Make brief notes. (TA+)

Plenary

• Recap the learning objectives and remind the children of different activities, e.g. visualisation, role play, prediction, and ask for feedback on each. *Which activities were most useful in helping you understand and enjoy the story?*
• *Would you like to read more about the Ruggles family?* Encourage the children to reflect on what they enjoyed and anything they found difficult or puzzling. Tell them that there are some other stories about the characters from *Tales of the Family from One End Street* that they could read themselves.

Assessment pointers

• AF6 (R): responses to questioning about the book as a whole show how well the children can reflect on the effect of texts on the reader.

Session 10

We are learning to …	Resources
• plan and write an adventure story • use storyboards or a planner to create a structure (PNS Strands 9.2) **Assessment Focuses** AF (W): 1	*Tales of the Family from One End Street* ITP: (4.8), 4.10, 4.11 PCM: 4.9

Shared teaching

• Share the learning objectives.
• Encourage the children to visualise characters from *Tales of the Family from One End Street* as you describe a scene. *The Ruggles children have arrived at the park and met up with their cousins. They have been told to go to the play park, but there is so much more to explore. What if the children all went off in different directions and had their own adventures in the park?* Explain that during the next four sessions the children will be planning and writing their own stories about what happens to the Ruggles children and display their stories so that everyone can read them.
• Show 'Park map and rules' (ITP 4.10) and explain that like Eve Garnett, they will base their ideas for stories on factual information. Point out some features on the map on ITP 4.10. *Does this map give you any story ideas?* Read the rules on ITP 4.10. *Do these rules give you any ideas? What would happen if one or two Ruggles children broke a rule?*
• Recall 'Adventure at the park' (ITP 4.8) to remind the children about the different characters in the story. Talk Partners discuss which characters they would like to write about.
• Look more closely at ITP 4.10. Encourage the children to use the map locations and the rules to Think-Pair-Share ideas for mischief or adventure. Share some suggestions.
• Use Modelled Writing to complete 'Adventure story plan' (PCM 4.9), taking suggestions from the children and demonstrating how to record ideas as brief notes. Use Think Alouds to talk through each question in turn, explaining your ideas, e.g. *I have chosen Kate and Peg because we don't know so much about them and I want to explain how Peg ended up with the bunch of roses.* Emphasise the use of notes to summarise ideas rather than writing complete sentences on the plan.

Independent and Guided

• The children plan their own adventure story involving characters from *Tales of the Family from One End Street*.

  ⬤⬤⬤ Complete PCM 4.9, referring to ITP 4.10 for ideas.

  ⬤⬤ As above. (TA+)

  ◉ Work as a group to plan the main story events in more detail. (T+)

Plenary

• Recap the learning objectives.
• Invite a few of the children to share their story plans. Praise examples of using the map and rules to come up with the 'Where' and 'Why' of the story.
• Show 'Writing adventure stories' (ITP 4.11). Discuss the success criteria and involve the children in adding further suggestions.
• Add the class story plan to the Learning Wall to refer to in Session 11.

Assessment pointers

• AF1 (W): plans show how far the children can generate imaginative and interesting ideas.

Session 11

We are learning to …	Resources
• write effective story openings • understand how to use direct speech effectively (PNS Strands 9.2, 9.4) **Assessment Focuses** AF (W): 5, 7	*Tales of the Family from One End Street* ITP: (4.11), 4.12 PCM: (4.9)

Shared teaching (1)

• Share the learning objectives.
• Refer to the class story plan on the Learning Wall. Remind the children of the notes they made on 'Adventure story plan' (PCM 4.9). Talk Partners compare plans and discuss how to start their stories. Stress that this is a new chapter for the book so there is no need to introduce the characters and setting; begin from when the children go off to play.
• Use Modelled Writing to compose an opening paragraph that explains which characters this adventure will focus on. Use 'Kate's adventure' (ITP 4.12) or create your own. Demonstrate how to use details from the book, e.g. *I remember what Kate is wearing, so I am going to use that.*
• Discuss vocabulary choices, e.g. *I'm going to use 'pursue' instead of 'chase', because that sounds more like Eve Garnett's style.*
• As you write, use Think Alouds to explain the choices you make and the rules you apply. Emphasise the process of reading through at regular intervals to check and edit what you have written.

Independent and Guided (1)

• The children write an opening paragraph for their stories.

  ⬤⬤⬤ Use PCM 4.9. Review writing to check for sense and accuracy.

  ⬤⬤ As above. (TA+)

  ◉ As above. (T+)

Shared teaching (2)

• Refer to the class story plan on the Learning Wall and explain that the next part of the story needs to describe the events that lead to the main problem. Talk Partners discuss ways of linking a series of sentences without using 'and then'. *How do authors add interest, excitement or comedy?* Take suggestions, e.g. varying sentence length, using dialogue, etc.
• Use Modelled Writing with ITP 4.12 or your own story to demonstrate various techniques in the next paragraph.
• *Picture a scene where one of the Ruggles children comes face to face with a 'posh' lady. How could you use direct speech to show the differences between them?* Take suggestions and write some examples of dialogue. Involve the children in applying rules of punctuation.

Independent and Guided (2)

• The children write the next part of their stories, including dialogue that shows what the characters are like, using the book for reference.

  ⬤⬤⬤ Refer to PCM 4.9.

  ⬤⬤ As above. (T+)

  ◉ As above. (TA+)

Plenary

• Recap the learning objectives.
• Ask a few of the children to share their stories so far. Recall annotated 'Writing adventure stories' (ITP 4.11). Encourage the children to provide feedback about whether the stories meet the success criteria.

Assessment pointers

• AF5, 7 (W): written outcomes will show how well the children are able to select vocabulary appropriate to particular characters and vary sentences.

We are learning to ...	Resources
• achieve different effects by changing the order of paragraphs in our stories • use connectives to make links between different parts of our stories (PNS Strands 10.1, 11.1) **Assessment Focuses** AF (W): 4	ITP: (4.11, 4.12), 4.13 PCM: (4.9)

Shared teaching

• Share the learning objectives and explain that before the children continue writing their own stories, they're going to review another example. Give out copies of 'Kate's adventure' (ITP 4.12). *You are going to read 'Kate's adventure', then change and improve it.*
• Read the story on ITP 4.12 as the children follow and encourage them to respond with questions or comments.
• Invite the children to suggest some possible alternatives for restructuring the story in a different way.
• Show 'Reordering paragraphs' (ITP 4.13) and read the alternative opening to 'Kate's adventure'. Explain the changes that have been made in this version. Explain that if you move sections or paragraphs around like this, you have to watch out for other changes that need to be made too. Encourage the children to suggest changes, such as adding connecting words and phrases to show how events are linked.
• Talk Partners discuss their opinions about opening the story by jumping straight to the ending. *Is it an improvement?* Take feedback and draw out pros and cons, e.g. it makes the story more intriguing, but it could be confusing to the reader.
• *Can you think of any other ways to reorder paragraphs in this story?* Encourage suggestions such as following Peg's story first, then returning to Kate's afterwards; or following both adventures simultaneously using connectives such as 'meanwhile'. Talk through which paragraphs would have to be moved or amended for each alternative.
• Reinforce the importance of connectives as you review the lists on ITP 4.13. Add further examples of your own and from the children's suggestions. Add these to the Learning Wall for the children to refer to.

Independent and Guided

• The children continue writing their stories and consider making changes to the order of paragraphs to make the story more interesting or exciting.

∞ Refer to annotated 'Adventure story plan' (PCM 4.9). Use a range of temporal connectives to make links between paragraphs.

∞ As above. (T)

◉ Follow the class story plan on the Learning Wall. Choose temporal connectives to show the links between paragraphs. (TA)

Plenary

• Recap the learning objectives.
  Ask a few of the children to share their stories so far. Recall annotated 'Writing adventure stories' (ITP 4.11). Ask the other children to look out for things that have been included in each story and comment on whether the stories meet the success criteria.
• Create a list of connectives to display on the Learning Wall. Remind the children to choose a variety of words as they write the next parts of their story.

Assessment pointers

• AF4 (W): written outcomes show how well the children are able to include temporal connectives to make links between paragraphs and indicate the passing of time.

We are learning to ...	Resources
• evaluate, edit and improve our writing • punctuate sentences accurately and effectively (PNS Strands 9.1, 11.2) **Assessment Focuses** AF (W): 1, 2, 3, 8	ITP: (4.11, 4.12) PCM: 4.10

Shared teaching (1)

• Share the learning objectives.
• Begin as Teacher in Role as Kate Ruggles. Using 'Kate's adventure' (ITP 4.12) as a guide, tell the children about your adventure in the park. Comment on what you were thinking and feeling. Encourage the children to ask questions for you to answer as Kate.
• Explain that the children are going to repeat this activity, focusing on the character from their own story. Organise pairs so that the children talk to a different character from their own. The pairs take turns to use Improvisation to tell their story in role and answer questions.
• Take feedback. *What have you learnt from telling your story in role? Has it given you new ideas to add to your story?*

Independent and Guided (1)

• The children complete first drafts of their stories and add details suggested by the improvisations.

∞ Focus on ways to make the adventure seem more real and develop characters in detail. (T)

∞ Make improvements to include more detailed descriptions.

◉ As above. (TA)

Shared teaching (2)

• Recall annotated 'Writing adventure stories' (ITP 4.11). Recap the success criteria and review how the children will know if their stories meet them. Discuss the evidence they should look for.
• Allow Think Time for the children to read their work and highlight anything they want to change or improve.

Independent and Guided (2)

• The children edit their stories to ensure they meet the success criteria, using 'Marking ladder' (PCM 4.10) as a tool for self-assessment. Pairs swap stories to provide peer assessment to complete PCM 4.10.

∞ Work independently to make the necessary changes.

∞ As above. (TA)

◉ Discuss PCM 4.10 as a group before editing stories. (T+)

Plenary

• Recap the learning objectives. *What changes did you make?*
• Remind the children that their stories are for the class to read. Discuss the best way to present them, e.g. as a class book or a wall display. *What else do you need to do to ensure your story is easy to read?*
• Allow time for the children to finalise their stories. Collect and display them in the agreed format on or near the Learning Wall.
• Encourage the children to read some stories independently. Provide sticky notes for them to give feedback on what they like in the stories.

Assessment pointers

• S&L: improvisations will show how well the children can create and sustain roles to explore and develop ideas.
• AF1, 2, 3, 8 (W): completed stories, peer and self-assessment show how well the children can write imaginative texts in a style appropriate to the task and that are structured correctly.

Session 14

We are learning to …	Resources
• read and enjoy a range of older stories (PNS Strands 8.1)	*Tales of the Family from One End Street*
Assessment Focuses	ITP: 4.14
AF (R): 7	PCM: 4.11

Shared teaching

• Before the session, gather together and display a selection of older 'classic' books (published before 1950) that will appeal to the children in your class. If possible, include *Mary Poppins* by P. L. Travers, *Swallows and Amazons* by Arthur Ransome, and other books referenced on 'Classic stories' (PCM 4.11). Aim to have at least one book for each pair of children.

• Share the learning objective. Challenge the children to recall exactly when *Tales of the Family from One End Street* was written. Refer the children to their books and help them to find the original publication date (1937).

• Introduce the last phase of this unit of work and explain that now they have read a book that was written over 70 years ago, they are going to find out more about other 'classic' stories. Explain that the children will use this information to plan what they might like to read next.

• Show 'Meet the Banks Family' (ITP 4.14). Read it as the children follow on screen and explain that this story was written just a few years before *Tales of the Family from One End Street.* Encourage the children to think about anything that is familiar before revealing the book's title. Encourage them to recall details if they have seen the film version.

• Ask Talk Partners to compare the Banks family with the Ruggles family. *Do you notice any differences?* Discuss the fact that the Banks family

has servants working for them and the children are looked after by a nanny. *Would you like to read this book yourself? Is there anything that would make it difficult?*

• Draw attention to the display of books. *Do you know any of these books?* Encourage the children to make links with film or TV versions, explaining that, in each case, the book came first.

Independent and Guided

• The children use PCM 4.11 to match book titles with plot summaries and identify story types to help them decide on their own reading preferences and make an informed choice about what to read next.

⚫⚫⚫ Use PCM 4.11. Work independently.

⚫⚫ As above. Work in pairs. (TA+)

⚫ As above. Discuss reading preferences in pairs, thinking about favourite books and types of stories. (T+)

Plenary

• Recap the learning objective and invite the children to share what they have discovered about their reading preferences. Encourage them to explain why they think they would like particular stories.

• Challenge the children to do some research at home or around the school. *Can you find out what the adults in your family or the school enjoyed reading when they were your age?* Discuss who to ask, e.g. parents, carers, grandparents, midday supervisors, other class teachers.

Assessment pointers

• AF7 (R): responses to questioning show how well the children understand social, cultural and historical contexts.

Session 15

We are learning to …	Resources
• reflect on what we enjoy reading and make choices about what to read next (PNS Strands 8.1)	ITP: 4.15 PCM: 4.12
Assessment Focuses	
AF (R): 5, 7	

Shared teaching

• Share the learning objective.

• Talk about books you enjoyed reading as a child. If possible, bring an old copy of a favourite classic children's story to share. Summarise the plot, explain what you liked and read a short extract as a 'taster'.

• Ask the children to share their findings about what other adults enjoyed reading. Make a list of titles and discuss any favourites.

• Set the scene for another story taster. *Imagine that you are allowed to go camping on an island on your own. The only way to get there is to sail your own boat and you must take everything you need with you.*

• Talk Partners consider what to take and the adventures they might have. Take feedback.

• Read 'Swallows and Amazons' (ITP 4.15) with the children following on screen. Encourage comments and questions. *Who is the 'nurse'? What do you think her job is?*

• Make comparisons with *Tales of the Family from One End Street. Do you think that the children from* Swallows and Amazons *would get on with the Ruggles children? What are the similarities and differences between them?*

• Focus on language used in ITP 4.15. *Is there anything that makes you think this story was written a long time ago?* Take suggestions of words and phrases, e.g. 'mother', 'be content to', 'nor', 'without leave from'.

• Discuss ways to work out meanings when language is unfamiliar. Draw out the idea that even though a story may seem difficult, it is worth persevering.

Independent and Guided

• The children explore older stories. Using the prompts on 'Choosing a book' (PCM 4.12), finding out when the story was written, reading the blurb and opening pages, then reading the first chapter.

⚫⚫⚫ Choose a classic story and read the opening chapter independently. Write comments on PCM 4.12.

⚫⚫ Choose a book with a partner. Work through PCM 4.12. (TA+)

⚫ As a guided reading group, work through PCM 4.12 for an allocated story. (T+)

Plenary

• Take feedback about books the children have been reading. *Why do you think that these books are still being read today?* Draw out the idea that they are well written and enjoyable and that they have exciting, original and interesting stories and characters.

• Discuss ways to make older texts more accessible, e.g. audio books, book groups. Encourage the children to continue reading their chosen texts independently.

• Recap the learning objective and review the unit as a whole. *What did you enjoy most? What did you learn while writing the story? What was most difficult?* Encourage the children to review their own progress. *What are you most proud of? What do you need to improve?*

Assessment pointers

• AF5, 7 (R): responses to questioning and independent work will show how well the children can relate texts to historical contexts and comment on use of language.

How Jim feels

Add notes about how Jim Ruggles feels at different points in the story.

Name: _____

On the holiday morning (page 44)

Jim feels _proud._

Because _he is going to be a stowaway._

Evidence _'The gang of the Black Hand would respect a stowaway ...'_

Jim realises the barges will be unattended (page 46)

Jim feels _____

Because _____

Evidence _____

_____

Jim hides in the pipe during the hail storm (page 47)

Jim feels _____

Because _____

Evidence _____

_____

Jim gets onto the barge (pages 49–50)

Jim feels _____

Because _____

Evidence _____

_____

During the voyage (pages 51–52)

Jim feels _____

Because _____

Evidence _____

_____

Jim realises the crane is going to lift up the pipe (pages 53–54)

Jim feels _____

Because _____

Evidence _____

_____

Jim is discovered (pages 54–56)

Jim feels _____

Because _____

Evidence _____

_____

Jim is in Mr Watkins's lorry (pages 57–60)

Jim feels _____

Because _____

Evidence _____

_____

Fold

Literacy Evolve Year 5 © Pearson Education 2009

The lorry ride home

Follow Jim Ruggles's lorry ride home and write how he feels.

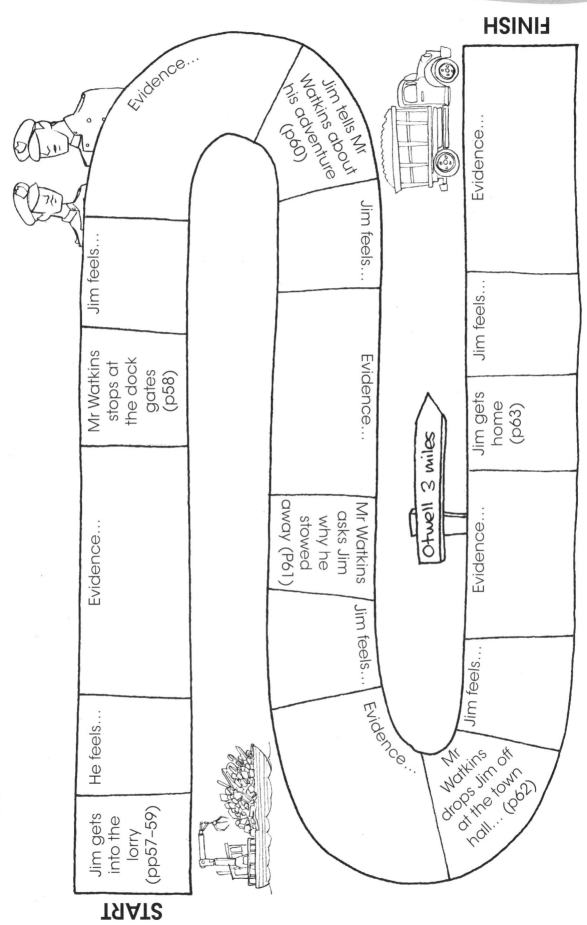

START

Jim gets into the lorry (pp57–59)

He feels…

Evidence…

Mr Watkins stops at the dock gates (p58)

Jim feels…

Evidence…

Jim tells Mr Watkins about his adventure (p60)

Jim feels…

Evidence…

Mr Watkins asks Jim why he stowed away (P61)

Jim feels…

Evidence…

Mr Watkins drops Jim off at the town hall… (p62)

Jim feels…

Evidence…

Jim gets home (p63)

Jim feels…

Evidence…

FINISH

Otwell 3 miles

Name: _____ Date: _____

Telegram

Read the telegram Mr and Mrs Ruggles received about John.

POST OFFICE TELEGRAPHS

Office of Origin and Service Instructions	Words	Sent
Sussex	22	At 4.23 p.m
	Charge	To Ruggles
Urgent	11D	By Lawrence

12 words

6D.

Every additional word

1½ D.

Every word telegraphed is charged for, whether in addresses or text.

TO { Mr and Mrs Ruggles
1, One End Street
Otwell

John	perfectly	safe;	returning	him	tonight
by	seven	o'clock	bus.		

FROM { Mr H. Lawrence

SUSSEX 4:23 p.m.

Name: _____   Date: _____

Literacy evolve

Adventure timetable

Complete the diary to show what happened in either Jim or John's adventure.

After breakfast, I _____

At 11 o'clock, I _____

At 12 o'clock, I _____

At 1 o'clock, I _____

In the afternoon, I _____

At Teatime, I _____

At 7 o'clock, I _____

Later that evening, I _____

The Ruggles's day out

1. Read the posters.

WHITSUN BANK HOLIDAY

Come to the great
CART HORSE PARADE
in Regents Park, London
(nearest underground station: Baker Street)

Come and see hundreds of the city's finest
cart horses and decorated carts.

A free spectacle for all the family to enjoy!
First round of judging: 9:30pm
Grand Parade: 1:00pm

**TRAVEL TO LONDON BY TRAIN
BANK HOLIDAY SPECIAL**

Tickets valid from 7am to 4pm only.
Otwell to London, Victoria
Return tickets 4 shillings

Trains run on the hour, every hour.

Children up to 14 years 2 shillings
(Infants travel free)

2. Answer the questions.

a. Where do the family have to get to?

_____

b. How much will it cost for the Ruggles to go by train?

_____

c. The journey from Otwell to London takes 1½ hours. What time will the
   Ruggles family need to set off?

_____

d. How much will the day cost?

_____

Old money

Use the information to work out the total cost of the Ruggles's day out.

Ruggles's receipt	
currant bun	1d
comic	2d
cinema ticket	4d
ice cream sundae	6d
train ticket to London	4/-

Farthing

¼d (farthing)
one quarter of a penny
the smallest coin

Half penny (ha'penny)
½d (half penny)
half a penny
(pronounced 'hape-ny')

Penny
1d (penny)
basic unit of money
240 pennies in a pound

Threepence
3d (threepence)
3 pennies (pronounced 'thruppuns')

Sixpence
6d (six pence)
6 pennies
40 sixpences in a pound

Shilling

1/- or 1s (shilling)
12 pennies
20 shillings in a pound

Florin
2/- or 2s (2 shillings)
24 pennies
10 florins in a pound

Half crown
2/6 (2 shillings and sixpence)
30 pennies
8 half crowns in a pound

Crown

5/- (5 shillings)
60 pennies
4 crowns in a pound

Pound
£1 (pound)
No pound coins
£1 notes and £5 notes

4.6

Name: _____   Date: _____

At the play park

1. Write notes and questions about what happened to the different characters in Chapter 6.

Name	What happened?	What do you want to know?
Lily Rose		
Jo		
Peg		
Pamela		
Anthony		

2. Write what happened to the other cousins who went to the play park.

> _____
>
> _____
>
> _____

Character cards

Find a person with the same card. Discuss what you enjoyed about your trip to London.

Adventure story plan

Plan an adventure story in the park about one or more Ruggles characters.

Who?
_____
_____

Where?
_____
_____

Which rules are broken?
_____
_____

The problem
_____
_____

Build-up to problem
_____
_____

Solution to problem
_____
_____

Name: _____   Date: _____

Marking ladder

Use the marking ladder to check your work. Then check your partner's work.

My partner's comments

My comments

I have written about a character from the book.	
I have included details to show that my story is set in the park in the 1930s.	
I have organised my story into opening, build-up, problem, solution and ending.	
I have used paragraphs and connectives to structure my story.	
I have chosen words and phrases for dramatic effect.	
I have used language to make my characters sound different when they speak.	

Classic stories

Write the title and author in the book blurbs. Guess the type of book.

Alice in Wonderland by *Lewis Carroll*
Little House on the Prairie by *Laura Ingalls Wilder*
The Hobbit by *J.R.R. Tolkien*

The Railway Children by *E. Nesbit*
The Secret Garden by *Frances Hodgson Burnett*
Treasure Island by *Robert Louis Stevenson*

When their father disappears, Roberta, Phyllis and Peter have to start a new life in the country. The railway beside their new house plays an important part in the family's future.

Title: _____

By: _____

Type: _____

Alice follows a rabbit down a rabbit hole and finds herself in a world full of fantastical characters and strange events. In a world where nothing is what it seems.

Title: _____

By: _____

Type: _____

A tale of pirates, villains and shipwreck. Jim Hawkins finds the secret to a pirate's treasure and sets out on his first sea voyage.

Title: _____

By: _____

Type: _____

The story of a family travelling across the prairies of the USA to set up a new home on the wild American frontier where bears roam free.

Title: _____

By: _____

Type: _____

Mary Lennox is sent to live with her uncle in a big, lonely house in Yorkshire. She discovers that there are secrets both inside and outside the house.

Title: _____

By: _____

Type: _____

Bilbo Baggins, persuaded by a wizard called Gandalf, sets off on a difficult and dangerous quest to get the treasure that was stolen by the dragon, Smaug.

Title: _____

By: _____

Type: _____

Name: _____ Date: _____

Choosing a book

Answer the questions about a classic story.

Book title: _____

Author: _____

First published: _____

Before you start reading

What are your first impressions? _____

_____

What do you think you will find difficult? _____

_____

Read the first page

Is there anything that puzzles you? _____

_____

Can you read all the words? Did it make sense? _____

_____

Does the taster make you want to read more? Why? _____

_____

Ask for another opinion

Find someone else who has read this book. What did they think?

_____

Read the first chapter

Would you like to read more now? Why? _____

_____

What puzzled you? _____

_____

Narrative Unit 5

MAGIK CIRCUS – film (Film narrative)

Medium term plan (3 weeks)	
Phase	**Learning Objectives**
Phase 1: Watching the film and investigating the text type (4 days)	• Children can explore and describe mood, characters and settings from the film. • Children can identify different film techniques that are used. • Children can write a story opening based on the film, using complex sentences.
Phase 2: Capturing ideas, writing in role and analysing the text (4 days)	• Children can use drama activities to analyse different aspects of the two characters. • Children can track characters' thoughts and moods through the film. • Children can write direct and reported speech.
Phase 3: Story-boarding, writing the story of the film and creating a multimedia presentation (7 days)	• Children can plan their story using a story-board. • Children can retell the story orally using notes. • Children can write their own version of the story, using varied sentences and dialogue. • Children can review, edit and improve their own work and respond to a partner's work and comments. • Children can create multimedia presentations for their stories.

Narrative Unit 5
MAGIK CIRCUS

Big picture

The children watch the short film *Magik Circus,* in which there is no spoken dialogue. They discuss film techniques, especially how these are used to convey mood and character. They explore characterisation in greater depth, through the use of drama activities to imagine the possible dialogue that might take place between the two characters. They explore writing direct and reported speech. They plan and then write their own version of *Magik Circus* and create presentations of the story.

Prior learning

This unit assumes that the children can already:
- identify the different contributions that music, words and images make in short films or TV programmes
- identify how different characters might think, feel and speak
- use storyboards to plan and structure stories
- use paragraphs in their work
- write complete short stories with a clear sequence of events.

Key aspects of learning

Communication: Work collaboratively to role-play and to share and comment on each other's work.
Creative thinking: Generate ideas about the mood of the film; use effective language to convey this; portray the story of the film creatively.
Empathy: Speculate about the characters' feelings through role play.

Enquiry: Ask questions about the film; speculate about the characters.
Evaluation: Evaluate and improve their own and each other's work using success criteria.

Progression in narrative

In this unit the children will:
- find evidence of characters changing and discuss possible reasons, what it shows about the character and whether the change was expected; recognise that characters may have different viewpoints
- plan and tell stories to explore narrative viewpoint; retell the story from the point of view of another character
- plan and write complete stories; organise more complex chronological narratives into several paragraphs
- extend ways to link paragraphs using adverbs and adverbial phrases
- aim for consistency in character and style in their writing.

Cross-curricular links

Art: The children could sketch scenes from the film, using colour to depict the contrasting moods and settings.
Design and Technology: The children could design and make moving model structures to create their own circuses or fairgrounds.
ICT: The children use various aspects of ICT to present their stories.

Viewing time

5 minutes 20 seconds approx.

PHASE 1: WATCHING THE FILM AND INVESTIGATING THE TEXT TYPE (4 DAYS)

Session 1

We are learning to ...	Resources
• use evidence to evaluate a visual presentation (PNS Strands 7.1)	*Magik Circus* (film) ITP: 5.1 PCM: 5.1
Assessment Focuses AF (R): 2, 3, 6	

Shared teaching

- Share the learning objective. *Where are stories found? Do they only appear in books? Where else do you hear, see or read them?* (E.g. films, TV, magazines, computer games, etc.) Make a note of the children's ideas to begin the Learning Wall. Explain that in this unit, the children will watch and investigate a short film, using their knowledge of stories to help.
- Show 'First impressions of *Magik Circus*' (ITP 5.1) and explain that the children are going to watch the film and then jot down the first ideas they have about it. Point out that there are no 'correct answers', but they will need to support their ideas by referring to parts of the film.
- Begin to play the film, but pause on the title '*Magik Circus*' as it appears. Ask the children to Think-Pair-Share predictions about the film from the title. *What kinds of images does the word 'circus' conjure up?* Add the children's ideas to the Learning Wall.
- Watch to the end of the film, reminding the children to be aware of their first impressions.

Independent and Guided

- The children write their first impressions independently, referring to specific parts of the film where possible, then share ideas in pairs.
- 🔵🔵🔵 The children jot down and then organise their ideas. (T+)
- 🔵🔵 Use 'First impressions' (PCM 5.1).

🔘 As above. (TA+)

Plenary

- Show ITP 5.1 and ask for feedback. Agree on what to add to the 'Likes' and 'Dislikes' sections for the whole class. Use the opportunity to check the children's overall understanding of the story.
- *What thoughts and questions do you have about the film?* Add points to ITP 5.1 and encourage the children to look out for the answers over the forthcoming sessions.
- Ask the children to suggest what rating to give the film from their first impression. *Why did you choose that rating?*
- Recap the learning objective for the session. *When you shared your ideas, did you refer to specific parts of the film?*

Assessment pointers

- AF2 (R): feedback from pairs and independent work show how well the children understand the story.
- AF3, 6 (R): independent work will show how far the children understand the purpose and viewpoint of the film.

Session 2

We are learning to ...	Resources
• explore how a film director creates mood and atmosphere (PNS Strands 7.5) **Assessment Focuses** AF (R): 3, 6	*Magik Circus* (film) ITP: 5.2 PCM: 5.2

Shared teaching

• In pairs, the children play Just A Minute. The first child in the pair has one minute to recall the story of the film. The second child has one minute to recall their first impressions.

• Share the learning objective. Discuss what is meant by mood and atmosphere. *How can mood and atmosphere be created in films?* Encourage the children to suggest sounds (including music, voice, and silence), movements, gestures, facial expressions, and settings.

• *What different moods and atmosphere can you remember from the film?* The children Think-Pair-Share ideas.

• Watch *Magik Circus* from the beginning until Marker 1. *What atmosphere and mood is the director creating here? How does it make you feel?* Discuss the setting, music, sounds, etc.

• Show 'Target board' (ITP 5.2). *Which words best describe the film so far?* Work with the children to drag the words to different zones of the target, placing the most relevant words at the centre.

• Talk Partners discuss 'what if' questions related to the film opening. *What if it was daylight? What if the music was rock music?* Take feedback and make comparisons with creating an atmosphere or mood in a written text, recalling work from previous units.

• Watch from Marker 8 until the end of the film. *How has the mood and atmosphere changed? How do you know?*

• Show ITP 5.2 and repeat the activity for the end of the film, reordering the words appropriately.

• Watch the film from Marker 7 until Marker 8. Explain that the children will be exploring the mood and atmosphere in this part of the film themselves.

Independent and Guided

• The children work in pairs to select words to describe the mood and atmosphere between Marker 7 and Marker 8 of the film.

ᴄᴏᴏ Create a 'Target board'. Write words in different zones, using a thesaurus to find suitable words.

ᴄᴏ Use 'Target board' (PCM 5.2) and a thesaurus to find additional alternative words to add. (T+)

◉ Use PCM 5.2. (TA+)

Plenary

• In groups, the children compare targets. Encourage them to discuss and agree whether they have identified the mood correctly. *What interesting descriptive words did you use?*

• Recap the learning objective.

• Write a question on the Learning Wall: *Can you describe the frog genie?* Provide sticky notes for the children to add descriptive words before Session 3.

Assessment pointers

• AF3 (R): responses to questioning and group work show how well the children have understood the mood and atmosphere of the film.

• AF6 (R): responses to questioning shows how far the children can comment on how the film made them feel at certain points and how the director created this effect.

Session 3

We are learning to ...	Resources
• infer the director's perspective from the different techniques used, e.g. colour, camera angles, different shots (PNS Strands 7.2) **Assessment Focuses** AF (R): 3, 6	*Magik Circus* (film) ITP: 5.3 PCM: 5.3

Shared teaching

• Recall Session 2, referring to how the director created mood and atmosphere in *Magik Circus*. Explain that in this session, the children will look in more detail at filming techniques used to create different effects and viewpoints.

• Share the learning objective and check the children's understanding of the term 'perspective' (viewpoint or opinion).

• Ask the children to consider the frog genie character. Draw a 'target board' on a large sheet of paper or on the whiteboard. Discuss the sticky notes on the Learning Wall, on which the children wrote words describing the frog genie. Agree where to place each word. *Which words accurately sum up his character?* Encourage the children to refer to the film to support their responses. *Do you think the director tries to make us view the frog genie in a certain way? How does the director make the character demonstrate these qualities?*

• Show 'Film terms glossary' (ITP 5.3). Discuss examples of each film technique.

• Watch *Magik Circus* again. The children make notes about how the frog genie is presented and any film techniques they notice being used. Talk Partners compare ideas, then take feedback. *Did you notice any close-ups of the frog genie? How did this affect your view of the character? Did you notice any other techniques being used?*

• Show ITP 5.3 again for reference during the independent activity.

Independent and Guided

• In pairs, the children study the use and effect of different techniques throughout the film.

ᴄᴏᴏ Use 'Film techniques' (PCM 5.3). Consider how different camera angles, cut and fade are used in the film. (T+)

ᴄᴏ As above. Consider how close-up, mid and long shots are used in the film.

◉ Rewatch *Magik Circus*. Explore how colour and light are used. (TA+)

Plenary

• Form small groups, consisting of at least one pair from each of the independent activity groups. The children give each other feedback about how the different techniques are used and discuss how these affect the viewer and the viewpoint of the film.

• Recap the learning objective and as a class, discuss the children's findings and draw some conclusions about how film techniques can influence how we view events in the film, e.g. 'seeing' things through a particular character's eyes. *What do you think this tells you about the director's point of view.*

Assessment pointers

• S&L: group work will show how well the children can adopt group roles and share information.

• AF3, 6 (R): group and class discussions show how far the children are able to make inferences and understand the director's viewpoint.

Session 4

We are learning to ...	Resources
• use and discuss visualisation techniques • write effective story openings • identify and write complex sentences (PNS Strands 8.2, 9.2, 11.1) **Assessment Focuses** AF (W): 5, 6, 7	*Magik Circus* (film) ITP: 5.4, 5.5

Shared teaching

• Share the learning objectives. Explain that in this session the children will be writing the opening of *Magik Circus* based on ideas developed from watching the film.

• Explain how well-written stories create pictures in your head. Explain that this is visualisation and that we all visualise things slightly differently. Talk Partners discuss whether they have ever read a book and then seen it as a film or on TV. *Was it as you visualised?* Share ideas about why the film may or may not be as they visualised it.

• Display 'Simple to complex' (ITP 5.4). *What is a complex sentence?* Click one of the simple sentences to display a more complex one including a sub-clause.

• Watch the film from the beginning until Marker 1, asking the children to focus on how they might put it into words. Explain that they will need to use language effectively, so that someone reading their sentences can visualise the opening of the film clearly.

• Start the film again and pause on the first shot of the night sky and circus. *What can you see? What can you hear? How does it make you feel? How could you create that mood and atmosphere in words?*

• Refer to ITP 5.4. Review how complex sentences add further details to help a reader visualise the scene better.

• Focus on the example with a continuous tense verb at the beginning of the sub-clause: 'Interrupting the silence, ... '. Ask the children to write as many different descriptive endings for this sentence as they can.

• Repeat for each of the other complex sentences, taking suggestions for how they could be varied. Encourage the children to choose interesting and descriptive vocabulary.

• Use Modelled Writing to demonstrate writing the story opening as a paragraph. Use the first paragraph of '*Magik Circus*' (ITP 5.5) if desired.

Independent and Guided

• The children write their own version of the story opening.

  Use at least three complex sentences.

  Use at least two complex sentences. (TA+)

  Work in a group. Use one complex sentence. (T+)

Plenary

• Recap the learning objectives.

• Ask some of the children to share their writing with the class. Ask the other children to close their eyes as they listen to the story openings. *Did the writer choose effective vocabulary to convey the scene? Did you notice any complex sentences?*

• Keep the children's story openings for use in future sessions.

Assessment pointers

• AF5, 6, 7 (W): written outcomes show how far the children can use varied sentence structure including complex and simple sentences, accurate punctuation, and select appropriate and interesting vocabulary.

PHASE 2: CAPTURING IDEAS, WRITING IN ROLE AND ANALYSING THE TEXT (4 DAYS)

Session 5

We are learning to ...	Resources
• ask questions about characters using quality questions • use drama and role play to empathise with characters (PNS Strands 1.3, 4.1) **Assessment Focuses** AF (R): 2, 3	*Magik Circus* (film) ITP: 5.6 PCM: 5.4

Shared teaching

• Share the learning objectives and explain that the outcome of this unit will be to write a version of *Magik Circus* including images, a soundtrack and a voiceover. But before the children can start writing, they need a better understanding of the characters.

• Talk Partners discuss who the characters in the story are, then share ideas as a class. *Does everyone agree?* Reflect on the fact that there are only two characters, yet one of those appears in three forms (lamp/genie/frog).

• Rewatch the film. Ask the children to focus on the characters and their behaviour. Pause at Marker 1 and ask the children to comment on the girl's feelings at this point. Encourage them to watch out for other key moments where her feelings may change.

• As a class, use Thought Tracking to investigate the girl's feelings at different points in the film: when she is counting the money in the tin; when she first sees the lamp; when she sees the frog genie's ideas for an act; after the performance at the end.

• Complete 'The circus girl' (ITP 5.6), making links between her character and the plot. *What questions would you like to ask her?*

• Set up a whole-class Hot-Seating activity to question the girl character. Choose a child to play the role of the girl or answer questions as Teacher In Role. Remind the children to use quality questions.

• Repeat the Thought Tracking process for the other main character (lamp/genie/frog). Focus on the changes in his character throughout the story and the effect this has on the plot.

Independent and Guided

• The children explore different aspects of the lamp/genie/frog character.

  Complete 'Exploring character' (PCM 5.4), focusing on the genie.

  Complete PCM 5.4, focusing on the frog. (T)

  Prepare questions to ask the genie character in a Hot-Seating activity. (TA+)

Plenary

• Recap the learning objectives.

• *What have you learnt about the characters in* Magik Circus*? How has working in role helped your understanding?* Allow Think Time, then ask the children to write their thoughts on sticky notes. Add these to the Learning Wall.

• *Do you have any more questions about the characters?* Add these to the Learning Wall.

Assessment pointers

• S&L: thought tracking will show how well the children can understand and empathise with characters.

• AF2 (R): independent work shows how well the children have inferred information about the characters from the visual text.

• AF3 (R): responses to questioning show how far the children can understand the characters and make deductions about their motives.

We are learning to …	Resources
• use and reflect on drama techniques to explore characters and story • use and reflect on visualisation, empathy and prediction techniques (PNS Strands 4.1, 8.2) **Assessment Focuses** AF (R): 2, 3	*Magik Circus* (film)

Shared teaching

• Share the learning objectives. Recap what is meant by visualisation (being able to picture something in our heads). *What do we mean by empathy?* Explain that this means being able to 'put oneself in another person's shoes' and imagine their feelings'.

• Rewatch *Magik Circus*. Pause at Marker 4, where the frog genie produces the snapping plant. Study the characters' facial expressions. *What do you think they would say? What gestures do they make?*

• Annotate the film clip by drawing speech and thought bubbles. Ask the children to make suggestions for text to enter into the speech and thought bubbles for the frog genie.

• Explain that the children will work in three groups, each focusing on a different part of the film to predict the characters' thoughts and speech. Continue to watch the film from Marker 4 until the end. Pause at appropriate points (Marker 6 and Marker 9) to identify what each group should focus on during independent work and to discuss each scene briefly.

Independent and Guided

• In pairs, the children act out their small scene and Freeze Frame crucial moments. They 'put themselves into a character's shoes' to empathise and decide what might be said and thought at that point. If possible, photograph the freeze frames to use in Session 8.

🔵🔵🔵 Focus on both characters' thoughts and speech at Marker 9. (T+)

🔵🔵 Focus on the girl's thoughts and what she might say at Marker 6.

🔵 Focus on the girl's thoughts at Marker 4. Identify whether her thoughts are different from what might be said. (TA)

Plenary

• Ask pairs within the same group to share their freeze frames. Encourage the children to explain why they chose particular words or phrases for what the characters thought and said. Ask pairs to compare their outcomes and give feedback, using Two Stars and a Wish.

• Take feedback. *Were your ideas similar? Did the other pair come up with anything which surprised you?*

• Select a few pairs from each group to perform their freeze frames to the class.

• Recap the learning objectives and discuss what has been learnt about the characters. *How did working in role help? Did you find out anything new by working in role?*

Assessment pointers

• S&L: freeze frames will show how far the children can create roles and empathise with characters.

• AF2 (R): responses during shared teaching will show the children's depth of understanding of the characters.

• AF3 (R): independent work in role will show how far the children can make inferences about how characters may feel and what they may say.

We are learning to …	Resources
• use evidence to say how a character changes • make inferences about what a character is thinking and feeling (PNS Strands 7.1, 7.2) **Assessment Focuses** AF (R): 2, 3, 6	*Magik Circus* (film) ITP: 5.7 PCM: 5.5

Shared teaching

• Allow the children Think Time to recall Session 7. *Did the characters' thoughts and feelings stay the same throughout the story?*

• Share the learning objectives. Discuss how a character's feelings will often change during a story to create interest.

• Explain that the children are going to track the mood of the frog genie. Show 'Mood graph' (ITP 5.7). Discuss the y-axis. *How might you describe the feeling at the top of the graph?* (ecstatic, delighted, thrilled) Ask for suggestions for the range of different feelings.

• Discuss the x-axis. *What does this show?* (the main events in the film)

• Watch *Magik Circus*, pausing after each of the scenes on the x-axis. *What is the frog genie's mood here? How do you know?* Encourage the children to make notes. At the end of the film, discuss the frog genie's mood at each point to get a consensus of opinion. *Where shall I plot that on the graph?*

• Join the points plotted on ITP 5.7 with a line to complete the graph. *What do you notice?* Think, Pair, Share to establish that the frog genie's mood sinks throughout the film.

• Review the peaks and troughs. *What do these show us? Can you give reasons?* Encourage the children to refer to events in the story.

Independent and Guided

• While watching *Magik Circus,* the children plot the mood of the circus girl character at the main points in the film, then analyse their graphs.

🔵🔵🔵 Use 'Mood graph' (PCM 5.5). Add notes to explain the peaks and troughs. Compare the graph to the frog genie's graph. Explain any patterns.

🔵🔵 Complete PCM 5.5. Add notes to explain the peaks and troughs. (TA+)

🔵 Complete PCM 5.5. Discuss the peaks and troughs in pairs, referring to events in the film. (T+)

Plenary

• Recap the learning objectives and take feedback. Use a different colour to plot the children's findings for the circus girl's mood on ITP 5.7. Ask the higher-ability group to explain what they noticed when comparing the moods of the two characters. Encourage them to give reasons.

• *How is the director using the characters in this story?* Note how the story structure affects the characters in very different ways.

Assessment pointers

• AF2, 3 (R): independent work will show how far the children understand the characters and how they might think and feel based on different parts of the film.

• AF6 (R): responses to questioning show how far the children understand that the director has created a contrast between the two characters which helps to maintain interest.

Session 8

We are learning to ...	Resources
• understand how to use direct speech effectively • understand the difference between direct and reported speech • understand and use punctuation for speech accurately (PNS Strands 9.4, 11.2) **Assessment Focuses** AF (W): 6	*Magik Circus* (film) ITP: 5.8, 5.9 PCM: 5.6

Shared teaching (1)

• Share the learning objectives. Explain that this session will focus on using and punctuating speech. *Why do authors include speech? Why does it need special punctuation? What do we mean by dialogue?*
• Explain that the children will use ideas from the freeze frames from Session 6 to write dialogue between the characters.

Independent and Guided (1)

• Either provide photographs of the freeze frames from Session 6, or ask the children to sketch the scene and add speech bubbles to it.

  ㅇㅇㅇ Write speech bubbles for both characters at Marker 9. (T)

  ㅇㅇ Write a speech bubble for the girl at Marker 6.

  ㅇ Write a speech bubble for the girl at Marker 4. (TA)

Shared teaching (2)

• Show 'Direct and reported speech' (ITP 5.8). Discuss what is meant by 'direct' and 'reported' speech. *Speech marks are used in direct speech but not in reported speech.*

• Drag the sentences into the table. *Is this direct or reported speech?* Point out the use of a comma before the end speech mark.
• Draw attention to words shown in red on ITP 5.8 that change for reported speech. *What kinds of words are these?* (verbs and pronouns)
• Discuss alternative verbs for direct speech, e.g. said, explained, whispered, etc. Add these to the Learning Wall.
• Watch the film from Marker 4 to Marker 6. Pause when the characters are interacting. Discuss what they could be saying. Use Modelled Writing to create a conversation. Encourage the children to suggest accurate punctuation.
• Show 'Writing direct speech' (ITP 5.9) and agree success criteria.

Independent and Guided (2)

• Pairs develop a dialogue starting from their freeze frame picture.

  ㅇㅇㅇ Use some direct and reported speech. (T+)

  ㅇㅇ Use direct speech.

  ㅇ As above. Use 'Writing speech' (PCM 5.6) to structure dialogue. (TA+)

Plenary

• Allow time for pairs to provide peer assessments in relation to the success criteria on ITP 5.9. Ask the children to show thumbs up, down or half way to indicate whether they achieved the success criteria.
• Recap the learning objectives. Ask the children to recall their first impressions of the film. *Have your impressions changed?*

Assessment pointers

• AF6 (W): independent work, responses to questioning, peer and self-assessment show how far the children use speech marks accurately.

PHASE 3: STORYBOARDING, WRITING THE STORY OF THE FILM AND CREATING A MULTIMEDIA PRESENTATION (7 DAYS)

Session 9

We are learning to ...	Resources
• recall the structure of a narrative using a storyboard • write storyboards to create a structure (PNS Strands 7.3, 9.2) **Assessment Focuses** AF (R): 4; AF (W): 3	*Magik Circus* (film) ITP: 5.10, 5.11 PCM: 5.7, 5.8

Shared teaching (1)

• Explain that during the final phase of this unit, the children will be writing the story of *Magik Circus*. Explain that the outcome will be to create a multimedia presentation.
• Share the learning objectives.
• Ask the children to recap the film. Talk Partners play Just a Minute, taking turns to retell the main events of the story.
• Allow the children time to make notes, then discuss the main events as a class. Agree what should appear in the written story.
• Rewatch *Magik Circus*. Ask the children to choose frames to represent each of the main events identified.
• Show 'Film storyboard' (ITP 5.10). Compare the still images with the main events identified by the children. *How well do these images match the events you chose?*
• Create a storyboard by dragging the images on ITP 5.10 into order. Add a description below each image, e.g. opening, problem, solution, ending, etc. to build the story structure.

Independent and Guided

• The children create their own storyboards, drawing stick figures to represent the characters and writing notes to give an outline of the story's structure.

  ㅇㅇㅇ Use 'Storyboard 1' (PCM 5.7). Identify six main parts of the film. Categorise these by film structure, e.g. opening, problem, etc.

  ㅇㅇ As above. (T+)

  ㅇ Complete 'Storyboard 2' (PCM 5.8). (TA+)

Shared teaching (2)

• *What do we need to do to write a good story?* Ask the children to Think-Pair-Share ideas.
• Show 'Writer's toolkit' (ITP 5.11). Click on each bullet point in turn and discuss the points. Link these to the children's personal targets where possible.
• Encourage the children to refer to this in the next few sessions to support them during extended writing of the film narrative.

Plenary

• Explain that ITP 5.11 provides the children with their success criteria and they should use these prompts to ensure that their story is successful.
• Recap the learning objectives. Agree that a good way to start planning would be to tell the story orally first. *What might the next learning objective be?* Make notes of suggestions on the Learning Wall, e.g. 'Improve our oral retelling of the narrative, using the toolkit for support.'

Assessment pointers

• AF4 (R): responses to questioning show how far the children can comment on the structure of visual texts.
• AF3 (W): independent work shows how well the children are able to sequence and structure information and events.

We are learning to ...	Resources
• tell a story using notes • improve oral retelling, using the toolkit for support • use storyboards or a planner to create a structure (PNS Strands 1.1, 9.2) **Assessment Focuses** AF (R): 4	ITP: (5.10, 5.11) PCM: (5.7, 5.8), 5.9

Shared teaching

• Share the learning objectives, including the one set by the children during Session 9. *How will the storyboard help you?* Point out that it is a reminder of the main structure, but the children will need to add details to make the story interesting.
• Use annotated 'Film storyboard' (ITP 5.10) to demonstrate how to retell the story orally in a simple way. *How could I improve it? What can you use to ensure a successful story?*
• Recall 'Writer's toolkit' (ITP 5.11) to remind the children what a successful story needs.
• Give the children 'Story prompts' (PCM 5.9). Allocate small groups one element to focus on and explain that you are going to retell the story again. The children need to make notes of good examples.
• Retell the story including more details. Ask the children to listen and collect evidence for their allocated element on PCM 5.9.
• Allow groups Think Time to discuss their notes.
• Review each element of PCM 5.9 in turn. Ask each group for feedback. *How did the beginning draw the audience in? Which words helped you visualise the setting? How did the dialogue help to describe the characters?* Ask for more suggestions. Encourage the children to make notes about each element for reference when writing.

Independent and Guided

• In pairs, the children take turns to rehearse and retell the whole story, using PCM 5.9 and ITP 5.11 as prompts. They note ideas on 'Storyboard 1' (PCM 5.7) or 'Storyboard 2' (PCM 5.8) completed in Session 9.
  ○○○ Use PCM 5.7.
  ○○ As above. (T)
  ○ Use PCM 5.8. (TA+)

Plenary

• Allow time for the children to tell their story to a new partner. Partners review the story, using PCM 5.9 as a 'checklist', adding notes of good examples.
• Recap the learning objectives.
• Discuss the improvements the children have made to their stories. *How did the toolkit help you? How will your annotated storyboards help your writing?*

Assessment pointers

• S&L: oral independent work shows how well the children are able to structure and sequence ideas effectively, using interesting language.
• AF4 (R): group work and responses to questioning show how well the children understand the story structure.

We are learning to ...	Resources
• plan and write a story based on a film • use varied sentence structures and adverbial phrases to enhance our writing (PNS Strands 9.2, 11.1) **Assessment Focuses** AF (W): 5, 6	Magik Circus (film) ITP: (5.5)

Shared teaching

• Explain that the children will be working on a written version of the film *Magik Circus*, using the story openings they wrote in Session 4.
• Share the learning objectives.
• Recall annotated '*Magik Circus*' (ITP 5.5) or read through the first paragraph of the modelled writing. *What made this a successful story opening?* Reflect on the language choices, use of complex sentences and punctuation. Remind the children how they used the film (visual text) to support the writing.
• Watch the film from the beginning to Marker 1 again. The children Think-Pair-Share ideas for the first scene. Encourage them to make a note of sentence ideas and include at least one adverbial clause.
• Take suggestions and add ideas to Screen 1 of ITP 5.5. Edit and improve the text, focusing particular attention on areas of common difficulty.
• Watch the film from Marker 1 to Marker 2. Encourage the children to notice details of events. *What falls off the bed?* (the teddy)
• Use Modelled Writing to develop this part of the story. Go to Secreen 2 and use the second paragraph of ITP 5.5 as a model. Point out how to use descriptive language to reflect the mood and capture the air of restlessness. Demonstrate the use of adverbial clauses, paying

particular attention to how to write them, e.g. Throwing aside the covers, she gingerly peeked through the caravan window. *What effect do they have?*
• Draw out some particular issues or pointers for the class as a whole, based on assessments in previous sessions.
• Review the model text. *Is it successful? How do we know?* Watch the appropriate section of the film again to check that the written text reflects the visual text.

Independent and Guided

• The children watch the film from Marker 2 until Marker 3 and write the story independently. Groups compare their work and reflect on how the same theme can be presented slightly differently. The children give peer assessments of each other's work using Two Stars and a Wish. Support the children with an identified need. (T+/TA+)

Plenary

• Recap the learning objectives. Take feedback from the children, sharing their two stars and a wish. Encourage the children to share examples they think are particularly good. *What do you like about this sentence? Why do you think it is effective?* Add ideas to ITP 5.5.
• Explain that in Session 12, the children will continue their stories focusing on how to use speech and punctuation successfully in their writing.

Assessment pointers

• S&L: group work will show how far the children can express and respond to opinions.
• AF5, 6 (W): written outcomes will show how far the children are able to use varied sentences and punctuate them correctly, including commas to demarcate adverbial phrases and sub-clauses.

Session 12

<table>
<tr><td>

We are learning to ...
- review the effectiveness of our own and each other's work
- plan and write a story based on a film
- use varied sentence structures and adverbial phrases to enhance our writing
- understand and use punctuation for speech accurately (PNS Strands 9.1, 9.2, 11.1, 11.2)

Assessment Focuses
AF (W): 1, 2, 6, 8

</td><td>

Resources
Magik Circus (film)
ITP: (5.5), 5.12
PCM: (5.7, 5.8)

</td></tr>
</table>

Shared teaching

- Share the learning objectives. Explain that the next two sessions will be extended writing sessions for the children to complete their stories.
- Watch *Magik Circus* from Marker 3 until Marker 6. *What is different about this part of the film from the part written so far?* (the two characters interact) Remind the children of the work they did on this in Session 8. Talk Partners discuss how to write and punctuate speech. *What can you remember about writing speech?*
- Explain that although the characters don't speak in the film (they mainly use gestures), in the written versions the children will need to use speech to add interest.
- Recall annotated '*Magik Circus*' (ITP 5.5). Use Modelled Writing to add the next part of the film narrative to ITP 5.5 using dialogue. Explain when and why you are using direct and reported speech, e.g. *"Watch this!" said the frog genie* or *The frog genie told the girl to watch his next trick.* Which sounds best?
- Use Modelled Writing to demonstrate how to edit the writing by taking a sentence and reordering the clauses, rewording it, adding more description and effective punctuation, etc.
- Show 'Writing a film narrative' (ITP 5.12). Discuss the success criteria

and agree which points will be important for writing this part of the film. *Are there any points you would like to add or change?*

Independent and Guided

- The children work independently to write the next part of the *Magik Circus* story (up until Marker 6). Encourage the children to use their completed 'Storyboard 1' (PCM 5.7) or 'Storyboard 2' (PCM 5.8) for support during the period of extended writing. Check progress against the agreed success criteria and give immediate feedback to the higher ability group about progress and improvements needed. Support the children with an identified need. (T+/TA+)

Plenary

- Recap the learning objectives.
- Recap the work on editing. Encourage the children to reread their writing and edit it using a different colour pen or pencil. *Can you improve the sentence structure? Is the punctuation and spelling correct? Are your descriptions effective?*
- Ask pairs to swap books, then peer assess whether their partner's editing was effective.
- Ask for volunteers to share examples of using direct and reported speech. *Why did you use direct or reported speech? What punctuation did you need to use? Did you need to change any spellings?*

Assessment pointers

- S&L: pair work will show how sensitively the children can give and respond to opinions.
- AF1, 2 (W): written outcomes will show how far the children can produce imaginative writing, relevant ideas and appropriate narrative style.
- AF6, 8 (W): written outcomes show how far the children can use correct spelling, speech and other punctuation correctly.

Session 13

<table>
<tr><td>

We are learning to ...
- review the effectiveness of our own and each other's work
- write imaginative endings (PNS Strands 9.1, 9.2)

Assessment Focuses
AF (W): 3, 4

</td><td>

Resources
Magik Circus (film)
ITP: (5.5, 5.12)

</td></tr>
</table>

Shared teaching

- Recap Session 12 and give feedback on the children's writing. Recall 'Writing a film narrative' (ITP 5.12) and share some good examples of particular aspects from the children's work, e.g. good use of direct speech, effective editing, good use of language to create mood and atmosphere. If possible, scan and display the writing or read stories aloud, pausing at appropriate points to discuss effective work.
- Share the learning objectives. Explain that in this session, the children will complete their stories.
- Show the final paragraph of '*Magik Circus*' (ITP 5.5) and discuss what is wrong with this passage of text (no paragraphs). Invite the children to suggest where the paragraph breaks should go and edit the text accordingly.
- Talk Partners review the stories they have written so far and discuss their use of paragraphs. *How did you decide where a new paragraph was necessary? Are any further paragraph breaks needed?*
- Discuss how *Magik Circus* ends. Watch the film from Marker 6 until the end of the film. Talk Partners discuss ideas for portraying the end of the film in writing. *How can we show in writing that the story is finished?* Point out that writing 'The End' is not good style. Take suggestions for alternatives.

- Use Modelled Writing to create an ending by adding to ITP 5.5.

Independent and Guided

- The children finish writing the story of *Magik Circus*, (from Marker 6 to the end of the film) using what they have learnt about writing endings and checking that they have used paragraphs. Circulate and review the children's writing, giving immediate feedback about progress and improvements needed. Support the children according to needs identified in Session 12. (T/TA)

Plenary

- Recap the learning objectives.
- In pairs, ask the children to read each other's story endings and give feedback to their partner. *Does the story sound finished? How could it be improved?* Encourage the children to review whether paragraphs have been used effectively to organise the story.
- Recall ITP 5.12. Discuss each point in turn, asking the children to show thumbs up, down or halfway to indicate how confident they are about whether their writing has met the success criteria. *What do you need to improve?*

Assessment pointers

- S&L: pair work will show how sensitively the children can give and respond to opinions.
- AF3 (W): written outcomes show whether the children can organise stories with a clear opening, middle and ending.
- AF4 (W): peer and self-assessment show how well the children have used appropriate paragraph breaks to structure their writing.

We are learning to ...	Resources
• evaluate writing using a marking ladder (PNS Strands 9.1)	*Magik Circus* (film) ITP: (5.5, 5.12), 5.13 PCM: 5.10, 5.11
Assessment Focuses AF (W): 1, 4, 5, 7	

Shared teaching (1)

• Give feedback on some of the children's completed stories. Share good examples of writing, focusing especially on story endings.
• Ask the children to comment on what they think makes the various story endings successful. *Why is this a good ending? What do you like about it? Does it surprise the reader?* Recall 'Writing a film narrative' (ITP 5.12). Discuss how the stories meet the success criteria.
• Share the learning objective. Explain that the marking ladder will provide a detailed checklist of features that each story should contain.
• Show 'Marking ladder' (ITP 5.13). Demonstrate how to check the points on the marking ladder against one of the children's stories or the model writing on annotated '*Magik Circus*' (ITP 5.5).

Independent and Guided

• In pairs, the children complete marking ladders to assess their writing. If appropriate, the children use coloured pencils or highlighters to underline words, phrases and sentences which illustrate the points on the marking ladder and a different colour to identify words and phrases which they think could be improved.
⦿⦿⦿ Use 'Marking ladder 1' (PCM 5.10).
⦿⦿ As above. (TA)
⦿ Use 'Marking ladder 2' (PCM 5.11). (T+)

Shared teaching (2)

• Demonstrate how the story could be used as a narration or voiceover for the film *Magik Circus*, by reading a good example aloud while the film plays. *How could we bring the speech alive?* Discuss the use of expression to add interest when reading aloud.
• Rewatch *Magik Circus*. Ask the children to read their own story quietly to themselves as they watch.
• Encourage the children to consider how well their own story fits the film. *Are there any parts of your writing you would like to change?* Allow Think Time and then take feedback as a class.

Plenary

• Recap the learning objective. *Was your writing effective? Did the marking ladder help you assess your own and your partner's writing?*
• Based on the peer responses on the marking ladder and the children's own evaluations after watching the film, ask Talk Partners to identify points to focus on next time they write a story. Ask the pairs to record these ideas on sticky notes to add to the Learning Wall.
• Encourage the children to choose the most important point for them and write it in their books as an individual target.

Assessment pointers

• AF1, 4, 5, 7 (W): peer and self-assessments show how well the children are able to write imaginative texts, structuring paragraphs and sentences appropriately and using effective vocabulary.

We are learning to ...	Resources
• understand the importance of audience and purpose • use ICT to create a multimedia presentation (PNS Strands 9.2, 12.2)	ITP: 5.14, 5.15 PCM: 5.12
Assessment Focuses AF (W): 2	

Shared teaching (1)

• Explain that the final activity for this unit is to create a multimedia presentation based on *Magik Circus*, using parts of the children's written stories as on-screen text or voiceovers.
• Share the learning objectives. *What is meant by multimedia?* Show 'Multimedia presentation' (ITP 5.14) as an example. *What different media are being used?* (text, images) *What other media or effects could be added?* (animation)
• Talk Partners discuss ways in which ITP 5.14 differs from the film and their written stories. Take feedback. *Who is the audience for the presentation? What is its purpose?*
• Using appropriate software, demonstrate how to create presentation slides, adding titles, backgrounds, colour, special effects for written text, voiceover commentaries, sound effects, slide transitions, etc.

Independent and Guided (1)

• In pairs or small groups, the children choose one part of the film to focus on. They decide on the audience and purpose for their multimedia presentation, then plan it using 'Multimedia presentation storyboard' (PCM 5.12). They sketch out the scenes and make notes to identify the sequence and effects to include. If possible, the children then use ICT to create the slides or do a more complete paper-based version. Support the children with an identified need. (T+/TA+)

Shared teaching (2)

• When the children have completed their presentation, ask pairs to share their work with another pair.
• Encourage the children to give peer assessment. *What works? What doesn't work? Can you make suggestions for editing?*

Independent and Guided (2)

• The children edit and revise their presentations based on the peer feedback. Pairs join together to form small groups and take turns to explain their audience and purpose, then show their presentation. Support the children with an identified need. (T/TA)

Plenary

• Ask the children for feedback on effective presentations, what worked and why. *Did the presentation and text convey the story to the audience?*
• Recap the learning objectives and review the unit as a whole.
• Show 'Review of the unit' (ITP 5.15). Invite the children to select words to describe their feelings about the unit.
• Discuss what the children have learnt and what supported their learning. *Which were the most and least useful activities? What is your next step? What do you need to do to improve in the future?*

Assessment pointers

• S&L: pair work will show how sensitively the children can give and respond to questions.
• AF2 (W): pair and group work show how well the children are able to produce a text that is appropriate to the task, purpose and audience.

First impressions

Write your first impressions of *Magik Circus*. Refer to parts of the film to explain your reasons.

Likes

_____
_____
_____

Dislikes

_____
_____
_____

Thoughts and questions

_____
_____
_____

Star rating (why?)

_____
_____
_____

Literacy Evolve Year 5 © Pearson Education 2009

Target board

Write the words on the target to describe the mood in *Magik Circus*.

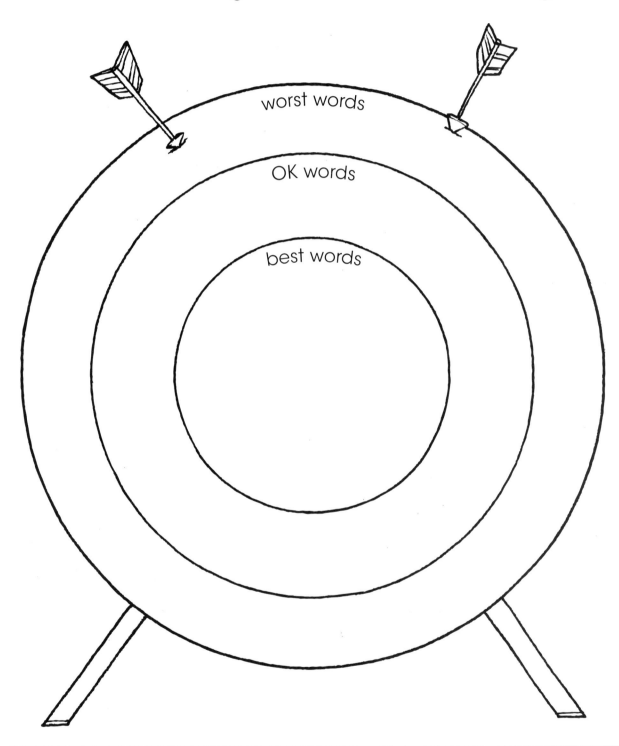

worst words

OK words

best words

sinister   cheerful   sorrowful   strange   playful

entertaining   serious   amusing   curious   unusual

Film techniques

Write examples of the different film techniques and their effects.

Technique	Example	Effect
Close-up		
Mid shot		
Long shot		
Fade		
Cut		

Exploring character

Complete the profile for one of the characters from *Magik Circus*.

Name: _____
_____

Likes: _____
_____

Dislikes: _____
_____

Fears: _____
_____

Dreams: _____
_____

How does the character change during the film?
_____
_____

What different sides of the character do you see?
_____
_____

Mood graph

On the graph plot the mood of the circus girl at different points in the film.

Feelings

(😊 / 😐 / 😞)

Key events in the story

opening | lamp and girl enter the tent | genie appears | genie shows tricks | frog appears | circus performance

Writing speech

Write a conversation between the circus girl and the frog genie.
Then write the conversation as reported speech.

_____

_____

_____

_____ said the girl.

_____

_____

_____

_____ replied the genie.

Storyboard 1

Sketch the main events of *Magik Circus* and make notes to describe them.

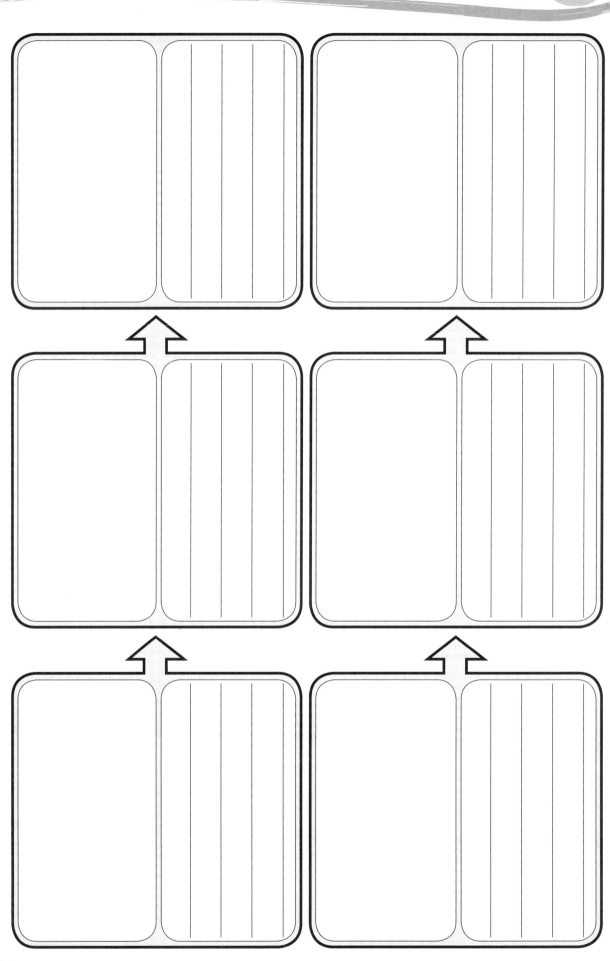

Storyboard 2

Sketch the main events of *Magik Circus* and make notes to describe them.

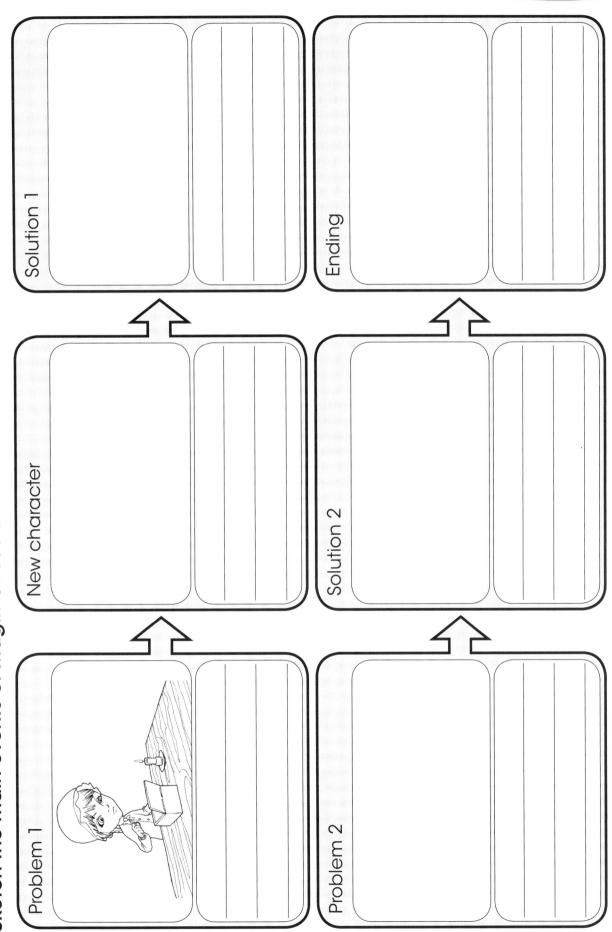

Problem 1

New character

Solution 1

Problem 2

Solution 2

Ending

5.8

Name:

Date:

Literacy evolve

Literacy Evolve Year 5 © Pearson Education 2009

Story prompts

Make notes about your teacher's retelling. Then ask a partner to make notes about your retelling.

	Teacher's retelling	My retelling
Interest for listener		
Story structure, e.g. beginning, middle, end		
Opening line		
Setting description		
Character introduction		
Dialogue		
Powerful words		
Gestures		
Tone of voice		

Literacy Evolve Year 5 © Pearson Education 2009

Name: _____ Date: _____

Marking ladder 1

Use the marking ladder to check your work.

My partner's comments

My comments

My opening grabs the reader's attention.	I have introduced and resolved a problem.	Paragraphs help structure my story.	I have chosen words and phrases carefully for effect.	I have used some complex sentences.	I have developed my characters through their speech, thoughts and actions.

Marking ladder 2

Use the marking ladder to check your work.

My partner's comments

I have an interesting opening.	I have introduced and resolved a problem.	I have written in paragraphs.	I have used interesting, descriptive words.	I have used full stops and capital letters correctly where needed.	I have included and used speech marks correctly.

My comments

Multimedia presentation storyboard

Add notes to plan your presentation

Screen 1

Picture: _____

Text: _____

Screen 2

Picture: _____

Text: _____

Screen 3

Picture: _____

Text: _____

Screen 4

Picture: _____

Text: _____

Screen 5

Picture: _____

Text: _____

Screen 6

Picture: _____

Text: _____

Narrative Unit 6

NEWS AND ADVERTS – film (Media scripts)

Medium term plan (2 weeks)	
Phase	**Learning Outcomes**
Phase 1: Watching and evaluating a scripted performance (2 days)	• Children can explore how scripts are used for different purposes on TV and other media. • Children can use a variety of clues to identify the audience and purpose of different scripts.
Phase 2: Watching and analysing scripted news broadcasts (4 days)	• Children can perform from a written script. • Children can compare how scripted broadcasts present the same theme. • Children can plan and write a script for presentation using a flowchart. • Children can analyse how different film techniques are used to support the words.
Phase 3: Writing and performing a script (4 days)	• Children can work in groups to write their own script. • Children can use complex sentences in their writing. • Children can perform and record their own scripts in groups. • Children can evaluate each other's final scripted performances.

Narrative Unit 6

NEWS AND ADVERTS

Big picture

This unit links the work children have done previously on play scripts with their non-fiction writing. The children explore how scripts are used for a range of presentations in the media, such as on TV news and information programmes. They watch examples of scripted presentations and compare features, looking at how they are structured and the film techniques used. They also compare how the same theme can be presented in differently depending on audience and purpose. The children complete the unit by working in groups to write their own scripted presentations and then performing and if possible, filming them.

Prior learning

This unit assumes that children already know:

• plays are divided into sections called scenes
• every speech by a character starts on a new line, without using speech marks
• each speech starts with the character's name, followed by a colon
• stage directions are used to show actions or how characters are to speak and may be written in brackets or italics.

Key aspects of learning

Communication: Working in groups to plan, write, perform and record their script, each taking on different roles as part of a team.

Enquiry: Asking questions about the scripted presentations they watch; finding out more about their topic to include in their presentation.
Evaluation: Evaluating and improving their own and each other's work.
Information processing: Researching ideas to include in their scripts linked to another subject area.

Progression in narrative

In this unit the children will:

• identify the features of scripted presentations
• identify and then use different film techniques and stage directions to enhance the information being presented
• write well-structured and suitably set out scripts
• identify how formality and detail may vary depending on the target audience and can write a suitable script aimed at a chosen audience.

Cross-curricular links

Science/Geography/History/RE/PE/PHSCE: The focus of the children's scripts could link to another subject area, e.g. if their presentation is about how to keep healthy, this could be linked to Science and, PE.
ICT: The children could use digital video cameras to record and edit their presentations.

Viewing time

4 minutes approx.

PHASE 1: WATCHING AND EVALUATING A SCRIPTED PERFORMANCE (2 DAYS)

Session 1

We are learning to ...	Resources
• use evidence to evaluate a visual presentation • identify how scripts can be used in a variety of different situations (PNS Strands 7.1, 7.3) **Assessment Focuses** AF (R): 2, 5, 6	*Born Free Foundation appeal* (film) ITP: 6.1 PCM: 6.1, 6.2

Shared teaching

• Introduce the unit by asking the children what they already know about scripts, referring to previous work they have covered, e.g. scripts written in previous years, plays produced within the school, etc. Remind the children that these plays had a script. *What is meant by a script? Why are scripts used for plays?* Ask the children to Think-Pair-Share ideas.
• Share the learning objectives. *Where else might scripts be used?* Ask Talk Partners to discuss, then take feedback (advertisements, news broadcasts, weather forecasts, radio announcements, TV programmes). Write suggestions to start the Learning Wall.
• *Why is it necessary to have a script for these?* Make links to the reasons that plays have scripts discussed earlier. *Are there any similarities?*
• Watch *Born Free Foundation appeal. What type of clip is this? Who is the audience for this film? What is its purpose?* Talk Partners compare their answers.
• Show 'Evaluating clips' (ITP 6.1) and collect the children's ideas and add notes. Discuss what is meant by each heading in turn.
• Watch *Born Free Foundation appeal* again.

Independent and Guided

• The children evaluate the clip to answer questions about the film.
  [OOO] Complete 'Evaluating clips 1' (PCM 6.1).
  [OO] As above. (T+)
  [O] Complete 'Evaluating clips 2' (PCM 6.2). (TA+)

Plenary

• Show ITP 6.1 again. Make notes in the remaining boxes as a class. Ask the lower ability group about the information given. Ask the middle ability group about the effects used (zoom, fade, camera angle, voiceover, speaking directly to camera, gestures, etc). Ask the higher ability group about the effect on the audience, including the language used. *Is it formal, informal, chatty, technical, humorous, informative?* Encourage the children to refer to specific parts of the clip to support their answers.
• Recap the learning objectives. *What effect did the film have on you? How did it make you feel?*
• If possible, arrange for the children to evaluate another scripted performance using PCM 6.1 or PCM 6.2, either by watching a TV programme for homework, using an ICT session to view a clip online or watching a school's broadcast in another subject area.

Assessment pointers

• AF2 (R): written outcomes show how far the children are able to retrieve key information from film clips.
• AF5, 6 (R): responses to questioning show how well the children can identify the purpose and viewpoint of film clips.

Session 2

We are learning to ...
- use a variety of different clues to identify the audience and the purpose
- compare the similarities and differences between scripts for different purposes
(PNS Strands 7.2, 7.3)

Assessment Focuses
AF (R): 5, 6

Resources
Born Free Foundation appeal (film)
ITP: 6.2
PCM: 6.3

Shared teaching (1)
- Recall the list of different presentations from Session 1 that would use a script. If necessary, refer to the Learning Wall to prompt the children.
- Share the learning objectives. Explain that the focus of this session will be the importance of audience and purpose for a range of different scripts.
- Rewatch *Born Free Foundation appeal*. Recap the audience and purpose discussed in Session 1. *What clues do we have to tell us who the audience and purpose are?* Ask the children to Think-Pair-Share ideas.
- Take feedback and agree that there are clues in the type of language used (e.g. simplistic for younger children), the use of formal or informal language, the tone used by the presenter (e.g. authoritative), the topic covered and the way it is presented.
- Show 'Mystery clips' (ITP 6.2). Listen to the example script extracts and invite the children to drag the headings to match the extracts. *How did you know which was which?* Draw out the link between how the language and tone used help to identify the type of presentation, which in turn will help to identify the audience and purpose.

Independent and Guided
- In groups, the children compare different script extracts looking for clues about the intended audience and purpose. If appropriate, and suitable ICT facilities are available, the children could also watch video clips of other scripted presentations on computers and expand the task to include these in their comparisons.

  OOO Use 'Audience and purpose' (PCM 6.3). Explore 'Script 4' and 'Script 5'. (TA)

  OO As above. Explore 'Script 2' and 'Script 3'.

  O As above. Explore 'Script 1'. (T+)

Shared teaching (2)
- Arrange for Envoys from each group to visit other groups to share the findings about the scripts compared. Ensure that each group hears from envoys who worked on different scripts, so that the children are able to make comparisons between all the scripts on PCM 6.3.
- Discuss the findings as a class and agree the audience and purpose for each script.

Plenary
- Recap the learning objectives. *What did you learn from reading all of the different scripts? Why is the audience and purpose so important?* Explain to the children that Session 3 will focus on why these types of presentation need to be scripted.

Assessment pointers
- AF5, 6 (R): independent work and responses to questioning show how well the children can identify the purpose and viewpoint of extracts, commenting on the use of language to support their ideas.

PHASE 2: WATCHING AND ANALYSING SCRIPTED NEWS BROADCASTS (4 DAYS)

Session 3

We are learning to ...
- work in groups to peform scripts, taking different roles
- perform a scripted scene
- compare different performances of the same script
(PNS Strands 3.2, 4.2, 8.3)

Assessment Focuses
AF (R): 1

Resources
BBC News broadcast (film)
ITP: (6.1), 6.3

Shared teaching (1)
- *Why do we need scripts for different types of presentation?* (E.g. so that the presenters say everything necessary and all the facts are covered clearly; to consider audience and purpose.)
- Share the learning objectives. Explain that the children will perform a script, then watch a recording of the real performance and compare.
- Show 'BBC News script' (ITP 6.3). Discuss any layout features the children recognise, such as stage directions.

Independent and Guided (1)
- In groups of three, the children perform the script, using printouts of ITP 6.3, taking turns to act the roles of presenter, reporter and expert. They use the stage directions and think about how they speak should in each role. Support the children with an identified need. (T/TA)

Shared teaching (2)
- Ask a confident group to perform the script for the class. If possible, use a video camera to film the performance to make direct comparisons against the actual BBC News performance later on.
- *What do you notice about how the group performed?* Encourage the children to refer to the script when making comments, e.g. how well

stage directions were followed, whether the presenter, reporter and expert roles were or should be played differently.
- Ask questions to draw out similarities and differences between this script and a play script. *How did you know when it was your turn to speak?*
- Recall 'Evaluating clips' (ITP 6.1). Discuss the headings in reference to the BBC News script.

Independent and Guided (2)
- The children explore the BBC News script to find evidence of various features described in ITP 6.1.

  OOO Highlight evidence on copies of ITP 6.3. Focus on language use and its effect on the audience, making annotations as appropriate.

  OO As above. Focus on the audience, purpose and effects used. (T+)

  O Focus on the main information given. (TA+)

Plenary
- Explain that you are going to show the children a video of the script they have just read. *What do you expect to see? How do you expect it to look?* Encourage Talk Partners to share their expectations.
- Watch *BBC News broadcast*. *Was the performance as you expected?* If you recorded the children's dramatisation earlier, show this and compare the performances. Note that if they are very alike, this is due to a successful script.
- Recap the learning objectives. *What makes a successful script for a presentation?* Ask the children to write ideas on sticky notes and add the notes to the Learning Wall.

Assessment pointers
- AF1 (R): drama performances show how far the children are able to read and perform a script.

We are learning to ...	Resources
• understand how common themes can be presented for different audiences and purposes (PNS Strands 8.3) **Assessment Focuses** AF (R): 5	*BBC News broadcast* (film) *Newsround broadcast* (film) ITP: 6.4 PCM: 6.4, 6.5

Shared teaching

• Share the learning objective and explain that the children will be learning how the same theme can be presented differently for different audiences and purposes.

• Recap discussions on audience and purpose from previous sessions.

• Show 'Mobile phone issues' (ITP 6.4). Ask the children to suggest any issues surrounding mobile phones that they can think of.

• Click on the hotspots to reveal various issues.

• Explain that the children are going to explore these issues further using Improvisation. Allocate small groups a different topic from the six on 'Improvisation ideas' (PCM 6.4). Ask the children to create short Improvisations to perform for the rest of the class. Encourage the other children to guess the audience and purpose for each group's improvisation.

• *What did you learn from this task?* Agree that the improvisations showed that the same theme (mobile phones) can be covered in different ways to meet different audiences and purposes.

• *What would have helped to improve your performances?* Identify that a script would have been useful. Encourage the children to explain why.

• Watch *BBC News broadcast*.

• Explain that the children are going to compare this with another broadcast. Review 'Comparing news clips' (PCM 6.5), discussing each section to ensure the children understand what to look for.

• Watch *Newsround broadcast*. Allow Talk Partners time to discuss their initial reactions.

Independent and Guided

• In pairs, or independently, the children watch *BBC News broadcast* and *Newsround broadcast*, finding similarities and differences between the two clips. Replay the clips as often as necessary, or provide groups with laptops to enable the children to review the clips themselves if possible.

 Complete PCM 6.5.

 As above. (T)

 Complete the first three columns of the table. (TA)

Plenary

• Recap the learning objective and share the children's findings from the comparison of the two news broadcasts. *What was the same in each report? What were the main differences in the news report for children?* Encourage the children to support their ideas by referring to the broadcasts.

Assessment pointers

• S&L: improvisations will show how well the children can create and sustain roles to explore and develop ideas.

• AF 5 (R): written outcomes show how well the children can identify how the language used reflects the purpose of the script.

We are learning to ...	Resources
• work in a group to plan and write a script for presentation • achieve different effects by changing the order of sections in a script plan (PNS Strands 3.1, 10.1) **Assessment Focuses** AF (W): 3	*Newsround broadcast* (film) ITP: 6.5 PCM: 6.6

Shared teaching

• Share the learning objectives.

• Watch *Newsround broadcast* again. Pause at Markers 2, 3, 4 and 5 to discuss what is happening.

• Show 'News broadcast flow chart' (ITP 6.5). Discuss how the flow chart reflects the film's structure. Make links to previous non-fiction units on reporting and ask the children to identify any similarities.

• *Could the structure of the presentation be changed?* Ask the children to Think-Pair-Share ideas about the effect of reordering the flow chart.

• Take feedback, then play the segments of *Newsround broadcast* in a different order, e.g. Marker 2 to Marker 3, Marker 4 to Marker 5, Marker 1 to Marker 2, Marker 5 until the end, Marker 3 to Marker 4. Repeat in another order. *What is the effect of changing the order?*

• Agree that the introduction needs to stay at the beginning, but the rest of the report could be reorganised. Link this to writing e.g. *In a written report, each segment would be a paragraph. The paragraphs can be moved around within the report.*

• Explain that the children are going to work in groups to plan their own scripted presentations. Make appropriate cross-curricular links to work in other subject areas such as history, geography, science or PHSE.

For example, to fit with geography work on water, the children could prepare a presentation about water conservation to encourage people to save water.

• Remind the children that to be successful, they need to listen to others in the group, put forward ideas, support each other and work together to make decisions. If necessary, review rules for group interaction.

Independent and Guided

• Small groups work together to plan a scripted presentation. The children agree the topic, audience and purpose, then complete a flow chart to create a clear structure for their presentation. They use sticky notes to write details about each section of the script, then move these around on the flow chart to identify the best order.

 Design a flow chart to match the number of sections that will be used in the presentation script. (T)

 Use 'Presentation flow chart' (PCM 6.6) to plan a scripted presentation with five sections.

 As above. (TA+)

Plenary

• Recap the learning objectives and ask some of the groups to share their progress. *Have you planned a structure for your presentation? How could you reorder the structure for effect?* Remind the children that they will need to write paragraphs for each section.

Assessment pointers

• S&L: group work will show how well the children can adopt group roles, drawing ideas together and promoting effective planning.

• AF3 (W): script plans show how far the children can sequence sections effectively.

We are learning to ...	Resources
• work in a group to plan and write a script for presentation	*Newsround broadcast* (film)
• explore how a film maker uses film techniques to create tension (PNS Strands 3.1, 7.5)	ITP: 6.6, 6.7, 6.8 PCM: (6.6), 6.7
Assessment Focuses AF (W): 2, 7	

Shared teaching

• Share the learning objectives and explain that the children will build on their knowledge of scripts and film effects to help them write successful scripts for their own presentations.
• *What do you remember about film techniques from previous units?* Encourage the children to explain any techniques they suggest.
• Watch *Newsround broadcast* from Marker 2 until Marker 3. Explain that a voiceover is used to add details to the pictures seen by the viewer. Point out the close-up of the gorilla's eyes. *Why has this close-up been chosen?* Discuss how it enhances the words.
• Watch *Newsround broadcast* from Marker 3 until the end. The children record any effects they notice, then compare these with Talk Partners.
• Show 'Dramatic effects' (ITP 6.6) and click to reveal more information. Discuss when each one is used in the film. *How does it affect the viewer?* Explain that the children should include some of these effects when writing their own scripts.
• *What other features will a successful script include?* Allow Talk Partners time to discuss ideas, then take feedback.
• Discuss 'Writing a script' (ITP 6.7). Add any additional success criteria the children suggest.

• Distribute 'Scriptwriter's checklist' (PCM 6.7). Explain that the children will need to use this to help them write a successful script for their presentation. Display a copy on the Learning Wall.
• Use Modelled Writing to demonstrate how to begin writing a script. Use 'Editable script' (ITP 6.8) or your own ideas. Encourage the children to make suggestions for improvements and any stage directions or dramatic effects which could be included.

Independent and Guided

• Using computers if possible, groups work together to write the introduction to their scripted presentation based on their flow charts or notes on 'Presentation flow chart' (PCM 6.6). The children use Role Play to test their ideas where necessary.
- **ᴏᴏᴏ** Complete PCM 6.7. Try to include all aspects of the 'Try to' section.
- **ᴏᴏ** Complete PCM 6.7. (TA+)
- **ᴏ** As above. (T+)

Plenary

• Groups swap and peer assess introductions according to the success criteria on ITP 6.7. *What did you find most effective?*
• Allow time for groups to edit their work based on the feedback.
• Recap the learning objectives. *Have you written a successful script opening using dramatic effects?* Ask for thumbs up, down or half way to indicate levels of confidence.

Assessment pointers

• S&L: group work will show how well the children can adopt group roles and express opinions.
• AF2, 7 (W): peer and self-assessment show how well the children can produce texts appropriate to the purpose and audience, using effective or technical vocabulary.

PHASE 3: WRITING AND PERFORMING A SCRIPT (4 DAYS)

Session 7

We are learning to ...	Resources
• work in a group to plan and write a script for presentation	ITP: (6.7), 6.9 PCM: (6.6, 6.7)
• identify and write complex sentences (PNS Strands 3.1, 11.1)	
Assessment Focuses AF (W): 4, 5, 6	

Shared teaching

• Share the learning objectives and explain that today the children will be focusing on sentence construction.
• *What is a complex sentence?* Show 'Complex sentences' (ITP 6.9). Recall that a complex sentence has a main clause and another clause, called a subordinate clause, which depends on the main clause for its meaning. Discuss how the order of clauses can be changed.
• Talk Partners read the sentences on ITP 6.9 and improve them by adding a subordinate clause. Encourage the children to use connectives and add further detail to join the sentences together into a paragraph. Make changes to ITP 6.9 then click to reveal the example text and explain that complex sentences are more powerful.
• Explain that the children should include complex sentences in their scripts to retain the interest and attention of viewers. Draw their attention to the use of commas within the sentence. Discuss how this helps the reader or presenter read the sentence.
• Recall 'Writing a script' (ITP 6.7). Discuss the success criteria and add any additional ideas the children suggest. Encourage them to highlight the matching points on 'Scriptwriter's checklist' (PCM 6.7) and remind them that they will need to focus on these when writing the next parts of their scripts.

Independent and Guided

• Groups continue to write paragraphs for their scripted presentations, referring to flow charts or annotated 'Presentation flow chart' (PCM 6.6) and PCM 6.7. Half way through the session, the children act out their scripts, sticking rigidly to what they have written so far. They use this to identify any missing information and where more detail is needed.
- **ᴏᴏᴏ** Include at least three varied styles of complex sentence. (T+)
- **ᴏᴏ** Include at least two complex sentences.
- **ᴏ** Include at least one complex sentence. (TA+)

Plenary

• Invite groups to share complex sentences. Ask lower ability children to explain why they are complex sentences; ask middle ability children to identify the main and subordinate clauses; ask higher ability children to explain the effect the sentence has.
• *What has worked for you as a group today? What tips would you give for writing scripts?* Allow Think Time, then take feedback.
• Recap the learning objectives and discuss the next steps. *What do you need to do to complete your scripts?* Encourage the children to make notes on PCM 6.6 and PCM 6.7.
• Before Session 8, review the scripts to provide feedback for possible improvements and identify a group for guided support.

Assessment pointers

• S&L: group work will show how far the children can engage with others, draw ideas together and promote discussion.
• AF4 (W): written outcomes show how far the children are able to use paragraphs to organise scripts cohesively.
• AF5, 6 (W): written outcomes show whether the children can write varied complex sentences.

We are learning to ...	Resources
• work in a group to plan and write a a script for presentation	ITP: (6.7)
• review the effectiveness of our own and others' work	PCM: (6.6, 6.7)
• punctuate sentences accurately and effectively (PNS Strands 3.1, 9.2, 11.2)	
Assessment Focuses	
AF (W): 1, 2, 3, 4	

Shared teaching

• Share the learning objectives. Explain that by the end of this session, the groups need to have completed their scripts. They will review another group's finished script, then have the chance to make the final edits to their presentation.

• Provide any feedback from reviewing the children's scripts. Encourage the children to make notes of good ideas to improve their presentations.

• *How can we achieve dramatic effects in scripts?* Agree that different film techniques (zoom, fades, etc.), use of dramatic gestures and facial expressions and use of the voice and language are all ways of achieving dramatic effects. Explain that the focus of this session will be on how to use punctuation within scripts to support these dramatic effects.

• Write a sentence with no punctuation. *What do you notice?* Invite a child to add some punctuation, e.g. commas, full stop, question mark, exclamation mark, etc. Encourage the children to Think-Pair-Share how the chosen punctuation changes the way the sentence is read. Repeat for different punctuation and example sentences.

• Recap the importance of audience and purpose. Remind the children

that this will affect the language (formal or informal), vocabulary, and different effects used.

• Refer to the success criteria on annotated 'Writing a script' (ITP 6.7). Remind the children that their finished scripts should cover all these aspects.

Independent and Guided

• Groups complete their scripted presentations, including appropriate punctuation in the scripts to achieve the dramatic effects intended. The children refer to their flow charts or 'Presentation flow chart' (PCM 6.6) and your feedback for improvements.

⊙⊙⊙ Use 'Scriptwriter's checklist' (PCM 6.7) to assess writing. Address all the points, including the 'Try to' section. (T)

⊙⊙ Use PCM 6.7. Address as many points as possible.

⊙ As above. (TA)

Plenary

• Ask groups to swap scripts. Each group evaluates their partner group's script against PCM 6.7 and makes suggestions for edits to improve it.

• Allow time for the groups to edit their scripts to make any changes.

• Recap the learning objectives. *How can you tell if your script really works?* Agree that the true test of a good script is to see it in action. Explain that in Session 9 each group will be performing their script.

Assessment pointers

• S&L: group work will show how far the children can engage with others, draw ideas together and promote discussion.

• AF1, 2 (W): written outcomes will show how far the children are able to produce imaginative scripts, appropriate to audience and purpose.

• AF3, 4 (W): written outcomes will show how well the children can organise and sequence texts.

We are learning to ...	Resources
• perform scripts using appropriate dramatic techniques and expression	ITP: 6.10
• understand the impact of theatrical effects (PNS Strands 4.2, 4.3)	
Assessment Focuses	
AF (R): 1, 3	

Shared teaching

• Share the learning objectives and explain that the children are going to find out how successful their scripts are when they are dramatised. Depending on the resources available, explain how the session will be organised. If possible, allow the children to use digital video cameras to film the performances themselves and add the effects in their scripts. Pair groups together, so that one acts as a technical crew while the other performs. If technical equipment is not available, the children will need to improvise, e.g. use pictures with voiceovers, and prepare to present their rehearsed scripts to the class in Session 10.

• Explain that they will need to think carefully about the roles within their group. Show 'What's my role?' (ITP 6.10). Discuss each role (director, camera person, stage crew, presenter, reporter, expert) and agree what their jobs are. Take feedback of other roles the children may wish to include.

• Discuss how to make final preparations for the performance. *What props do you need?* Refer back to the news broadcasts watched in previous sessions for ideas. Encourage the children not to waste valuable time on props unless they really enhance the performance. Provide large sheets of material or sugar paper to display behind the presenters as backdrops.

• If necessary, brief the children on how to use any technical equipment appropriately. Arrange for the children to use a quiet room for filming to avoid background noise.

• Remind the children to follow their scripts.

Independent and Guided

• Groups practise and perfect their presentations, before filming and editing to ensure that all of the effects in their scripts are included. If only one video camera is available, film each group's presentation in turn. Support the children with an identified need. (T+/TA+)

Plenary

• Ask the children to reflect on how they worked together as a group. *What went well? What could be improved? What might you do differently next time?* Ask the children to share feedback with each other on the roles they performed.

• Discuss the children's reflections on their performance as a group. *Have you achieved your targets?* Provide feedback about each group's achievements.

• Recap the learning objectives. Explain that during the final session of the unit, the children will be watching and evaluating the performances of each group's scripted presentation.

Assessment pointers

• S&L: presentations will show how well the children can talk in extended turns to convey ideas.

• AF1 (R): drama performances will show how far the children are able to read aloud expressively and to convey meaning.

• AF3 (R): drama performances will show how far the children can interpret information from texts.

We are learning to …	Resources
• evaluate a performance • evaluate writing using success criteria • evaluate writing using a marking ladder (PNS Strands 4.3, 9.1) **Assessment Focuses** AF (R): 6; AF (W): 2, 6, 7	PCM: 6.8

Shared teaching

• Refer to the Learning Wall. Ask the children to Think-Pair-Share what they have learned during the unit. Take feedback and make a list of all the points the children recall.

• Share the learning objectives and explain that this will be an evaluation session, where the children measure their achievements against the success criteria set in the scriptwriter's toolkit. Provide 'Marking ladder' (PCM 6.8) to support the children. Discuss any questions the children have about PCM 6.8.

• Pair up groups that have not yet worked together to act as peer response groups. The groups will need a copy of each other's scripts. Explain that as they watch all the presentations, the children should focus on their allocated peer response group's performance and make notes to discuss with their group later.

• Show all the performances filmed in Session 9 or watch the groups perform their scripted presentations. Invite each group to give a brief explanation of their film or presentation, including the intended audience and purpose.

Independent and Guided

• Peer response groups evaluate each other's work, using PCM 6.8. The children consider whether the script and performance are appropriate for the intended audience and purpose. If possible, provide groups with access to laptops to replay the finished films as necessary. After the peer-assessment, the groups review the comments received, then self-assess their own work. Circulate to ensure that each group's marking is fair and balanced. Support the children with an identified need. (T/TA+)

Plenary

• Invite the children to share something they liked about another group's script or performance. Encourage them to be specific. *What dramatic techniques or language did they use? What effect did that have on the audience?* Encourage the children to comment on the authors' purpose and viewpoint.

• Recap the learning objectives. Ask the children to give feedback on the process of writing a script. *What did you enjoy most in this unit? What did you learn while watching the films and writing and performing the scripts? Did you like working in a group? What was most difficult?*

• Encourage the children to review their own progress. *What are you most proud of? What do you need to improve?* Add a list of suggestions to the Learning Wall to complete the unit.

Assessment pointers

• S&L: group work will show how far the children can evaluate the features of their own and other's speech.

• AF6 (R): responses to questioning will show how well the children can comment on authors' purposes and viewpoints and the overall effect of the text.

• AF2, 6, 7 (W): peer and self-assessment show how well the children are able to produce texts appropriate to the audience and purpose, using effective vocabulary and accurate punctuation.

Evaluating clips 1

Complete the table about a film clip. Support your answers with evidence.

Name of clip: _____

Audience	
Purpose	
Effects used e.g. zoom, fade, voiceover, gestures	
Information given	
Effect on the audience	

Evaluating clips 2

Tick the answers you think are true about a film clip. Explain how you know.

Name of clip: _____

Audience
adults ☐
parents ☐
men ☐
women ☐
older people ☐
young people ☐
other: _____ ☐

Notes
_____
_____
_____
_____

Purpose
to give information ☐
to persuade ☐
to entertain ☐
to explain ☐
other: _____ ☐

Notes
_____
_____
_____

Effects used
zoom ☐
fade ☐
voiceover ☐
presenter making gestures ☐
other: _____ ☐

Notes
_____
_____
_____

Information given
List the main information given ☐
other: _____ ☐

Notes
_____
_____

Effect on the audience
interested ☐
amused ☐
shocked ☐
surprised ☐
other: _____ ☐

Notes
_____
_____
_____

Audience and purpose

Write the audience and purpose for each script.

Script 1

Good evening and welcome to the *News at Ten*. Coming up on tonight's programme: high winds cause chaos across Britain; record sales as the new Mega games console is launched; and why one British woman is on her way to Hollywood.

Audience: _____

Purpose: _____

_____

_____

Script 2

Hi there! This is your guide to using the new Mega games console. Check out our new podcast to get all the information and tricks you'll need to beat your friends online. Then you can become the next Mega Gamer.

Audience: _____

Purpose: _____

_____

_____

Script 3

Experience the thrills! Control the action! Live the dream – with the new Mega games console! The best in gaming technology with all new interactive features. Prepare to be amazed! Coming soon!

Audience: _____

Purpose: _____

_____

_____

Script 4

It's estimated that as many as four in five families now have video or computer games consoles, and three in ten have two or more. Tonight we'll be investigating what effect these hi-tech devices have on those that use them.

Audience: _____

Purpose: _____

_____

_____

Script 5

Well, as we've seen on the news, it's been particularly windy for this time of year. But that's all about to change. Those winds will be dying away towards lunchtime tomorrow and instead we'll be facing icy temperatures and the possibility of some snow on higher ground.

Audience: _____

Purpose: _____

_____

_____

Information about Lebanon

Read the information to find out more about Lebanon.

Lebanon

Lebanon is a small, mountainous country in the Middle East. The people of Lebanon come from lots of different religious groups and this has caused serious problems in the past.

Key facts

Population: approximately four million
Capital: Beirut
Main language: Arabic
Main religions: Islam and Christianity

Beirut

The capital city of Lebanon is Beirut, on the Mediterranean coast. During the civil war it was split into two sections, east and west, with Muslims on one side and Christians on the other. The two sides were separated by the Green Line and the area in the middle was called no man's land. The buildings were all damaged by the constant fighting and it wasn't safe for anyone to live there.

Civil war

In 1975 civil war broke out in Lebanon and lasted until 1990. Different groups of people wanted to take control of the country. They had their own militias to protect them and fight their enemies. The country was divided, with different groups controlling the north and south. During the civil war a great number of people were hurt or killed.

Beirut

Questions about Lebanon

Use 'Information about Lebanon' to answer the questions.

a. Where is Lebanon?

b. What is the capital city of Lebanon?

c. What sea is Beirut near?

d. What groups make up the Lebanese population?

e. When did the civil war in Lebanon start and finish?

f. Why did the civil war start?

g. How was Beirut separated during the civil war?

h. How did the civil war affect Beirut?

Improvisation ideas

Choose an idea and create an improvisation that is suited to the audience and purpose.

IDEA 1

Topic: how to use mobiles
Audience: people who have never used a mobile before
Purpose: to explain how to use one

IDEA 2

Topic: world mobile phone network
Audience: business people
Purpose: to explain how their phones can be used wherever they go

IDEA 3

Topic: MP3 music players on mobiles
Audience: teenagers
Purpose: to encourage them to buy a phone with an MP3 player

IDEA 4

Topic: dangers of using mobiles when driving
Audience: drivers
Purpose: to warn drivers about safety issues

IDEA 5

Topic: text message bullying
Audience: school children
Purpose: to raise awareness of the issue

IDEA 6

Topic: mobile accessories
Audience: mobile owners
Purpose: to encourage them to buy new accessories

Comparing news clips

Compare the two news clips and complete the table.

	Clip 1: _____	Clip 2: _____
Presenter's language, gestures and tone		
Information given		
Supporting films		
Filming effects e.g. zoom, cut		
Onscreen titles		
Formality e.g. presenter's dress and tone		

Literacy Evolve Year 5 © Pearson Education 2009

Presentation flow chart

Use the chart to plan a presentation.

Topic: _____

Audience: _____

Purpose: _____

Scriptwriter's checklist

Use this checklist to help you write a script for your presentation.

Checklist

- Are your audience and purpose clear? ☐
- Have you included a cast list? ☐
- Have you set the scene and given background information? ☐
- Is your language choice suitable for your audience and purpose? ☐
- Have you correctly organised the script, e.g. name, colon (:) and speech without speech marks? ☐
- Are your stage directions clear, in italics and placed in brackets? ☐
- Have you used punctuation to create dramatic effects? ☐
- Have you described a range of special effects you would like to use? ☐
- Have you used the correct tense? ☐

Try to:
- use a variety of sentence structures, including complex sentences
- include interesting sentence openers
- choose technical vocabulary that supports your topic.

Marking ladder

Check another group's script and performance. Then check your own work.

Our group's comments

We have included a cast list.

We have set the scene and given background information.

Our language is suitable for the audience and purpose.

We have correctly organised the script.

Our stage directions are clear, in italics and placed in brackets.

We have used punctuation to create dramatic effects.

We have described a range of different special effects we would like to use.

We have used the correct tense.

Peer group's comments

Poetry Unit 1

MICHAEL ROSEN / CHARLES CAUSLEY (Poetic voice)

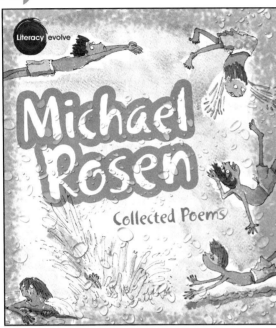

Medium term plan (2 weeks)	
Phase	**Learning Outcomes**
Phase 1: Poems that use different styles (6 days)	• Children can identify how and why poets use language to create particular effects. • Children can find evidence in a poem to explain what is happening. • Children can use drama techniques to explore events and issues in a poem.
Phase 2: Composing poems in different styles (2 days)	• Children can draft a whole-class poem in free verse style. • Children can draft and revise their own work.
Phase 3: Drafting and revising poems with different styles (2 days)	• Children can write their own poems in different styles. • Children can plan, draft and revise their own poems. • Children can use ICT to present their poems.

MICHAEL ROSEN/CHARLES CAUSLEY

Big picture

The children read poems by Charles Causley and Michael Rosen and also watch performance poems by Michael Rosen. The children discuss the authors' style, including use of rhyme / free verse, vocabulary choices, subject matter and the narrator's voice. With close reference to the text, they discuss the effect of these on the reader. The children then draw on personal experience and use a poem by Michael Rosen as a model to create a shared poem. They then experiment with a different poetic style (following Charles Causley) to create a rhyming poem. Finally, the children establish success criteria for a rhyming nonsense poem and write a draft of their own poem. They share their poem with a partner and redraft, before finalising it for an audience.

Prior learning

This unit assumes that the children can already:
- use drama techniques to explore issues, behaviour and feelings
- comment on the impact of particular words and phrases on the audience, with some awareness of how poets can vary these
- create their own poems, planning what to write and making choices about the words and phrases they use.

Key aspects of learning

Creative thinking: Contribute ideas and vocabulary for a shared poem. Find inventive uses of language and imagery for their own poems.

Empathy: Empathise with thoughts and feelings expressed in a poem, both stated and implicit.

Problem-solving: Use clues from a text to solve a mystery.

Self-awareness: Draw on personal experience and feelings to contribute to a group poem.

Progression in poetry

In this unit the children will:
- discuss poets' possible viewpoint, explain and justify own response and interpretation
- compare different forms and describe impact
- invent nonsense words and situations, and experiment with unexpected word combinations
- write free verse; use or invent repeating patterns; attempt different forms, including rhyme for humour.

Cross-curricular links

Art and Design: The children could create a mural using images from their own nonsense poems.

ICT: The children could use ICT to write and present their final poem.

PSHE: Follow-up work to the poem *Harrybo* could include work on feelings of sadness.

PHASE 1: POEMS THAT USE DIFFERENT STYLES (6 DAYS)

Session 1

We are learning to ...	Resources
• group words according to their spelling patterns • explore how authors use rhyme and choose words for comic effect (PNS Strands 6.3, 7.5) **Assessment Focuses** AF (R): 5	*Year 5 Poetry Collection* ITP: P1.1, P1.2 PCM: P1.1

Shared teaching

- Share the learning objectives for the session and explain that in this unit the children will read poems in different styles, starting with rhyming poems by Charles Causley.
- Read *I Saw a Jolly Hunter* by Charles Causley (page 10). *Is this a funny poem, a serious one, or both? What view does the poet seem to have about the hunter?*
- Talk Partners discuss why Charles Causley has used the word 'jolly' so many times in the poem. *What effect does this have? What different meanings does the word have?*
- Take feedback. Discuss the meanings of 'jolly', e.g. cheerful 'a jolly hunter'; very 'jolly good'; something familiar 'jolly old safety catch'. Explain that the last two meanings are colloquial and mostly used in speech. *What sort of person would use the word 'jolly' in this way?* (E.g. an upper class retired military person.) *What other use of language gives you clues about what the hunter is like?* (E.g. the way words are missed out sometimes: 'Sight of jolly prey'; 'Hunter jolly dead'.)
- Show 'I Saw a Jolly Hunter' (ITP P1.1). *What patterns are there in how the poem is set out?* (E.g. a pattern of four-line stanzas with alternate longer and shorter lines, the shorter ones being indented, etc.)
- Beat out the regular rhythm this pattern makes. Explain that this is a traditional style for telling a story in a poem called a ballad.
- Highlight the rhyme words on ITP P1.1. *Which rhyme words look the same as each other?* ('gun' / ' sun'; 'hare' / 'care'). *Which don't?* ('prey' / 'way' ; 'gone' / 'on'; 'dead' / 'said') *Why is this?* (They have the same sounds, different spellings.)
- Show 'Rhymes' (ITP P1.2). *What else makes a good rhyme in a poem?* Add suggestions.

Independent and Guided

- The children work in pairs to investigate rhyming words.

  OOO Use a rhyming dictionary to write another opening stanza, using the same pattern and the word 'jolly', e.g. I saw a jolly sailor / in a jolly coat / sailing at the seaside / in his jolly boat.

  OO Use a rhyming dictionary to list as many different rhyming words as possible for the *-ed* sound as in 'dead' and 'said'. Rewrite the poem's final line using some of these words. (TA+)

  O Use 'Rhyming words' (PCM P1.1). (T+)

Plenary

- Pairs present their examples of alternative rhymes, lines and stanzas. *Which ones meet the success criteria for using rhyme?*
- Recap the learning objectives. *What have you learned about Charles Causley's use of word play for comic and dramatic effect? What have you learned about how he uses rhyming words?*

Assessment pointers

- AF5 (R): responses during shared teaching will show how far the children understand the use of language for comic effect and the use of rhyme in the poem.

We are learning to ...
- use evidence in a poem to explain what happens
- explore how authors use words for dramatic effect
  (PNS Strands 7.1, 7.5)

Resources
Year 5 Poetry Collection
ITP: P1.3

Assessment Focuses
AF (R): 5

Shared teaching
- Share the learning objectives and explain that in this session, the children will be looking at another rhyming poem by Charles Causley.
- Read and enjoy *Green Man in the Garden* by Charles Causley (page 11).
- Take feedback. *Did anything puzzle you? What did you like? What did you dislike? What patterns did you pick out?*
- Talk Partners list the similarities and differences between *Green Man in the Garden* and *I Saw a Jolly Hunter,* e.g. it is a story in a similar ballad form; it uses the same pattern of rhymes; it is more scary, less funny; it has speech in it, printed in italics; it doesn't repeat the same word many times; it has more old-fashioned language.
- Show 'Green Man in the Garden' (ITP P1.3). Discuss the use of language in lines such as: 'Of sycamore your horns' and 'Of bark your dancing shoes'. *How would we normally write this?* (E.g. Your horns are made of sycamore, etc.) *Why has Charles Causley changed the word order? What effect does it have?* Annotate the text.
- Talk Partners discuss language used to describe the green man in Stanzas 2 and 3.
- Take feedback. *When the green man speaks in Stanza 4, why does the author say 'he creaked' rather than 'he croaked'?*
- Take feedback. Discuss traditional tales of the green man: a creature

who is half human, half tree, who is supposed to live in the woods and who tempts people to follow him. *How do we use the word 'green' today?* (E.g. to mean something natural that fits well into its environment.)
- The children Think-Pair-Share ideas about what might have happened before the poem starts and what might happen afterwards, using evidence in the poem to back up your ideas.

Independent and Guided
- The children work in pairs to write what happens before, or after, the poem, using evidence from the poem. Write in the first person and use similar language to the poem.

  OOO Write another stanza using the same style to continue or end the story. (T)

  OO Write two or three paragraphs in narrative form which could be the beginning of the story.

  O Write a paragraph to say what happens next in the story. (TA)

Plenary
- Share beginnings, endings or continuations for the story. *Which ones fit in best with the language of the original poem? Which seem the most likely, given the events in the poem?*
- Recap the learning objectives.

Assessment pointers
- AF5 (R): responses during the shared teaching will show how far the children understand the use of language for dramatic effect.

We are learning to ...
- use questions to explore how authors use words for dramatic effect
- use evidence in a poem to explain what happens
  (PNS Strands 1.3, 7.1)

Resources
Year 5 Poetry Collection
PCM: P1.2

Assessment Focuses
AF (R): 5

Shared teaching
- Share the learning objectives and explain that the children will look at a third poem by Charles Causley. This one is also a rhyming poem in ballad style, but is written in a slightly different way from *I Saw a Jolly Hunter* and *Green Man in the Garden.*
- Bring into class an old rag-doll, one shoe, a round money box and a crumpled note which has been smoothed out. Explain that all these objects are clues involving a missing person, a young girl called Lulu.
- Read *What has happened to Lulu?* by Charles Causley (page 4).
- Ask the children to Think-Pair-Share ideas about what has happened to Lulu. Encourage the children to back up their theories with evidence from the poem.
- Take feedback, e.g. Lulu has run away from home; Lulu has been kidnapped; Lulu has been injured in a burglary and wandered off, etc.
- Read *What has happened to Lulu?* again. Review evidence in the poem to back up each theory *Why was the rag-doll left behind? Why did Lulu only have one shoe on? Who took her money-box? Who wrote the note and what did it say? Whose car engine was heard? Who cried out late last night?*
- Take feedback. *Who do you think is speaking in the poem?* (E.g. a

brother or sister, someone younger or older than Lulu.) *Would it be useful to interview this person about Lulu's disappearance?*
- Discuss how the poem is structured and why the poem itself does not give any answers as to what has happened to Lulu, e.g. it is written in the form of different types of questions; there are 9 questions in the 6 stanzas, 5 'why' questions and 4 'what' questions; it is spoken by a character who does not know what has happened and is trying to find out.

Independent and Guided
- In pairs, the children work together to compose a written response to the poem.

  OOO Draft a letter from Lulu to her sibling saying what has really happened to her and why.

  OO Draft the note that was left behind in Lulu's bedroom. (T+)

  O Use 'Asking about Lulu' (PCM P1.2) to draft more questions to ask the mother to try to solve the mystery of Lulu's disappearance. Use different question types, e.g. 'what', 'why', 'where', 'when', 'how'. (TA+)

Plenary
- Recap the learning objectives. Set up a Hot-Seating activity to answer questions in the character of Lulu's mother or Lulu's sibling.
- Share drafts of notes and letters. *Now you have heard all the evidence, what do you think happened to Lulu?*

Assessment pointers
- S&L: hot-seating will show how far the children can sustain roles to explore ideas.
- AF5 (R): identification of language features and comments on word choices show how far the children understand how authors use words for dramatic effect.

We are learning to ...	Resources
• explore how authors use words for dramatic effect • understand and use punctuation for speech accurately (PNS Strands 7.5, 11.2) **Assessment Focuses** AF (R): 5	*Year 5 Poetry Collection* *Rodge Said ...* (film) ITP: P1.4 PCM: P1.3

Shared teaching

• Share the learning objectives for the session and explain that the children will be looking at a different style of poem.
• Read *Rodge Said ...* by Michael Rosen (page 6). *What did you think of the poem?*
• Watch *Rodge Said ...* to see Michael Rosen perform the poem.
• Discuss how the performance and written poems vary. *What was different about hearing the poem read aloud by Michael Rosen as compared to reading it to yourself? How did he bring the language of the poem to life?* (E.g. using a different voice, stressing certain words, etc.) Add feedback to 'Rodge Said ...' ITP P1.4.
• Discuss the language used in the poem. *Does it sound like the language used by teachers and pupils in everyday school life? How does Michael Rosen achieve this?* Annotate ITP P1.4. Add a list of the language features in the poem to the Learning Wall. These could include direct speech; colloquial words ('or something'); words associated with adults ('we don't want that sort of thing going on here / thank you very much'); present day language ('Teachers – they want it all ways'); nickname ('Rodge'); use of line breaks to emphasise words ('Rodge said ... / Teachers').
• Talk Partners discuss whether *Rodge Said ...* has patterns of rhyme and rhythm like Charles Causley's poems.
• Take feedback and explain that the style of *Rodge Said ...* is free verse,

which doesn't use rhyme or regular rhythm. *What patterns are there in* Rodge Said ... ? Add comments to ITP P1.4, e.g. the reversal of the opening lines at the end of the poem; the reversal of the teacher's attitude in the two conversations.
• Discuss how speech is set out in the poem, e.g. Rodge's words telling the story are in single speech marks; Rodge's words to the teacher and the teacher's words to Rodge are in double speech marks.

Independent and Guided

• In pairs the children use Improvisation to act out the conversation between the teacher and Rodge, adding more dialogue. They then write some more conversation for the poem, setting it out using speech marks as in the poem.
⊙⊙⊙ Write a reply from the teacher in free verse style.
⊙⊙ Use the first two lines and write some more speech for Rodge. (TA+)
⊙ Use 'Another thing' (PCM P1.3). (T+)

Plenary

• Share free verse poems or further conversations for Rodge. *Are they in the same style as Michael Rosen's?* Refer to the list of language features on the Learning Wall.
• Choose a selection of the children's work for display. Look at the way speech marks are used. *Is it clear whose words are being quoted?*
• Recap the learning objectives.

Assessment pointers

• S&L: improvisations will show how well the children can understand a character through gesture and movement.
• AF5 (R): written poems will show how far the children can identify authors' language choices and responses to shared teaching will show an understanding of the use of speech marks.

We are learning to ...	Resources
• use drama to explore the issues in a poem • explore how authors use words for dramatic effect (PNS Strands 4.1, 7.5) **Assessment Focuses** AF (R): 5	*Year 5 Poetry Collection* *I'm the Youngest in our House ...* (film) ITP: P1.5

Shared teaching

• Share the learning objectives. Explain that the children will be looking at another poem in free verse by Michael Rosen.
• Watch *I'm the Youngest in our House ... What did you like about the performance? How did it make you feel?*
• Read *I'm the Youngest in our House ...* by Michael Rosen (page 4). *Have you had arguments like that at home? What did you say? What did your parents say? What did your brother or sister say?*
• Discuss the poet's use of language. *How is language used for dramatic and comic effect in* I'm the Youngest in our House ... ? (E.g. the speakers repeat words and sentences; the use of comic images 'my brother – all puffed up'; the use of capitals for the last line, to suggest the narrator shouting.)
• Discuss similarities and differences between the features of language in *I'm the Youngest in our House ...* and *Rodge Said ...* e.g. use of direct speech; use of colloquial words ('shuttup'); use of words associated with adults ('You heard what your mother said'); use of present day language 'So it goes like this'; use of nickname 'stinks'; use of line breaks to emphasise words, 'I say,' / 'Shuttup stinks'; there are more speakers; only single speech marks are used; capital letters and italics are used for emphasis in the speech.

• Take feedback and add to 'Features of poems' (ITP P1.5). Save for future reference.

Independent and Guided

• In groups, the children create performances of *I'm the Youngest in our House ...* .
⊙⊙⊙ Create a performance, improvising more dialogue to be included at the end. (TA+)
⊙⊙ Divide the poem into parts for different speakers and perform it. (T+)
⊙ Use 'Performance script 1' (PCM P1.4) to perform the poem.

Plenary

• Share performances of the poem.
• Recap the learning objectives. Evaluate how useful it was to act out the poem to explore what it is about and how it uses language.

Assessment pointers

• S&L: drama pieces will show how far the children can sustain roles and scenarios to explore the poem.
• AF5 (R): responses to shared teaching will show how far the children are able to identify and make simple comments on features of authors' language.

We are learning to ...	Resources
• use drama to explore the issues in a poem • explore how authors use words for dramatic effect (PNS Strands 4.1, 7.5) **Assessment Focuses** AF (R): 5	*Year 5 Poetry Collection* *Harrybo* (film) PCM: P1.5

Shared teaching

• Share the learning objectives and explain that the children will be looking at another poem in free verse by Michael Rosen.
• Read *Harrybo* by Michael Rosen (pages 10–11). *How does the poem make you feel?*
• Watch *Harrybo* to see Michael Rosen perform this poem. *How does Michael Rosen bring the dialogue between the boys to life? What tone of voice does he use at different times? What facial expressions?*
• Talk Partners discuss the poem and the performance of it. *What do you think of the way the boys behave towards Harrybo? Does the poem remind you of any situations you've been in? How is the situation in this poem different from* Rodge Said ... *or* I'm the Youngest in our House ... ?
• Take feedback. Discuss how *Harrybo* deals with a sadder, more serious situation than in the other Michael Rosen poems read in this unit: the death of Harrybo's grandad, how he is upset by it and how the other boys try to support him.
• Explore the poem in more detail. *Are there parts of the poem that are funny too? Which bits made you smile? What language used in the poem makes it serious as well as funny? Why does Michael Rosen use*

very simple words and sentences? (E.g. this is the kind of language the boys would use.) *Why do the boys start talking about random things like the red shoe horn, trainers, etc.?* (E.g. because they don't know what to say in this situation but they want to distract Harrybo, to stop him crying.) *How do they talk differently to Harrybo from how they usually would?*

Independent and Guided

• In groups of four, act out the situation described in *Harrybo*.
  ooo Use the text as a script. Continue the situation by creating extra dialogue; use similar simple language to create a scene that is sad but also funny. (T+)
  oo Use 'Performance script 2' (PCM P1.5).
  o Use Improvisation to create a similar situation where someone has come to school upset because of bad news and his or her friends try to cheer the person up. (TA+)

Plenary

• Recap the learning objectives.
• Share and evaluate drama presentations by different groups. *How do these compare to the way Michael Rosen performed the poem? Did acting out the poem help you to explore the issues involved? How?*

Assessment pointers

• S&L: drama pieces will show how far the children can sustain roles and scenarios to explore the poem.
• AF5 (R): responses to shared teaching will show how far the children are able to identify and make simple comments on features of authors' language.

PHASE 2: COMPOSING POEMS IN DIFFERENT STYLES (2 DAYS)

We are learning to ...	Resources
• evaluate, edit and improve our writing • write free verse poems (PNS Strands 9.1, 9.3) **Assessment Focuses** AF (W): 1, 7	*Year 5 Poetry Collection* ITP: P1.6

Shared teaching

• Share the learning objectives and explain that the children are going to write a poem as a whole class in the style of Michael Rosen.
• Read and enjoy *Chivvy* by Michael Rosen (page 5). *How did the poem make you feel? Did any of it sound familiar?*
• Allow Think Time for the children to note down things that their parents often say to them, e.g. *You're getting too big for your boots, You're not going out looking like that*, etc.
• Talk Partners share their parents' sayings. *Are any of them similar?*
• Take feedback. Discuss the language used in *Chivvy*. *How do most of the lines after the first one begin?* (with a verb, because they are mostly commands)
• Use Modelled Writing to create a class poem on 'Grown-ups' (ITP P1.6). Add to the draft. Encourage the children to suggest lines beginning with verbs.
• When the list of sayings is long enough (there are 18 in *Chivvy*, not counting the last line), discuss how the poem could be improved.
• Take feedback and refer to *Chivvy*, e.g. *Michael Rosen has put some sayings one after the other which contradict each other, e.g. 'Speak up / Don't talk with your mouth full'; 'Pull your socks up / Stand up straight',* etc. *How can we add to, or rearrange our poem to achieve the same effect?* Revise the draft on ITP P1.6.

• Discuss improvements that could be made to the ending, referring to *Chivvy* again, e.g. the final parents' saying contradicts all the other ones. *How could the class poem end in the same way?* (E.g. *Well, if you don't know yourself, I'm not going to tell you*, etc.) Revise the ending and save on ITP P1.6 for the children to view.

Independent and Guided

• Groups draft free verse poems in the style of Michael Rosen, using the class poem on ITP P1.6 as a model.
  ooo Write about things that parents do not say to their children, e.g. *Remember to play your music as loud as you like.* Start with 'Parents never say'. (T)
  oo Write about things that children say to parents, e.g. *Are we there yet?* Start with: 'Kids say things like'.
  o Edit and improve the whole-class draft poem. Add more sayings to the middle section and remove others if desired. (TA+)

Plenary

• Recap the learning objectives.
• Share and evaluate draft poems from different groups. *Did they use language in the same way that Michael Rosen's poem does? How could they be improved?*

Assessment pointers

• AF1 (W): draft poems will show how far the children can choose relevant ideas and establish and maintain a viewpoint.
• AF7 (W): vocabulary used to support the content and style of poems will show how far the children are able to select appropriate and effective words.

We are learning to ...	Resources
• evaluate, edit and improve our writing • write free verse poems (PNS Strands 9.1, 9.3) **Assessment Focuses** AF (W): 1	*Year 5 Poetry Collection* ITP: P1.7

Shared teaching

• Share the learning objectives and explain that the children are going to write a poem as a whole class in the style of Charles Causley.
• Read *As I Went Down Zig Zag* by Charles Causley (pages 8–9). *What does the poem remind you of?* Explain that it is about a steep footpath called Zig Zag near where Charles Causley used to live. *What other poems or poets does this remind you of? What do you like or dislike about the poem? What patterns or puzzles can you find in it?*
• Take feedback. Clarify unfamiliar vocabulary, e.g. 'kine' (cattle), 'leaven' (yeast, to make bread rise when baked), 'delve' (search).
• Show 'As I Went Down Zig Zag' (ITP P1.7). Use Modelled Writing to draft a new version of the first stanza, e.g. *As I went down Zig Zag / The clock striking one, / I saw a man wearing / A hamburger bun.*
• Talk Partners use rhyming dictionaries to give suggestions for another two lines to complete Stanza 2. Take feedback and add suggestions to the draft poem. Repeat for Stanza 3.
• Review the draft of the three stanzas and discuss how it could be improved. *Do the rhymes work? Do the lines flow well together? Does the draft sound like the original poem?* Save the revised draft on ITP P1.7 for the children to view.

Independent and Guided

• In groups, the children continue the whole-class poem using rhyming dictionaries.
- **ooo** Write new lines for Stanzas 9 to 12. (TA)
- **oo** Write new lines for Stanzas 6 to 8.
- **o** Write new lines for Stanzas 4 and 5. (T)

Plenary

• Recap the learning objectives.
• Take feedback and use suggestions from groups to complete the poem on ITP P1.7. *Does the new version use language in the same way as the original? How could the drafts be improved further?* Make final changes and perform the completed poems, assigning groups different stanzas to read. Save the poem for use in session 9.

Assessment pointers

• AF1 (W): draft poems will show how far the children can choose and develop relevant ideas.

PHASE 3: DRAFTING AND REVISING POEMS WITH DIFFERENT STYLES (2 DAYS)

We are learning to ...	Resources
• evaluate, edit and improve our writing • write rhyming poems (PNS Strands 9.1, 9.3) **Assessment Focuses** AF (W): 1	*Year 5 Poetry Collection* ITP: (P1.2, P1.7) PCM: P1.6, P1.7

Shared teaching (1)

• Share the learning objectives and explain that in the next two sessions, the children will be writing their own poems in different styles. The first one they will write will be their own rhyming nonsense poem.
• Recap the rhyming poems by Charles Causley read during the unit so far: *I Saw a Jolly Hunter, Green Man in the Garden, What Has Happened to Lulu?* and *As I Went Down Zig Zag.*
• Review the features of these poems, e.g. the use of ballad form; the use of nonsense language; the use of rhyme.
• Recap the success criteria for a good rhyming poem using 'Rhymes' (ITP P1.2).
• Reread 'As I Went Down Zig Zag' (ITP P1.7) and discuss the whole-class version of the poem. *Did this meet the success criteria for a good rhyming poem? Is there anything we can do to improve it?*

Independent and Guided (1)

• The children work independently to draft a rhyming nonsense poem.
- **ooo** Use *As I Went Down Zig Zag* as a model. (T)
- **oo** Complete 'Rhyming poem 1' (PCM P1.7).
- **o** Complete 'Rhyming poem 2' (PCM P1.6). (TA)

Shared teaching (2)

• Talk Partners share their first drafts and offer feedback. *Does your partner's draft meet the success criteria? If not, how could they improve it?* Take feedback and share Two Stars and a Wish.

Independent and Guided (2)

• The children finish their rhyming poems, making changes according to their partner's feedback. Support the children with an identified need. (T/TA)

Plenary

• Talk Partners share final drafts of their poems. *What do you like about their poems? How have they improved them? What changes did they make?* Share examples of successful poems with the whole class. *How could we share our poems with a wider audience?* (E.g. perform the poems for other classes or display the poems on the school intranet.)
• Recap the learning objectives.

Assessment pointers

• S&L: pair work will show how sensitively the children can give and respond to opinions.
• AF1 (W): work with talk partners and draft poems will show how far the children are able to choose relevant ideas and to develop these in detail.

We are learning to ...	Resources
• evaluate, edit and improve our writing • write free verse poems • use ICT to effectively present poems (PNS Strands 9.1, 9.3, 12.2) **Assessment Focuses** AF (W): 1	*Year 5 Poetry Collection* ITP: (P1.5) PCM: P1.8

Shared teaching (1)

• Share the learning objectives and explain that the children will write their own free verse poems in the style of Michael Rosen.
• Recap the poems by Michael Rosen read in this unit: *Rodge Said ... , I'm the Youngest in our House ... , Harrybo* and *Chivvy.*
• Explain that many of Michael Rosen's poems are about what happened to him, or to his friends, when they were growing up and they often include a recount of a particular incident.
• The children Think-Pair-Share an incident that happened to them or a friend at home or at school. Choose an incident that they remember well and make a few notes about what happened. Talk Partners then retell their stories.
• Share some incidents with the whole class.

Independent and Guided (1)

• The children work independently to write a recount of the incident shared with Talk Partners.

ooo Write out the recount as a rough free verse draft. (TA+)

oo Write the recount as prose.

o Complete 'Drafting a recount' (PCM P1.8). (T+)

Shared teaching (2)

• Review the features of free verse poems saved on 'Features of poems' (ITP P1.5) in Session 5, e.g. no use of rhyme or regular rhythm; use of line breaks to emphasise words; use of direct speech; use of colloquial words; use of present day language. Discuss how the children could apply these features to their poems.

Independent and Guided (2)

• The children work independently to finish their poems or transform their notes into free verse. When the children are ready, use ICT to bring final drafts up to presentation standard. Support the children with an identified need. (T/TA)

Plenary

• Recap the learning objectives.
• Talk Partners share their poems and offer feedback
• Take feedback. *What did you like about your partner's poem? What did they do well? What could be improved?*
• Review the unit. *Which poems did you particularly enjoy reading or writing? Did you prefer a particular style as a whole? Do you want to read more of their poems?*

Assessment pointers

• S&L: pair work will show how sensitively the children can give and respond to opinions.
• AF1 (W): final poems will show how far the children can choose relevant ideas, elaborate them through language choices and also how far they are able to establish and maintain a viewpoint.

Rhyming words

1. Write the missing words.

 W <u>h e r e</u>

 W _ _ _

 H _ _ _

 H _ _ _

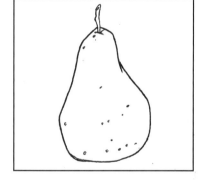 P _ _ _

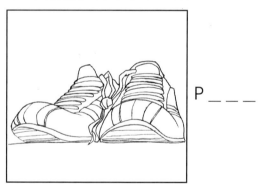 P _ _ _

2. Write the words into the table. Add more words with the same sounds.

-air	-ear	-are	-ere

Asking about Lulu

Write questions to ask Lulu's mother. Then imagine you are Lulu's mother and answer the questions.

What _____ _____ ?

Answer: _____ _____

Why _____ _____ ?

Answer: _____ _____

Where _____ _____ ?

Answer: _____ _____

When _____ _____ ?

Answer: _____ _____

How _____ _____ ?

Answer: _____ _____

Who _____ _____ ?

Answer: _____ _____

Literacy Evolve Year 5 © Pearson Education 2009

Another thing

1. **Put speech marks around the conversation between Rodge and the teacher.**

> ## poem based on *Rodge said ...*
> *Michael Rosen*
>
> Rodge said,
> Teachers – that's another thing about them,
> You're walking slowly down the corridor
> or something
> when they stop you and say,
> Haven't you got somewhere to go to?
> And you say, Yes.
> And they say,
> Well get a move on then!
> But if you're trying to get somewhere quickly,
> They say, What's the mad rush?
> Just slow down a bit.
> Teachers – that's another thing about them,
> Rodge said.

2. **Continue the conversation between the teacher and Rodge.**

"What's the mad rush? _____

Just slow down a bit" _____

And you say _____

_____

_____

_____

_____

_____

Performance script 1

Perform the script in a small group. Add some more stage directions to show how the characters speak. Add more lines.

Script based on *I'm the youngest ...*

Scene 1
(Brothers' bedroom)

Cast
Narrator
Brother
Mum
Father

Narrator:	I'm the youngest in our house, so it goes like this. My brother comes in and says
Brother:	Tell him to clear the fluff out from under his bed.
Mum:	Clear the fluff out from under your bed.
Father:	You heard what your mother said.
Narrator:	What?
Father:	The fluff. Clear the fluff out from under your bed.
Narrator:	There's fluff under his bed, too, you know.
Father:	But we're talking about the fluff under *your* bed.
Mum:	You will clear it up, won't you?
Brother:	*(all puffed up)* Clear the fluff out from under your bed, clear the fluff out from under your bed.
Narrator:	*(angry)* Shuttup stinks. YOU CAN'T RULE MY LIFE!

_____

_____

_____

Performance poem 2

Create a performance of the situation in the script. Add stage directions to show how the characters speak and behave.

Script based on *Harrybo*

Narrator:	Once my friend Harrybo came to school crying. We said …
All:	What's the matter? What's the matter?
Narrator:	And he said …
Harrybo:	My granddad's died.
Narrator:	So we didn't know what to say. Then I said …
Michael:	How did he die?
Harrybo:	He was standing on St Pancras station waiting for the train and he just fell over and died. *(starts crying again)*
Narrator:	He was a nice man, Harrybo's granddad. He had a shed with tins full of screws in it. Mind you, my gran was nice too. She gave me and my brother a red shoe horn each. Maybe Harrybo's granddad gave Harrybo a red shoe horn. Dave said …
Dave:	My hamster died as well.
Narrator:	So everyone said …
All:	Shhhh.
Dave:	I was only saying.
Narrator:	And I said …
Michael:	My gran gave me a red shoe horn.
Narrator:	Rodge said …
Rodge:	I got a pair of trainers for Christmas.
Harrybo:	You can get ones without laces.
Narrator:	And we all said …
All:	Yeah, that's right, Harrybo, you can.
Narrator:	Any other day, we'd've said: 'Of course you can, *we* know that, you fool.' But that day we said: 'Yeah, that's right, Harrybo, yeah, you can.'

Rhyming poem 1

Complete the rhyming poem. The second and fourth lines in each stanza should rhyme. Then draw pictures.

As I went down Zig Zag

    Skating on my **board,**

I saw _____

_____

As I went down Zig Zag

    Racing on my **bike,**

    I saw _____

_____

As I went down Zig Zag

    Rolling on my **blades,**

I saw _____

_____

So if you'd keep your senses,

    The point of my **rhyme**

Is when you go down Zig Zag

    Make sure you take your **time!**

Rhyming poem 2

Complete the rhyming poem. The second and fourth lines in each stanza should rhyme. Then draw pictures.

As I went down *loop the loop* _____

    Skating on my **board,**

I saw _____

_____

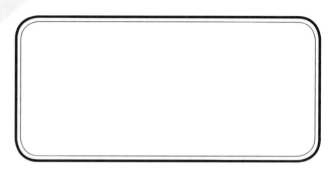

As I went down _____

    Racing on my **bike,**

I saw _____

_____

As I went down _____

    Rolling on my **blades,**

I saw _____

_____

As I went down _____

    Speeding on my **scooter,**

I saw _____

_____

So if you'd keep your senses,

    The point of my **rhyme**

Is when you go down _____

_____

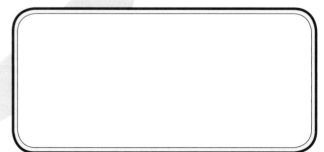

Drafting a recount

Add notes to plan your recount of an incident.

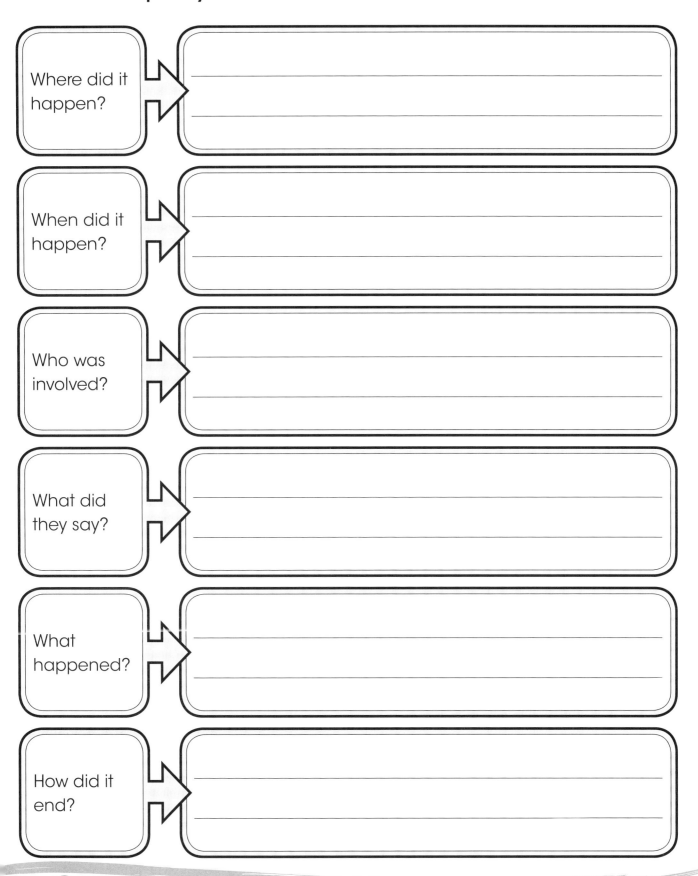

Where did it happen?

When did it happen?

Who was involved?

What did they say?

What happened?

How did it end?

MICHAEL ROSEN / CHARLES CAUSLEY (Narrative)

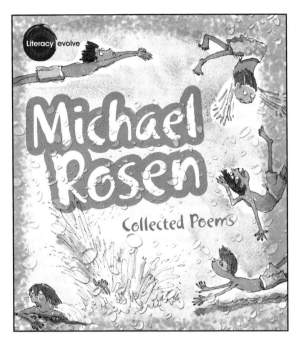

Medium term plan (2 weeks)	
Phase	**Learning Outcomes**
Phase 1: Familiarisation with the genre: narrative poems (3 days)	• Children can use drama and role play to explore issues and events in a poem. • Children can identify how poets use language to create dramatic effects. • Children can perform a poem using choral speaking.
Phase 2: Shared composition of a narrative from a poem (1 day)	• Children can find evidence in a poem to explain what is happening. • Children can write a whole-class narrative based on a poem.
Phase 3: Independent composition of a narrative from a poem (1 day)	• Children can write their own narrative based on a poem. • Children can evaluate, edit and improve their writing.
Phase 4: Narrative poems (2 days)	• Children can use drama activities to empathise with characters. • Children can identify how poets use language for comic effect.
Phase 5: Shared composition of a narrative poem (1 day)	• Children can write a narrative poem.
Phase 6: drafting and revising narrative poems (2 days)	• Children can write a narrative poem. • Children can evaluate, edit and improve their writing.

MICHAEL ROSEN/CHARLES CAUSLEY

Big picture

The children first focus on the poem *By St Thomas Water* by Charles Causley. They explore the events, characters and use of language through drama techniques, a choral reading and close reference to the text. The children then work together to create a whole-class narrative based on the poem. The children then explore Michael Rosen's poem *Top Board* and watch a performance of the poem. They are given the opportunity to discuss the characters and the use of language to create an effect on the reader. They then use the poem as a model for creating their own free verse narrative poems.

Prior learning

This unit assumes that the children can already:
- use drama techniques including working in role to explore issues, behaviour and feelings in a poem
- use evidence from the text to state what happened
- discuss poets' use of language and the effect of vocabulary, style and structure choices on the reader
- plan and write their own poems in different forms that engage the reader.

Key aspects of learning

Communication: Communicate orally and in writing; engage with the audience; create lively, thought-provoking poems.

Empathy: Empathise with the thoughts and feelings expressed in a poem, both stated and implicit. Comment on the use of empathy as a technique for understanding a poem.

Self-awareness: Express preferences, likes and dislikes. Draw on personal experience and feelings to contribute to poems.

Social skills: Work together to develop and rehearse a performance. Comment constructively on others' work.

Progression in poetry

In this unit the children will:
- discuss different forms and describe their impact on the reader
- in performance, vary pitch, pace, volume, expression and use pauses to create impact; use actions, sound effects and patterns
- use carefully-observed details and apt images to bring subject matter to life
- write free verse poems.

Cross-curricular links

ICT: The children could use ICT to write and present their final poem.
Music: The children could extend the work on choral reading into a class musical composition.

PHASE 1: FAMILIARISATION WITH THE GENRE: NARRATIVE POEMS (3 DAYS)

Session 1

We are learning to ...	Resources
• use drama to explore the issues in a poem (PNS Strands 4.1)	*Year 5 Poetry Collection*
Assessment Focuses	PCM: P2.1, P2.2, P2.3
AF (R): 2	

Shared teaching

- Share the learning objective and explain that in this unit, the children will read longer narrative poems by Charles Causley in the first week and poems by Michael Rosen in the second week. Explain that narrative poems tell stories, can be set in the past or in the present day and that they can be autobiographical or made up. *Can you think of any long narrative poems you have read?* Allow Think Time.
- Take feedback. Mention book-length story poems such as *Love that Dog* by Sharon Creech and explain that in the past stories were usually told in poetry form because it was easier for storytellers to remember them.
- Recap some of the features of Charles Causley's poetry from Year 5 Unit 1, e.g. they normally have a regular pattern of rhyme and rhythm, there is often something mysterious in them, they use old-fashioned language, etc.
- Read *By St Thomas Water* by Charles Causley (pages 5–7).
- Talk Partners discuss what they like or dislike about the poem. *Is there anything that you find puzzling?*
- Take feedback. Make lists of likes and dislikes about the poem and save these for display on the Learning Wall.
- Read *By St Thomas Water* again. *How old do you think the characters are? Are they related? Who is the oldest? Is the narrator a boy or a girl? Who is the leader?*

Independent and Guided

- In groups of three, the children use Improvisation to act out a scene from *By St Thomas Water*. Two children act while the third reads the relevant lines from the poem.
  - **OOO** Use 'Drama 1' (PCM P2.1). (T+)
  - **OO** Use 'Drama 2' (PCM P2.2).
  - **O** Use 'Drama 3' (PCM P2.3). (TA+)

Plenary

- Watch the improvisations (PCM P2.3, P2.1 and P2.2) so that the poem is read in order.
- Recap the learning objective.
- Review the lists of likes and dislikes about the poem on the Learning Wall. *Has anyone changed their mind about these as a result of the drama activity?* Evaluate the usefulness of the drama activity as a way of exploring the story of the poem. *What other drama techniques could be used?*

Assessment pointers

- S&L: improvisations will show how far the children can create and sustain roles to explore the poem.
- AF2 (R): contributions to the group drama work will show how far the children understand the events in the poem.

Session 2

We are learning to …	Resources
• find evidence in the poem of dramatic language • explore how authors use words for dramatic effect (PNS Strands 7.1, 7.5) **Assessment Focuses** AF (R): 5	*Year 5 Poetry Collection* ITP: P2.1 PCM: P2.4

Shared teaching

• Share the learning objectives and explain that the children will look at *By St Thomas Water* in more detail.
• Talk Partners remember as much of the poem as they can before rereading the poem. Show 'By St Thomas Water' (ITP P2.1) and discuss the extract. *What patterns can you see in the way the poem is written? Where is the word order in the poem different from normal?* (E.g. in Stanza 2.) *How would we normally write this?* (E.g. The grey flowers fell on the scuffed tombstone. The shell was silent; the water was cracked.) *Why has Charles Causley reversed the normal word order?* (E.g. to help with the rhyme and the rhythm; to stress different words and make the poem more dramatic; to create a pattern.) Highlight the points on ITP P2.1.
• Highlight the use of prepositions in the poem. *Why are these words given extra stress by being put at the start of lines?* (E.g. so we know exactly where the events of the poem take place.)
• Discuss how as well as telling us where the story happens, Charles Causley also describes the scene very dramatically using unusual adjectives, metaphors and similes. Highlight a few adjectives, e.g. 'scuffed', 'cracked'. Highlight the metaphor 'the beach of sky' and the simile 'like a crab' and discuss the images these create.

Independent and Guided

• The children work in small groups to analyse the language in *By St Thomas Water* using sticky notes to collect examples and to make notes.

  ooo Comment on some of the similes used, e.g. 'soft as the thunder', 'as clear as blood', 'as soft as smoke'. *Do you think they are effective? Why?* (T+)

  oo Comment on some of the adjectives used, e.g. 'thin', 'quick', 'creaking', 'crinkled', 'cautious'. *Do you think they are effective? Why?*

  o Use 'Adjectives' (PCM P2.4) to highlight the adjectives and then add others. (TA+)

Plenary

• Recap the learning objectives and take feedback. *What adjectives, similes or metaphors did you find? How did these create drama in the poem?* Highlight and add notes to ITP P2.1.
• Recap the lists of likes and dislikes of the poem on the Learning Wall. *Have any of these changed as a result of exploring the style and language of the poem?*

Assessment pointers

• S&L: group work will show how far the children can engage with others, draw ideas together and promote discussion.
• AF5 (R): independent and guided work will show how far the children are able to identify and make some comment on authors' language choices.

Session 3

We are learning to …	Resources
• perform a poem using choral speaking • say how useful performance is for understanding a poem (PNS Strands 4.2, 8.2) **Assessment Focuses** AF (R): 2	*Year 5 Poetry Collection* ITP: (P2.1)

Shared teaching (1)

• Share the learning objectives and explain that the children are going to create a choral performance of *By St Thomas Water*.
• Model annotating 'By St Thomas Water' (ITP P2.1) with suggestions for the performance, e.g. choose three soloists, one for each character and one as narrator; divide the rest of the class into four groups; Stanzas 3 and 5 can be spoken by the soloists and narrator; each pair of lines in Stanzas 1, 4 and 7 can be spoken alternately by groups one and two; each pair of lines in Stanzas 2, 6 and 8, apart from the last two lines of Stanza 8, can be spoken by groups three and four; the last two lines of Stanza 8 can be spoken by everyone.

Independent and Guided (1)

• The children use sticky notes to mark their lines on *By St Thomas Water* by Charles Causley (pages 5–7). They rehearse their lines in groups and as soloists to make sure they can be read fluently. Support the children with an identified need. (T/TA)

Shared teaching (2)

• Rehearse the choral speaking performance using PITP 2.1. Conduct the groups and soloists to co-ordinate the performance.
• Perform the choral reading and if possible record the choral reading as an audio file. Encourage the children to feed back on the performance. *What do you think worked well? How could we improve the performance?* Add suggestions to ITP P2.1.

Independent and Guided (2)

• The children work in performance groups, or as soloists, to add further sticky notes to *By St Thomas Water* to suggest how to improve their performance.

  ooo Add suggestions for using musical instruments to accompany the performance. (T+)

  oo Add suggestions to show how quickly or slowly to deliver the lines, and which words to stress.

  o Add suggestions to show how loudly or softly to deliver the lines. (TA+)

Plenary

• Take feedback of further suggestions for the choral performance and add them to ITP P2.1.
• Rehearse the performance incorporating these changes. Then perform and if possible record the performance.
• Recap the learning objectives for the session. *How useful has it been to explore the poem through a whole-class performance? Has it helped you to understand the poem more? How could we share our performance with other audiences?* (E.g. in an assembly, or by posting the recording on the school intranet.)

Assessment pointers

• S&L: poetry readings will show how far the children can shape their speech to engage listeners.
• AF2 (R): group work and choral performances will show how well the children are able to understand the poem and the effect the author is trying to achieve.

Session 4

We are learning to ...	Resources
• use evidence in a poem to explain what happens • write a narrative based on a poem (PNS Strands 7.1, 9.2) **Assessment Focuses** AF (W): 7	*Year 5 Poetry Collection* ITP: P2.2, P2.3 PCM: P2.5

Shared teaching

• Share the learning objectives and explain that the children are going to write about what happened before and after the incident described in *By St Thomas Water*.
• Show 'Characters' (ITP P2.2). Mind Map ideas about the characters in the poem (Jessie and the narrator). *What are their personalities like? What is the relationship between them? Is the narrator the young Charles Causley? Why are they at the graveyard?*, etc.
• Take feedback and add suggestions to PITP 2.2.
• Show 'Model opening' (ITP P2.3). Use Modelled Writing to create the opening of a prose narrative in the first person, using contemporary language about what happened before the incident in the poem.
• Talk Partners use Improvisation to explore the opening scene where Jessie tries to get the narrator (Charlie) to go fishing with her when they are meant to be at school.
• Watch some of the improvisations as a whole class. *Are the personalities of the two children portrayed well? Are there any details we could add to the opening?*
• Discuss the events of the poem in the light of this 'back story'. *How might Jessie persuade the narrator to steal a jam-jar from a grave and then dance around the tombstone? Why does the narrator cover his ears when he hears a voice? How does each child react after Jessie reads the lettering?*

Independent and Guided

• In pairs, the children write out the events described in the poem as a prose narrative, continuing the opening started as a whole class. They should not go beyond Stanza 7.
- **ᴑᴑᴑ** Experiment with writing in the third person. (T)
- **ᴑᴑ** Include some dialogue between Jessie and the narrator, 'Charlie'.
- **ᴑ** Use 'The story continued' (PCM P2.5). (TA+)

Plenary

• Pairs share narratives with another pair and give feedback. *Do the characters in the other pair's story behave like the ones in the story opening?*
• Take feedback and share successful examples.
• Reread the whole-class story opening and then listen to some of the narratives which successfully continue it.
• Recap the learning objectives. *What information from the poem did you use to write your story?*

Assessment pointers

• S&L: pair work will show how sensitively the children can express and respond to opinions.
• AF7 (W): independent and guided activities will show how well the children are able to use appropriate vocabulary.

Session 5

We are learning to ...	Resources
• evaluate, edit and improve our writing • write a narrative based on a poem • use ICT to effectively present poems (PNS Strands 9.1, 9.2, 12.2) **Assessment Focuses** AF (W): 1	*Year 5 Poetry Collection* ITP: P2.4 PCM: P2.6

Shared teaching (1)

• Share the learning objectives and explain that in this session, the children are going to continue the story of *By St Thomas Water* and write an ending for it.
• Read the final stanza of *By St Thomas Water* on page 7.
• Talk Partners share ideas about what has happened to Jessie and the narrator in the 'many a year' after the end of the poem. *Why might the narrator want to come back and listen to the voices of the dead now?*
• Take feedback. *How might the story have been concluded?*
• Show 'Story ending' (ITP P2.4) and consider the questions for how the story might end.

Independent and Guided (1)

• In the same pairs as Session 4, the children write an ending for their stories.
- **ᴑᴑᴑ** Experiment with using different points of view in the narrative, e.g. write the story from Jessie's viewpoint and then from 'Charlie's'.
- **ᴑᴑ** Try to write the ending so that the last words are those in the final two lines of the poem. (TA)
- **ᴑ** Use 'The story concluded' (PCM P2.6). (T+)

Shared teaching (2)

• Join pairs together to share their endings. Each pair offers feedback by giving Two Stars and a Wish.
• Take feedback and share two stars and a wish. *What did you like about their ending? How could they improve it?*

Independent and Guided (2)

• Pairs make changes to their endings according to the feedback they received .The children then use ICT to bring final drafts to presentation standard. Support the children with an identified need. (T/TA)

Plenary

• Share examples of story endings with the whole class. *How well do they fit in with the narrative in the original poem? What difference does it make to the story if one is in a poem form and the other one is in a narrative?*
• Display the writing alongside a copy of Charles Causley's poem.
• Recap the learning objectives. *What changes did you make to your poem?*

Assessment pointers

• S&L: pair work will show how sensitively the children can give and respond to opinions.
• AF1 (W): final drafts will show how far the children can use appropriate ideas and imaginative content.

Session 6

We are learning to …	Resources
• use drama and role play to empathise with characters • say whether using drama helps us understand a poem (PNS Strands 4.1, 8.2) **Assessment Focuses** AF (R): 2	*Year 5 Poetry Collection* *Top Board* (film)

Shared teaching

• Share the learning objectives and explain that the children will be reading a longer narrative poem by Michael Rosen.
• Recap some of the features of Michael Rosen's poetry from Unit 1, e.g. he mostly uses non-rhyming free verse; often writes about his own experiences as a child; deals with funny and serious situations.
• Read *Top Board* by Michael Rosen (pages 7–9).
• The children Think-Pair-Share responses to the poem. *Have you had any scary experiences like that at a swimming pool? Have you ever dived off the top board? How did you feel the first time? Was it the same as how the narrator describes it?*
• Take feedback. Discuss the feelings of the boy in the poem. Encourage the children to empathise with him and try to visualise what the experience was like from his point of view. *How does he feel when he is first asked to dive from the top board, when he does the dive, after the dive and when the teacher asks for five more?*
• Take feedback. *How will he feel in the next swimming lesson when he has to dive off the top board again?*
• Talk Partners Role Play the situation in the poem, making up their own dialogue and using body language such as facial expression, posture and gesture to show emotions.

• Watch some of the role plays. *How well do the improvisations capture the emotions of the scene? Does the dialogue sound like something the character would say?*

Independent and Guided

• In small groups, the children create performances of the poem.
  ∞∞∞ Perform the poem, then continue it by making up some more lines to describe Michael's next dive from the top board.
  ∞∞ Pairs perform the poem with one child as Mr Hicks and one as Michael. (TA)
  ◉ As above. (T+)

Plenary

• Watch the performances by the different groups. *What did you think they did well? What could they improve? How do you think it could be performed differently?* Show the film of Michael Rosen performing *Top Board*. *How does Michael Rosen's performance of the poem compare with your own? What are the similarities and differences?*
• Recap the learning objectives. Reflect on how acting out the poem helps us to share the feelings of the characters involved. *How useful was it to empathise with the boy in the poem, to visualise the scene through his eyes and to predict how he might feel later?*

Assessment pointers

• S&L: drama pieces will show how far the children can sustain roles to explore the poem.
• AF2 (R): group work and performances will show how far the children understand the poem and can empathise with the character.

Session 7

We are learning to …	Resources
• make notes on a text using evidence to support our ideas • explore how authors use rhyme and choose words for comic effect • explore how authors use words for dramatic effect (PNS Strands 7.1, 7.5) **Assessment Focuses** AF (R): 5	*Year 5 Poetry Collection* *Top Board* (film) ITP: P2.5, PCM: P2.7, P2.8

Shared teaching (1)

• Watch *Top Board* again.
• Talk Partners discuss Michael Rosen's performance of the poem. *What words and phrases does the poet stress? How does he bring out the scariness of the experience? How does he make it sound funny as well? Does he use any interesting body language such as facial expression, posture and gesture to go with his performance? How effective is it? Have you ever been in a situation like that at school or somewhere else? Can you describe how you felt?*
• Show 'Top Board' (ITP P2.5). Discuss how Michael Rosen uses language in the poem to create dramatic and comic effects. Highlight language features, e.g. some words are in capital letters ('WHAT?!'); similes used to describe actions ('like doing a handstand on nothing', 'like my belly was going into my legs', 'like someone walloping me in the face'). *Does the language make it easy to imagine yourself in that situation?*

Independent and Guided

• In small groups, the children use sticky notes to comment on

interesting language in *Top Board*. Add these to the Learning Wall for use in Session 9.
  ∞∞∞ Comment on any language features which you think make the poem more dramatic or funnier. (T)
  ∞∞ Use 'Question prompts 1' (PCM P2.7).
  ◉ Use 'Question prompts 2' (PCM P2.8). (TA)

Shared teaching (2)

• Show ITP P2.5 and take feedback, encouraging the children to support their ideas with reference to the poem. Highlight and annotate in response to suggestions from the groups. *Which parts of the poem use language in a dramatic way?* (E.g. the stanza beginning ' … the big clock'.) *Which parts use it in a more comic way?* (E.g. the ending.)
• Discuss any differences in the suggestions that the groups make. *Why do you think that?*

Plenary

• Recap the learning objectives.
• *How successful has Michael Rosen been in retelling the story of his first dive from the top board in a narrative poem? Were you able to share what the experience was like because of the way the story was told?*

Assessment pointers

• S&L: group work will show how far the children can engage with others, draw ideas together and promote discussion.
• AF5 (R): annotations to the poem show how far the children can identify features of authors' use of language and comment on it.

Session 8

We are learning to ...	Resources
• write a narrative poem (PNS Strands 9.3) **Assessment Focuses** AF (W): 7	*Year 5 Poetry Collection* ITP: P2.6, P2.7

Shared teaching (1)

• Share the learning objective and recap the story of *Top Board. What type of character do you think Michael is? Is he brave? How do you think the poem might change with a different character?*

• Show 'Caricature' (ITP P2.6). Explore the character on screen. *Who do you think this is? What do you think he might be like? Is he strong? How do you think he might feel?*

• Explain that the children are going to write an autobiographical poem based on this character. They are going to write about this character's P.E. lesson. *He calls it his P.T. lesson. What do you think P.T. stands for?* (physical training). *How do you think the character might feel about P.T.?* (physical torture)

• Show 'My P.T. lesson' (ITP P2.7). Read the character's diary entry about his P.T. lesson. *Were your predictions correct? Why do you think the character might not like P.T.? What do you think happened in the P.T. lesson?*

• Click 'Poem' and use Modelled Writing to create a free verse poem using ideas from the diary and the children's suggestions. *How can we turn this into free verse? Where should the line breaks come, so the stress falls on the key words? How could the language be made more dramatic?*

• Talk Partners visualise the situation. *How was the character feeling? How could you describe this? What would he say?*

• Take feedback and use suggestions to continue the poem.

Independent and Guided

• The children work in pairs to write about the character's feelings at the most dramatic point of the situation, using *Top Board* as a model.

∞ Write in free verse, including some similes.

∞ Write in prose, including some similes. (TA+)

◉ Write in prose from a given starting point in the class poem. (T)

Shared teaching (2)

• Take feedback. Add suggestions to complete the poem on ITP P2.7.

• Use Modelled Writing to draft the conclusion to the character's story and model how you would include it in the whole-class poem. Encourage the children to suggest ideas. Save the whole-class poem for use in Session 10.

Plenary

• Recap the learning objective. *Did you find it hard to make the narrative into a poem? How did you overcome these problems?*

• Reread the whole-class poem on ITP P2.7. *What do you like about our poem? Is there anything you would change? How?*

Assessment pointers

• AF7 (W): written work will show how far the children can choose appropriate vocabulary and use words for effect.

Session 9

We are learning to ...	Resources
• evaluate, edit and improve our writing • write a narrative poem (PNS Strands 9.1, 9.3) **Assessment Focuses** AF (W): 1	*Year 5 Poetry Collection* ITP: (P2.5)

Shared teaching (1)

• Share the learning objectives and explain that In the next two sessions, the children are going to write their own narrative poems in the same style as *Top Board*. Remind the children that earlier in this unit they looked at how Michael Rosen uses language in *Top Board*, to create dramatic and comic effects. *What do you remember about how the poem was written to help the reader imagine the situation he was describing?*

• Show annotated '*Top Board*' (ITP P2.5) and recap the features of the poem.

• Explain that like *Top Board*, the children's poems are going to be about something that happened in their lives. *Can you think of a scary or embarrassing situation? You need to remember it clearly. Do you remember what it felt like at the time? Maybe it was about something you'd never tried before or somewhere new.*

• Talk Partners share their ideas with each other and say which one they will choose to write about.

Independent and Guided (1)

• The children work independently to draft memories of the chosen experience in prose.

∞ Include some similes to describe what the experience felt like. (T+)

∞ Include some direct speech by another character in the narrative.

◉ Write about thoughts and feelings at the time in the first person. Use ICT and save the draft for use in Session 10. (TA+)

Shared teaching (2)

• Talk Partners share and offer feedback on their first drafts, giving their partner Two Stars and a Wish. *What worked well? What could be even better if worked on further?*

Independent and Guided (2)

• The children work independently to reflect on ther drafts and try to improve them based on two stars and a wish feedback. Support the children with an identified need. (T/TA)

Plenary

• Recap the learning objectives.

• Listen to some of the drafts. *How have you improved your draft as a result of the feedback? In what ways? What do you think works well?*

Assessment pointers

• S&L: pair work will show how sensitively the children can express and respond to opinions.

• AF1 (W): first drafts will show how far the children are able to choose and develop relevant ideas.

We are learning to …	Resources
• evaluate, edit and improve our writing • write a narrative poem (PNS Strands 9.1, 9.3) **Assessment Focuses** AF (W): 1	*Year 5 Poetry Collection* ITP: (P2.5, P2.7)

Shared teaching (1)

- Share the learning objectives and explain that in this session, the children will continue with their own narrative poems using the model of *Top Board* by Michael Rosen (pages 7–9).
- Explain that in the next stage of their writing, they will need to turn their drafts into free verse. *What are the features of free verse?* (E.g. It has no use of rhyme or regular rhythm.)
- Remind the children of the work done in Session 8. *How did we create the free verse poem based on the diary?* Show 'My P.T. lesson' (ITP P2.7) and reread the finished poem.
- Recap the process of creating the poem, e.g. *We wrote it in the first person and used speech marks for direct speech and we considered where the line breaks should come, so that stress falls on the key words.*

Independent and Guided (1)

- The children work independently to change their drafts into free verse narrative poems.

  [OOO] Use language to make the experience more dramatic and also maybe more humorous for the reader.

  [OO] Insert line breaks in the free verse so as to stress certain important words. (T+)

- **[icon]** Use ICT to change the draft into free verse. Experiment with different layouts. (TA+)

Shared teaching (2)

- Talk Partners share their poems and offer feedback. Encourage the children to refer to '*Top Board*' (ITP P2.5) for ideas of how to improve the poems.
- Take feedback. *What do you like about your partner's poem? What could be improved? Do you need any help?*

Independent and Guided (2)

- The children make the final changes to their poems in light of their partner's feedback. They then bring their poem up to final presentation standard. Support the children with an identified need. (T/TA)

Plenary

- Recap the learning objectives. Share examples of successful poems with the whole class. *What do you like about your poems? What did you find hard? How could we display or share our poems with other audiences?*
- Recap the unit as a whole. *Which poem did you most enjoy? What have you learnt from reading these poems? Would you like to read more of these poets' work?*

Assessment pointers

- S&L: pair work will show how far the children can listen and respond to others.
- AF1 (W): final poems will show how far the children are able to produce imaginative and thoughtful texts.

Drama 1

Act out the scene from the poem. Use the prompts to help you.

Extract from *By St Thomas Water*
Charles Causley

Who will be acting? Who will be the narrator?

'If we walk,' said Jessie,
'Seven times round,
We shall hear a dead man
Speaking underground.'
Round the stone we danced, we sang,
Watched the sun drop,
Laid our heads and listened
At the tomb-top.

Which actions do you want to show?
How will you show them?

Soft as the thunder
At the storm's start
I heard a voice as clear as blood,
Strong as the heart.
But what words were spoken
I can never say,
I shut my fingers round my head,
Drove them away.

Which lines will the narrator say?

How will the characters move?

How will the narrator say the lines? (softly, loudly, slow or fast)

'What are those letters, Jessie,
Cut so sharp and trim
All round this holy stone
With earth up to the brim?'
Jessie traced the letters
Black as coffin-lead.
'He is not dead but sleeping,'
Slowly she said.

How will you show the characters' feelings?

Drama 2

Act out the scene from the poem. Use the prompts to help you.

Extract from _By St Thomas Water_
Charles Causley

I looked at Jessie,
Jessie looked at me,
And our eyes in wonder
Grew wide as the sea.
Past the green and bending stones
We fled hand in hand,
Silent through the tongues of grass
To the river strand.

By the creaking cypress
We moved as soft as smoke
For fear all the people
Underneath awoke.
Over all the sleepers
We darted light as snow
In case they opened up their eyes,
Called us from below.

Many a day has faltered
Into many a year
Since the dead awoke and spoke
And we would not hear.
Waiting in the cold grass
Under a crinkled bough,
Quiet stone, cautious stone,
What do you tell me now?

> Who will be acting? Who will be the narrator?

> Which actions do you want to show?
> How will you show them?

> Which lines will the narrator say?

> How will the characters move?

> How will the narrator say the lines? (softly, loudly, slow or fast)

> How will you show the characters' feelings?

Drama 3

Act out the scene from the poem. Use the prompts to help you.

> How will you show the quick fish?

> Without the jam jar, the flowers fall on the tombstone. How can we show this?

> How does the sun move? How can we show this?

Extract from *By St Thomas Water*
Charles Causley

By St Thomas Water

Where the river is thin

We looked for a jam-jar

To catch the quick fish in.

Through St Thomas Churchyard

Jessie and I ran

The day we took the jam-pot

Off the dead man.

On the scuffed tombstone

The grey flowers fell,

Cracked was the water,

Silent the shell.

The snake for an emblem

Swirled on the slab,

Across the beach of sky the sun

Crawled like a crab.

> The characters are looking for a jam jar. How do they move?

> The characters are running through the church yard. How do they feel? How can we show this?

> The water moves like a snake. How can we show this?

Adjectives

Highlight the adjectives. Then fill in the spaces with other adjectives.

> ## Extract from *By St Thomas Water*
> *Charles Causley*
>
> By St Thomas Water
> Where the river is thin
> We looked for a _____ jam-jar
> To catch the quick fish in.
> Through St Thomas Churchyard
> Jessie and I ran
> The _____ day we took the jam-pot
> Off the dead man.
>
> On the scuffed tombstone
> The grey flowers fell,
> Cracked was the water,
> Silent the shell.
> The snake for an emblem
> Swirled on the _____ slab,
> Across the beach of sky the sun
> Crawled like a _____ crab.
>
> 'If we walk', said Jessie,
> 'Seven times round,
> We shall hear a dead man
> Speaking underground.'
> Round the _____ stone we danced, we sang,
> Watched the sun drop,
> Laid our heads and listened
> At the _____ tomb-top.

The story continued

Continue the story of what happens in the poem.

It was Jessie who 'borrowed' her brothers' fishing net that day we went down to St Thomas Water. We should have been in school and I didn't really want to go fishing. My mother would have been furious if she had found out! But Jessie persuaded me – as usual.

It was hard catching anything because the fish were so fast. Eventually Jessie managed it but we didn't have anywhere to put them. Jessie had forgotten a jam-jar, but she said she knew where to get one.

'Come on, Charlie,' she cried, 'We'll nick one from the graveyard. They won't mind!'

_____

_____

_____

_____

_____

_____

_____

_____

The story concluded

Continue the ending for the story in the poem.

Of course we were seen when we ran out of the churchyard.
My mother found out and banned me from playing with Jessie
again. I knew Jessie got into trouble too with her brothers for
leaving their fishing net behind.

_____

_____

_____

_____

_____

_____

_____

_____

_____

_____

_____

_____

_____

_____

_____

Question prompts 1

**Discuss the questions about *Top Board*.
Find the answers in the poem.**

Which lines
introduce the
background
to the story?

Which words
are spoken by
Mr Hicks?

Which lines
give the
narrator's
thoughts?

Where are
punctuation
marks used to
show feelings?

What different
senses are
used in the
description?

What was it
like standing
on the top
board?

What similes
describe the
dive into
the pool?

What effect
does the
ending of the
poem have?

Question prompts 2

Discuss the questions about *Top Board*.
Find the answers in the poem.

Which lines introduce the background to the story?

Which lines give the narrator's thoughts?

What was it like standing on the top board?

Which lines show what Mr Hicks says?

Which lines describe the dive into the pool?

Which other lines do you like in the poem? Why?

What do you think about the ending of the poem?

Poetry Unit 3

MICHAEL ROSEN / CHARLES CAUSLEY (Performance)

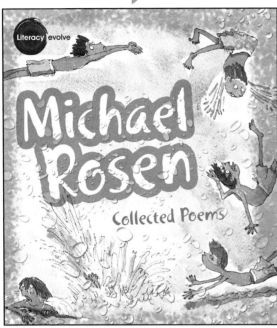

Medium term plan (1 week)	
Phase	**Learning Outcomes**
Phase 1: Choral and performance poems (2 days)	• Children can use drama to explore characters' feelings and behaviour in a poem. • Children can comment on the usefulness of drama techniques in understanding a poem.
Phase 2: Shared composition of a performance poem (1 day)	• Children can create a whole-class poem based on their own experiences. • Children can evaluate, edit and improve the whole-class poem.
Phase 3: Drafting and revising performance poems (2 days)	• Children can plan, draft and revise their own poems. • Children can perform their poems.

MICHAEL ROSEN/CHARLES CAUSLEY

Big picture

The children read two poems from the point of view of performance, discussing features such as rhythm, patterns and vocabulary. They work collaboratively to create performances and discuss what makes a good performance of a poem. They also watch performance poems by Michael Rosen. The children go on to consider what makes a good poem for performance, before collecting ideas for a class poem. Finally, the children create their own performance poem and plan, rehearse, perform and evaluate their poems.

Prior learning

This unit assumes that children can already:
- prepare a poem for performance, with some awareness of the features that make a poem good to perform
- discuss poets' use of language and how language is used for particular dramatic or humorous effects
- work together, taking on roles and responding to other's ideas
- create their own imaginative texts for a particular audience and purpose.

Key aspects of learning

Communication: Consider the audience when planning and rehearsing a performance; perform with confidence in front of an audience.

Creativity: Generate interesting ideas for shared and individual poems; come up with creative ways of performing poems.

Social skills: Work together to develop and rehearse a performance; comment constructively on other's work.

Progression in poetry

In this unit the children will:
- discuss the use of unusual or unfamiliar language choices; explore imagery including metaphor
- in performance, vary pitch, pace, volume, expression and use pauses to create impact; use actions, sound effects and patterns and dramatic interpretation
- use carefully-observed details and apt images to bring subject matter alive, including humour.

Cross-curricular links

History/Geography: The children could find out about other local customs and traditions.

ICT: The children could enhance their performance with a multi-media display; they could record and broadcast their performances.

Music: The children could develop their poems into musical compositions.

PHASE 1: CHORAL AND PERFORMANCE POEMS (2 DAYS)

Session 1

We are learning to ...	Resources
• explore and perform a poem • evaluate a performance (PNS Strands 4.2, 4.3) **Assessment Focuses** AF (R): 2	*Year 5 Poetry Collection* ITP: P3.1, P3.2

Shared teaching (1)

- Share the learning objectives and explain that in this unit, the children will read and perform poems by Charles Causley and Michael Rosen and then write and perform their own poems.
- Show 'Rhymes and chants' (ITP P3.1). Talk Partners discuss chants that they may have heard or sung in the playground.
- Read *Mary, Mary Magdalene* by Charles Causley (pages 2–3). Emphasise its strong rhythm, like a child's skipping rhyme. Explain that the poem is based on a custom in Launceston, Cornwall, where Charles Causley lived. There is a stone figure of St Mary Magdalene lying on her side under a tree. Locals say that if you throw a pebble and it lands on her back and stays there, it will bring you good luck.
- Show '*Mary, Mary Magdalene*' (ITP P3.2). Clap out the rhythm softly as you read the poem again. *Why has Charles Causley used this kind of rhythm?* (because it is about a children's game) *Who is the narrator?* (a girl) *How do you know?* (because of what she asks for)
- Talk Partners discuss anything puzzling in the poem or any patterns.
- Take feedback. Clarify puzzles and unfamiliar vocabulary, e.g. 'hose' (stockings); 'stony tree' (the statue is under a tree carved out of stone); 'spray' (the blossom on the stone tree).
- Discuss and highlight the patterns in the poem. (E.g. the repetition of 'Mary, Mary Magdalene' in alternate stanzas; the alternate stanzas are

in italics because they are Mary's answers; the second and fourth lines in each stanza rhyme; the poem goes full circle.)
- Discuss how the poem might be performed, emphasising similarities to a skipping chant. Add notes to ITP P3.2.

Independent and Guided

- In groups, the children discuss and make notes about how the poem can best be performed.

  ∞ Discuss how the poem can be divided up between soloists or groups. (T+)

  ∞ Discuss which actions could be performed.

  ◉ Make a list of props and sound effects that could be used in the performance. (TA+)

Shared teaching (2)

- Take feedback and add notes to ITP P3.2. Then rehearse and perform the whole poem as a class. If possible, record the performances.

Plenary

- Recap the learning objectives. *What did you like about the performances? Was the rhythm clear? Did the actions add to the performance? How? Has it added to the enjoyment of the poem?*

Assessment pointers

- S&L: group work will show how well the children can adopt group roles, drawing ideas together and promoting effective planning.
- AF2 (R): group work and performances will show how far the children understand the poem.

We are learning to ...	Resources
• explore and perform a poem • evaluate a performance (PNS Strands 4.2, 4.3) **Assessment Focuses** AF (R): 2	*Year 5 Poetry Collection* *If you don't put your shoes on ...* (film) ITP: P3.3

Shared teaching

- At the beginning of the session, challenge the children to get ready as you count up to 15.
- Watch *If you don't put your shoes on ...* *Why do you think the adult in the poem has made putting shoes on into a game? Have you ever done something similar with a younger child? Has anyone ever done something similar with you?*
- Share the learning objectives.
- Read *If you don't put your shoes on ...* by Michael Rosen (pages 2–3). *How many speakers are there in the poem?* (two) *Who are they? How do you know who is speaking?* (The indented line 'Mum where are my socks mum?', shows that it is a child speaking and we can deduce from this that all the child's responses are indented.) *Why do you think the poem is written like that? Does it sound like real speech?*
- Show 'If you don't put your shoes on ... ' (ITP P3.3). *How has Michael Rosen set the poem out?* (In free verse; each speaker is on a separate line; no punctuation within the lines, e.g. 'Fifteen we're off'; the numbers are mostly down the left-hand side; there are no speech marks.) *Why is the poem written like this?* (to give a feeling of the very monotonous countdown by the parent and the very hurried, panicky speech of the child)
- Remind the children of Michael Rosen's performance. *How could we perform the poem as a group?* Add notes to ITP P3.3.

Independent and Guided

- In groups, the children discuss how the poem can best be performed. Add sticky notes to the poem with suggestions.
- **CCC** Write out as much of the poem as possible as a play script, with names of speakers, setting and stage directions. (TA+)
- **CC** Annotate the poem with possible actions at different points.
- **C** Annotate the poem with the initials of who is speaking at different times. (T)

Plenary

- Take feedback from the group and add notes to ITP P3.3.
- Rehearse the poem and perform as a whole class. If possible, record the performance.
- Recap the learning objectives. *What worked well? What could be improved? Has the performance added to your enjoyment of the poem?*

Assessment pointers

- S&L: group work will show how well the children can adopt group roles, drawing ideas together and promoting effective planning.
- AF2 (R): group work and performances will show how far the children understand the poem and its structure.

PHASE 2: SHARED COMPOSITION OF A PERFORMANCE POEM (1 DAY)

Session 3

We are learning to ...	Resources
• evaluate, edit and improve our writing • write a performance poem (PNS Strands 9.1, 9.3) **Assessment Focuses** AF (W): 7	*Year 5 Poetry Collection* *If you don't put your shoes on ...* (film) ITP: P3.4, P3.5

Shared teaching

- Share the learning objectives and explain that the children are going to write a poem to perform as a whole class, but first they need to think about what makes a good performance poem.
- Reread *Mary, Mary Magdalene* by Charles Causley (pages 2–3) and watch *If you don't put your shoes on ...* .
- Show 'Performance poems' (ITP P3.4). *What features made these good poems to perform? Are there any you would like to add or change?*
- Explain that the children will use the same structure as in *If you don't put your shoes on ...* for the class poem.
- Talk Partners discuss possible ideas for the subject of a countdown poem such as Michael Rosen's, e.g. getting up, getting ready for school, eating your school dinner, getting changed after swimming, doing your homework, tidying your bedroom, etc.
- Take feedback and choose one subject for the poem.
- Show 'If you don't ... ' (ITP P3.5). Use Modelled Writing to create the opening of the poem. Encourage the children to suggest the next few lines as the countdown begins. Use Think Alouds to model selecting from, modifying or rejecting various ideas as you compose the poem, e.g. *I'm going to have the child say: One / I'm too tired / You shouldn't have stayed up late last night / Two / Just leave me a few more minutes,* etc.

Independent and Guided

- In groups, the children continue to compose possible lines for the class performance poem.
- **CCC** Continue the countdown up to 10, remembering to go into fractions after 9. (TA)
- **CC** Write another six steps in the countdown.
- **C** Write another three steps in the countdown. (T)

Plenary

- Take feedback and use the ideas to complete the class poem. *What would be a good final line for our poem?*
- Recap the learning objectives.
- Read the completed version of the class poem. Compare the completed draft with the success criteria on ITP P3.4. *Are all the criteria covered? How could the draft be revised to improve it?* Make improvements to the poem as appropriate and save it for use in Session 4.

Assessment pointers

- AF7 (W): contributions to the whole-class poem will show how far the children can use appropriate and effective vocabulary.

Session 4

We are learning to ...	Resources
• evaluate, edit and improve our writing • write a performance poem (PNS Strands 9.1, 9.3) **Assessment Focuses** AF (W): 1	*Year 5 Poetry Collection* ITP: (P3.3, P3.4, P3.5) PCM: P3.1, P3.2

Shared teaching (1)

• Share the learning objectives.
• Recall annotated 'If you don't ... ' (ITP P3.5). Reread the whole-class poem. *How could we best perform our poem? How will we show the interaction between the different speakers? What actions would be appropriate? What could we do to make it funny?* Refer to 'If you don't put your shoes on...' (ITP P3.3) for further suggestions and add notes to ITP P3.5.
• Use Forum Theatre to act out the whole-class poem. Encourage the children to direct the action. *What works well? Is the interaction between the speakers convincing? What improvements could be made to the performance? Could the actors use gesture more?*
• Watch the revised performance. *Do you think that was an improvement? What worked well? What did you like best about it?*
• Recap the success criteria using 'Performance poems' (ITP P3.4). *Are there any you would like to add or change?*

Independent and Guided (1)

• In groups, the children discuss and draft performance poems.
  ∞ Use 'Performance poems' (PCM P3.1). (T+)
  ∞ Draft a poem based on the countdown model of *If you don't put your shoes on ...*.

◎ Use 'If you don't ...' (PCM P3.2). (TA+)

Shared teaching (2)

• Join groups together to share their first drafts and use the success criteria to offer feedback. *Are there clearly defined parts for different speakers? Is the overall structure clear?*

Independent and Guided (2)

• Groups independently reflect on and try to improve their performance poems based on feedback from response groups. Support the children with an identified need. (T/TA)

Plenary

• Recap the learning objectives.
• Listen to some of the drafts which response groups think match the success criteria. *Have the drafts been improved as a result of the feedback given? How?*

Assessment pointers

• S&L: group work will show how well the children can adopt group roles and express opinions.
• AF1 (W): first drafts and revisions will show how far the children are able to choose and develop relevant ideas and content and also establish and maintain a viewpoint.

Session 5

We are learning to ...	Resources
• write and perform our poems • evaluate, edit and improve our writing (PNS Strands 4.2, 9.1) **Assessment and Focuses** AF (W): 1	ITP: (P3.4) PCM: P3.3, P3.4

Shared teaching (1)

• Share the learning objectives and explain that in this session, the children will continue to write their own performance poems. After that they will perform their finished poems to the whole class.
• Recall 'Performance poems' (ITP P3.4) and recap the success criteria.

Independent and Guided (1)

• The children work in the same groups to finish their performance poems. Support the children with an identified need. (T/TA)

Shared teaching (2)

• Recap the poetry performances the children have watched. *What techniques did Michael Rosen use? How did he make the poems come to life?*
• Model making a checklist of points to consider for an effective performance. *Does everyone know what lines to say and when? Does everyone know how to say their lines? Is everyone speaking clearly and not too quickly so that the audience can follow what they say? Is any music or sound effect used loud enough but not too loud? Can the audience see any action or miming clearly?*

Independent and Guided (2)

• The children work in the same groups to plan, rehearse and improve their performances, refering to the checklist for effective performance poems.
  ∞ Consider adding music or sound effects.
  ∞ Use 'Performance prompts 1' (PCM P3.3). (T+)
  ◎ Use 'Performance prompts 2' (PCM P3.4). (TA+)

Plenary

• Groups present their performance poem to the rest of the class. *Did the performances meet the success criteria? Did you find the interactions between the speakers convincing? Did you enjoy the performances? Were they funny? What did you like best?*
• Recap the learning objectives. *How could we share our performances with other audiences?*
• Recap the unit as a whole. *What did you enjoy most? What did you find difficult? What do you think you did best?*

Assessment pointers

• S&L: poetry performances will show how far the children can talk in imaginative and purposeful ways.
• AF1 (W): final poems will show how far the children can produce imaginative and interesting texts, suitable for performance.

Performance poems

Choose one of the ideas to write a poem in the style of Michael Rosen or Charles Causley. Use the examples to help you.

Write a poem about waiting for an adult to get ready.

> *If you don't get ready to take me to school before it gets to 8.30, I'll have to sign the late book – again!*
> *8.25. OK, I'm trying to find the car keys*

Imagine you are a dog. Write a poem about waiting to go for a walk.

> *If you don't take me for walkies before I bark six times ...*
> *I'll have to make a puddle on the floor – again!*
> *Woof! All right, I'm just watching the end of this TV show.*

Use the rhyme and rhythm from *Mary, Mary Magdalene* to write a short poem about a famous monument.

> *Oh mighty, mighty Big Ben*
> *Standing straight and tall*
> *Keeping the time for all to see*
> *London hears your call*

Write a new stanza for *Mary, Mary Magdalene* using the same rhyme, rhythm and first line.

> *I'll send you for your Christening*
> *A woollen robe to wear,*
> *A shiny cup from which to sup,*
> *And a name to bear.*

If you don't ...

Complete the performance poem in the style of Michael Rosen.

If you don't _____

If you don't _____ before I count to six

Then _____

One

_____

Two

_____

Three

_____

Four

_____

Five

_____

Five and a half

_____

Five and three-quarters

_____

Six

_____

See I did it.

Didn't I?

Performance prompts 1

Use the prompts to help you plan your performance. Make notes on your poem.

Parts

Who will say which part?

Which lines will you say together and which will you say alone?

Ending

How will you create an effective ending to the performance?

How do you want the audience to feel at the end?

Setting

What background, set or lighting will you have?

How will this improve the performance?

Props

What objects or costumes will you use?

When and how will you use these?

Expression

How loudly, softly, quickly or slowly will you say the words or lines?

What tone of voice will you use?

Movement

What actions or mimes will you use to go with the words or lines?

How will these help make the meaning clearer?

Performers

How many performers are there?

Which are groups and which are soloists?

Sound

What music or sound effects will you use?

When and how will you use these?

Performance prompts 2

Discuss the questions to help you plan your performance.

Which lines or words do you need to say quickly or slowly?

What action or miming will you include?

How will you divide up the poem into parts?

Who will read which part?

Which lines or words do you need to say loudly or softly?